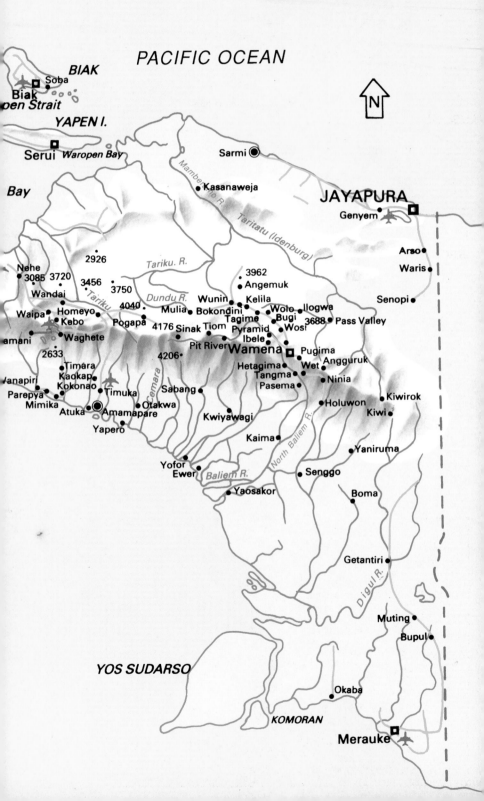

IRIAN JAYA

INDONESIAN

NEW GUINEA

IRIAN JAYA

Text and Photographs by

DR. KAL MULLER

PERIPLUS
EDITIONS
INCORPORATED

Periplus Indonesia Travel Guides

BALI
Island of the Gods

INDONESIAN NEW GUINEA
Irian Jaya

SPICE ISLANDS
The Moluccas

JAVA
Garden of the East

INDONESIAN BORNEO
Kalimantan

SULAWESI
The Celebes

SUMATRA
Island of Adventure

EAST OF BALI
From Lombok to Timor

UNDERWATER INDONESIA
A Guide to the World's Best Diving

KAL MULLER has explored, photographed and reported on some of the most fascinating places in the world. His work has appeared in dozens of books, including the stunning *Paradise on the Equator,* as well as *National Geographic, Geo* and other magazines. Muller was born in Hungary, speaks five languages (at last count) and now splits his time between Indonesia and his home in Mexico. For the last 15 years he has wandered the archipelago with 40 pounds of camera equipment, his notebook and his good-humored and inquisitive nature.

Published by Periplus Editions, Inc.

1442A Walnut Street #206
Berkeley, California 94709

*Sole distributer in United Kingdom
and Europe (excluding Holland)*

Robertson McCarta Ltd.
122 Kings Cross Road
London WC1X 9DS

*Sole distributor
in Indonesia*

c.v. Java Books
P.O. Box 55 JKCP
Jakarta 10510

Publisher: Eric M. Oey
Editor: David Pickell
Design: Peter Ivey

Library of Congress Catalog Card Number: 89-61135
ISBN 0-945971-06-0

Cover: *Dani huts in the Baliem Valley. By Kal Muller*
Frontispiece: *The mummified remains of chief Werapak Elosarek in Akima village. By Kal Muller*

Contents

PAGE 23

PAGE 45

PAGE 133

PAGE 107

PART III: *The Baliem Valley*

PART IV: *The Casuarina Coast*

PART V: *Appendix*

PAGE 41

TO IMBC FOR INSPIRATION ABOVE AND BEYOND

Many friends have generously given of their time to help with this book. Phil Reid, the best of travel companions. Paul Lundberg, crucial introductions and correcting errors. Beni Wanda, a Dani friend and best of guides. Wayne Knight, superb helicopter pilot. Long-term Roman Catholic priests. John Cutts, a most dynamic and intelligent son of Irian.

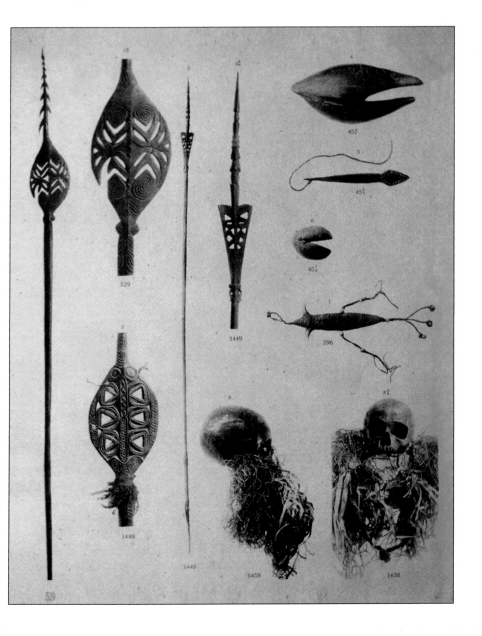

PART I

Introducing Irian Jaya

Irian Jaya, Indonesia's western half of the huge island of New Guinea, offers an unparalleled opportunity to witness peoples just now emerging from the Stone Age. Highland tribesmen still sport their traditional penis gourds, and have only recently traded their stone adzes for steel implements. Still practiced, too, are age-old and very sophisticated farming methods.

The mention of cannibalism here today only produces embarrassed smiles and shrugs, although reports from the southern lowlands suggest that several tribes still practice the ritual. One of the most famous victims may have been Michael Rockefeller, who disappeared after his boat capsized off Irian's southern shore in 1961. But he could just as well have been devoured by Irian's huge sea-going crocodiles — fearsome creatures that may exceed six meters in length.

The 1990s are the ideal time to visit Irian Jaya — though still exotic, a visit no longer means risking your life. The **Baliem Valley** in Irian's highlands lies less than an hour via a daily scheduled flight from **Jayapura**, the provincial capital on the north shore. The Baliem is home to the Dani peoples, who practiced ritual warfare with spears and arrows up until the 1960s, when the government stopped the fighting — almost. Even today, small-scale battles occasionally flare up, with fatalities running to a dozen or more. Steel axes have now joined the more traditional weaponry in hand-to-hand combat, but visitors need not worry — there's no danger to them from these ritual grudge-matches, which are precipitated by disputes over land rights, abducted women, stolen pigs and murdered tribesmen.

Wamena, the administrative center of the Baliem Valley, has an airport, hotels and restaurants, and an interesting market. From here, day hikes lead to traditional highland villages, salt-making pools, and audiences with the gruesome blackened mummies of deceased war chiefs. Longer treks can be made to the lofty, snow-tipped mountains and deep gorges spanned by shaky suspension bridges, through the homelands of seldom-visited tribesmen.

While these traditional peoples are Irian's top drawing card, other attractions clamor for attention. Wildlife fans will be fascinated by the island's great biological diversity. Some 1,500 varieties of birds are found here, including the fierce, flightless cassowary and the beautiful birds of paradise. The mammals are chiefly marsupials, except for the peculiar, hedgehog-like echidna, which lays eggs. Giant monitor lizards and snakes are also interesting, if less sought after, finds.

The variety of plant life on Irian ranges from mangrove swamps to alpine heaths. The jungles and wooded highlands harbor orchids, ferns and strange plants like the carnivorous *Nepenthes,* whose pitcher shaped leaves trap and digest insects.

Biak Island, a main stopover on Garuda's Los Angeles to Denpasar flight, makes a fine base from which to explore the islands off north Irian. The **Padaido Islands**, just off Biak, are fringed with shallow coral reefs. Intrepid explorers can then hire local boats to visit the traditional stilted fishing villages and snorkeling sites on **Supiori**, **Numfor**, **Serui**, and all the way across Cenderawasih Bay to **Roon Island** — reported to be the best diving spot in the world.

Irian still lies far from the beaten track. A visit requires planning, money and time. One doesn't just pop in on the spur of the moment on the way to Bali. Yet it is one of the few places on earth today where one can still experience true adventure.

Overleaf: *Sunset off Amamapare, a shipping center carved out of Irian's swampy south coast.*
Opposite: *A Dani tribesman entertains his fellows by playing a tune on a traditional mouth harp, fashioned of bamboo and string.*

GEOGRAPHY

Huge Island of Enormous Diversity

The island of New Guinea is enormous — 2,400 kilometers end to end and 740 kilometers at the shoulder (1,500 by 450 miles). These 800,000 square kilometers (310,000 sq. mi.) qualify it as the world's second largest island, just behind Greenland. The Indonesian province of Irian Jaya claims the western half of this untamed island; Papua New Guinea, an independent country, occupies the eastern half. Irian's 410,660 square kilometers (158,510 sq. mi.) make up a whopping 22 percent of Indonesia's total land area.

Nowhere else on earth are so many radically different ecological zones packed into such a tightly delimited space — from the towering, jagged peaks rising above the snow line to alpine grasslands, mossy montane and submontane forests, impenetrable foothill jungles, eucalyptus savannas, peat swamps filled with sago palms, and brackish lowland mangroves.

A 2,000 kilometer (1,200 mile) long cordillera of craggy mountains running the length of the island is New Guinea's most distinctive topological feature. The crests of the main divide top the the 3,000 meter mark (10,000 ft.) in many places, and a number of rocky peaks soar above 4,500 meters (15,000 ft.). There are small permanent snowfields and relict glaciers at the highest elevations, and cirques and moraines attest to a history of widespread glaciation.

Rugged highlands

Irian Jaya's highlands consist largely of sedimentary limestones, sandstones and shale of the Tertiary period. This rock has been uplifted and faulted on a massive scale by plate movements — the island's cordillera of mountains traces the line where the Sahul Shelf and the Pacific Ocean Plate meet.

The limestones are particularly impressive, and in many areas have weathered in the tropical climate to fantastically-shaped karst plateaus, spines and towers, especially in the Bird's Head region of western Irian. Volcanic rock is not common in the mountains, but in one of the few places an igneous intrusion has appeared — at Tembagapura in the Sudirman Mountains — the outcrop has proved to be incredibly rich in copper, gold and silver and is now the site of the world's most productive copper mine. (See "Tem-

bagapura" page 142.)

The mountain chain comprises four contiguous ranges. Straddling the Papua New Guinea border, the Wisnumurti (formerly Star) Range is crowned by Mt. Mandala at 4,760 meters (15,603 ft.), and Mt. Yamin at 4,595 meters (15,076 ft.). To the west, the Jayawijaya (Formerly Oranje) Range defines the southern edge of the Baliem Valley — here Mt. Trikora soars to 4,750 meters (15,580 ft.). To the west, Puncak Jayakesuma, or just Puncak Jaya — the pride of the

Sudirman (formerly Nassau) Range — reaches an official height of 4,884 meters (16,020 ft.), the highest elevation between the Himalayas and the Andes. The Charles Luis Range, west of the Paniai (formerly Wissel) Lakes, ends at the "Vogelkop" or Bird's Head Peninsula ("Kepala Burung" in Indonesian).

Rivers and coastal swamps

In drama second only to Irian's spectacular mountains are the steep, south-facing slopes that roll down from 3,000-4,000 meter (10,000-13,000 ft.) ridges to a vast ring of mangrove swamps at the shore. Blanketed by dense forests and scarred by landslides, these steep ridges of sedimentary rock yield within a few kilometers from the coast to gorges cut by short, powerful rivers. The narrow coastal strip, only 20 kilometers (12 mi.) wide southwest of Puncak Jaya, widens considerably to the east. The swamplands near the Papua New Guinea border are vast, reaching 300 kilometers (190 mi.) inland. Several rivers are navigable almost to the mountains.

Intrusions of dark gray diorite punctuate the southern slopes of the ranges between the Baliem Gorge and the Ok Sibyl. These hard, granite-like rocks yielded raw material for the inhabitants' stone axes.

The northern slopes of the mountains descend gradually to a set of convoluted east-west ridges and valleys, yielding to rivers

flowing north to the Pacific instead of the much closer Arafura Sea to the south. The Baliem River system is the only major river reaching to the south coast from the island's interior valleys.

Moving north out of the highlands and toward the Pacific Ocean is the broad Meervlakte or "Lake-Plains," a river basin 200 kilometers (650 mi.) east–west and 35 kilometers (110 mi.) north–south. This forested depression contains the Taritatu (formerly Idenburg) River flowing from the east and the Tariku (formerly Rouffaer) River from the west. The two eventually join to form the Mamberamo, the only waterway reaching far inland from Irian's north shore.

The island fringe

The seas around Irian are dotted with islands, some of note because of their historical importance as the sites of trading outposts or World War II battles. In the southeast, Yos Sudarso Island bears the name of an Indonesian admiral who died in the campaign to wrest Irian from Dutch control. Yos Sudarso is large — 170 by 100 kilometers (100 by 60 mi.) — but low, swampy and separated from the mainland only by a narrow channel.

Off the Bird's Head, Misool Island takes its name from a medicinal bark much prized by the Javanese. Salawati and the Raja Empat Islands dot the seas to the north, and a wide, irregular crescent of islands west of the Bird's Head ends with large Waigeo Island. North of Cenderawasih (Bird of Paradise) Bay, the seas give way to many small islands along with four sizable ones: Biak, Supiori, Numfor and Yapen.

Opposite: *Despite the tropical latitude, permanent snowfields cap the Sudirman Range near Puncak Jaya.* **Above, left:** *The mouth of the Timika River, which empties into the Arafura Sea.* **Above, right:** *Irian's lowland swamps in places reach 300 kilometers (190 mi.) inland.*

FLORA AND FAUNA

Beautiful, Bizarre and Deadly

Possessing as it does such a range of radically different ecological zones, it comes as little surprise that New Guinea's wildlife is so strange and diverse. The largest beast found here is a reptile — the huge saltwater crocodile. The largest land animal is not a mammal but a bird — the ostrich-like cassowary. Most of the island's indigenous mammals are marsupials, and one — the curious hedgehog-like echidna — lays eggs. As if this collection of oddities were not enough, Irian Jaya is also home to some of nature's most beautiful creatures — the fabulous bird of paradise.

A diversity of plant life

Irian has the richest concentration of plant life in all of Indonesia, and perhaps the world — including hundreds of species that are of medicinal importance and over 124 endemic genera. Altogether some 2,700 species of orchids are found here. The island also harbors some very strange plants. The gills of the fungi *Mycena* glow on the darkest nights — for reasons still unknown to scientists. Pitcher plants (*Nepenthes* sp.), whose leaves have evolved to form cups of enzyme-rich water, attract and digest insects. The bulbous base of the giant epiphytic anthouse plant (*Myrmecodia brassii*) found in the subalpine forests of the Kemabu Plateau is honeycombed with passageways — home for swarms of ants, frogs and lizards.

The lush vegetation of Irian is in fact a deceptive cover over poor soils badly leached by heavy rains and containing no rich volcanic material. Mangroves and nipa palms ensnarl the brackish estuaries of the coast. Upstream where the water is less salty, swamp forests replace the mangroves. Here is where the people of Irian harvest the edible sago palm, *Metroxylon* sp. Further inland, the forests are composed mainly of tropical evergreens. In the highland valleys, where slash and burn farming techniques are used, neglected terrain is quickly covered by a tenacious spear grass called *kunia* or *alang-alang*.

The lowland alluvial forests contain valuable timber reserves, making them a major target of the logging industry. The rainforest at altitudes of between 100 and 1,000 meters is also the richest in flowering plants. Irian holds the largest tracts of undisturbed low-

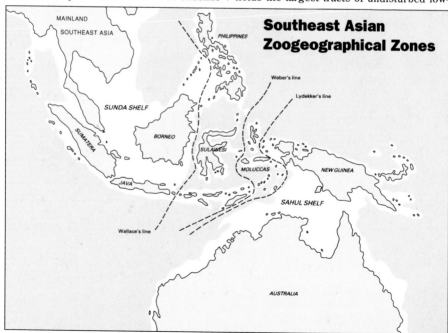

Southeast Asian Zoogeographical Zones

MAINLAND
SOUTHEAST ASIA

PHILIPPINES

Weber's line

Lydekker's line

SUNDA SHELF

SUMATERA

BORNEO

SULAWESI

MOLUCCAS

NEW GUINEA

JAVA

SAHUL SHELF

Wallace's line

AUSTRALIA

land rainforest in Southeast Asia, now that Kalimantan has been largely stripped. Indeed, Irian has the world's second-largest rainforest (after the Amazon), but as logging concessions cover the island, no one can be sure for how long.

At 1,000 to 2,000 meters (3,300 to 6,600 ft.), rainforest trees give way to temperate species encrusted with lichens and festooned with streamers of moss. From the 2,000 meter (6,600 ft.) mark up to the limit of tree growth at around 3,800 meters (12,500 ft.), one finds alpine forests of stunted conifers, shrubs, rhododendrons and rare tree ferns. Above this is a zone of heaths and tundra, then rock, snow and ice.

Naturalist Sir Alfred Wallace

Sir Alfred Russel Wallace opened the world's eyes to Irian's magnificent biological diversity. Between 1854 and 1862, Wallace sent a total of 125,660 specimens back to England, including a staggering 83,200 Coleoptera (beetles). A talented and scrupulously honest writer, Wallace estimates that he traveled 14,000 miles within the archipelago on some 60 to 70 separate journeys.

Wallace was the first to recognize the marked change in faunal types as one moves east of Bali from Asia to Australasia. The large area of biological overlap in between, including Sulawesi, the Moluccas, and Nusa Tenggara, is now called "Wallacea" in his honor. The fauna of New Guinea, lying on the Sahul Shelf and once connected to Australia by a land bridge, is typically Australasian. (See map page 16.)

During his eight years in the archipelago, Wallace spent a total of eight months in what is now Irian — three months on the shores of Doreri Bay, three months on Waigeo Island and two months in Aru. Approaching the coast for the first time, Wallace tingled with anticipation, knowing that "those dark forests produced the most extraordinary and the most beautiful of the feathered inhabitants of the earth" — the birds of paradise. He recalled that the first Portuguese to reach the area, tough, unromantic traders, "were presented with the dried skins of birds so strange and beautiful as to excite the admiration even of those wealth-seeking rovers."

'Birds of the gods'

Long before the world knew of the habitats and habits of the birds of paradise, their feathers enhanced the appearance of the rich and powerful. These brilliant feathers graced the headdresses of fierce janissaries at the 14th century Turkish court, and were *de rigueur* at the Nepalese court and those of

Below: *The tree kangaroo, Irian's largest mammal, has evolved an interesting mechanism to weather the island's heavy rains — its fur slopes downward from a peak on its shoulders.*

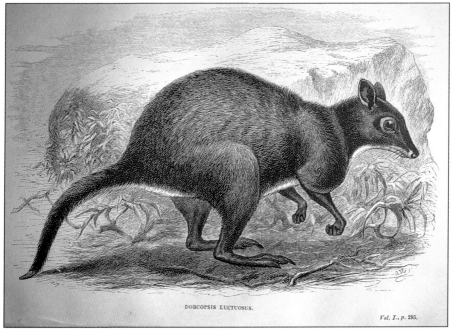

DORCOPSIS LUCTUOSUS.

Vol. I., p. 295.

other colorful potentates. In the 1880s, the Paris fashion world discovered the feathers and thousands of birds were slaughtered to adorn capes, hats and other extravagant accessories before the trade was banned in the 1920s. Unfortunately, the ban has been as full of holes as the smugglers' ocean is wide.

Malay traders called them *manuk dewata* — the gods' birds. The Portuguese, seeing no feet or wings on the skins, called them *passaros de sol,* "birds of the sun." A learned Dutchman, writing in Latin, coined the name, *avis paradiseus,* "bird of paradise."

A great body of myth has developed around these birds, and well into the 18th century Europeans still believed that the birds came from Paradise. After hatching,

they allegedly flew toward the sun whence they received their brilliant colors. They had no feet, and thus had to remain always in the air. This, it was believed, was to prevent them from soiling their plumage. It was also believed that the female laid her eggs and incubated them on the back of the male.

In 1598 the Dutch navigator Jan van Linschoten, wrote: "(N)o one has seen these birds alive, for they live in the air, always turning towards the sun and never lighting on the earth till they die, for they have no feet or wings." Even in 1760, Carolus Linnaeus, the famous Swedish taxonomist, christened the largest species *Paradisea apoda,* meaning "footless paradise bird."

All these myths were simply the result of

the native method of preserving the skins: the wings and feet were cut off, the body skinned up to the beak and the skull removed. The birds were hunted for centuries with bow and arrow, but more recently, poachers employ 30 by 15 meter mist nets to trap the hapless birds.

As a group, Paradisaeidae is characterized by a plumage unequalled by any other family of birds. In several species, large tufts of delicate, bright-colored feathers spring from each side of the body beneath the wings, forming trains or fans or shields. These "nuptial plumes" are seasonal, and for most of the year the birds are drab. The middle feathers of the tail are often elongated into "wires," twisted into fantastic shapes or adorned with the most brilliant metallic hues. Depending on the species, these accessory plumes spring from the head, the back or the shoulders. The color and luster of their plumage is the envy of all other feathered creatures.

Strangely, the plain old crows are their nearest relatives. Paradisaeidae comprises 42 species, of which 36 inhabit New Guinea and its neighboring islands. "The rarer sorts," writes Wallace, "were only found several days' journey in the interior, among rugged mountains, and the skins were prepared by savage tribes who had never even been seen by any of the coast people. It seems as if Nature had taken precautions that her choicest treasures should not be made too common and thus be undervalued."

Other colorful avifauna

New Guinea possesses some 1,500 species and subspecies of birds. Migratory birds transit here from North Asia, New Zealand and Australian during their respective winters. Although the birds of paradise set a high standard, there are other gems in the group — the Victoria crowned pigeon, or *goura,* for example, is no slouch in the show-off department. This large, New Guinea bird sports an overall bluish-grey coloration with a crest of delicate feathers. The anterior of the wings, the shoulders and sometimes the chest, are purplish.

Parrots, cockatoos, and lories brighten up the forests with red, yellow, and purple. Industrious bowerbirds decorate their large nests with bright objects such as flowers and berries, sometimes collecting small piles of objects of a single color.

The cassowary is a large, flightless bird with a nasty reputation. These ugly customers have powerful feet ending in large claws. This formidable weapon has disemboweled more than one human victim. The male cassowary incubates his mate's eggs.

Curious beasts

Marsupials dominate the list of mammals indigenous to Irian. Unlike placental mammals, young marsupials complete their gestation in an external pouch. Tree kangaroos, found in the lower mountain regions, are the largest of Irian's native, land-dwelling mammals. This animal displays a clever adaptation to Irian's torrential downpours. The grain of its fur points "downhill" from the peak of its shoulders, allowing the rain to run off in both directions. (See illustration page 17.)

Other marsupials include the bandicoot and the cuscus — a woolly, tree-dwelling creature with a prehensile tail. Unfortunately for this cat-sized beast, its fur is much appreciated by the locals for personal adornment and cuscus meat is considered a delicacy. The marsupial black-eared giant rat can grow to over 40 centimeters (16 in.) and weigh up to 2 kilos. Huge bats, called flying foxes because of their long snouts, roam the forests on 1.5-meter (5 ft.) wings seeking fruit.

The most unusual mammals in Irian are the spiny anteaters or echidnas (*Tachyglossus* sp. and *Zaglossus* sp.), which along with the Australian duck-billed platypus are the only mammals to lay eggs. When threatened, the spiny anteater sometimes rolls itself in a ball like a hedgehog.

Death adders and goliath frogs

The reptiles of Irian are led by the appropriately named death adder (*Oxyuranus scutellatus*). The venom of this snake will bring death in a few seconds unless the bitten limb is immediately chopped off. A high percentage of Irian's 100 snake species are poisonous, including all 17 species of sea-snakes. One of the most beautiful reptiles is the green tree python (*Chondropython viridis*), a harmless creature with jewel-like markings. Irian is home to 150 species of lizards, including 3-meter monitors, close relatives of the famous Komodo dragon.

Irian's estuarine crocodiles are a threat to life and limb. A 7-meter (23 ft.) specimen that had been terrorizing the Asmat village of Piramat was finally killed in 1970. This rogue beast had taken 55 human victims. Crocodile skins were an important Irianese export in late Dutch times and are becoming so again — there are now 25 crocodile farms in Irian.

There are more frogs in New Guinea than anywhere else, with well over 200 species, some hardy ones found up to 3,850 meters (12,600 ft.). The world's largest frog, the goliath frog (*Conrana goliath*), makes its home here. This 3.4 kilo (7.3 lb.) monster is bigger than a man's head.

Huge lake sawfish prowl Irian's Lake Sentani. This species, which can exceed 5.2 meters (17 ft.), feeds by striking at schools of fish with its saw-like snout, and then gobbling up the hapless victims disabled by the blows. Sentani locals believe their ancestral spirits live in these sawfish and refuse to eat them. Lake Yamur, at the base of the Bird's Head, is one of the very few places in the world that one encounters freshwater sharks.

The variety of insects on Irian is equally

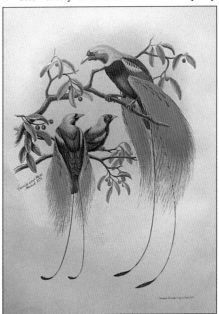

astounding. There are an estimated 75,000 butterfly and moth species, including the beautiful birdwing butterflies of the Arfak Mountains. Irian's 30,000 beetle species include interesting specimens like the capricorn beetle, built like a not-so-miniature tank, whose thumb-sized larvae are prized as food. Some 800 spider species include the formidable giant bird-eaters, whose size and aggressiveness allow them to reverse the usual order of prey and preyed upon.

Opposite: *Italian naturalist L. M. d'Albertis discovered several new birds during four trips to Irian in 1872-1877, including this sicklebill.*
Above: *The raggiana and other birds of paradise have been hunted for centuries for their plumes.*

PREHISTORY

Papuans and Austronesians in Irian

Prior to the arrival of the Portuguese in the early 16th century, there appear but scant references to Irian and its inhabitants. Frizzy-haired men and women appear on some of the friezes at Borobudur but these could just as well represent peoples from islands closer to Java. The *Negarakertagama,* a 14th century panegyric poem dedicated to the powerful East Javanese king of Majapahit, mentions two Irianese territories, Onin and Seran on the southwestern side of the Bird's Head peninsula, but direct control from Java must have been practically non-existent. It is certain however that *prahu*-borne trade between some of the Moluccan islands — perhaps even Java — and the western extremity of what is now Irian existed long before this. Items such as bird of paradise skins and missory bark, unquestionably of Irianese origin, were well-known trade items. And the Sultan of Tidore, for example, long claimed areas in and around west Irian.

The peoples of Irian, black-skinned, hirsute and frizzy-haired, are physically very distinct from Indonesians in the rest of the archipelago. Just when these so-called "Papuans" — relatives of the Australian aboriginals — first arrived in Irian is still a matter of conjecture. Another question involves their relation, if any, to the peoples of Africa. Are the widely scattered dwarf Negrito populations of Southeast Asia evidence of an early migration from the "dark continent," or rather the result of an independent evolution *in situ*?

What is known is that inland forest peoples, living on steep terrain and with little protein in their diet, evolve toward a more resilient dwarfism, where a high ratio of strength to body weight is essential for survival. It is also known that adaptation to high amounts of sunlight produces high melanin

concentrations in the skin. But these facts are of but little help in tracing man's arrival in Irian. And nature has obliterated most traces of New Guinea's earliest inhabitants.

There may also be a link connecting the "Java Man" of a half million years ago to today's Papuans. But in any event, it has been established that, much later, groups related to the Papuans and the Negritós were the true aboriginals of the Indo-Malayan archipelago — and the likely ancestors of today's Papuans.

The Papuan migrations

How did the Papuans reach New Guinea? The first clues date from the Pleistocene era, when periods of glaciation reduced sea levels 100 to 150 meters (300-500 ft.) below their present levels. The history of man and animals in insular Southeast Asia is intimately linked with the resulting submergence and emergence of two great continental shelves at opposite ends of the archipelago: the Sahul in the east and the Sunda in the west. But at no time was there a land bridge stretching all the way across what is now Indonesia — vast stretches of open water had somehow to be crossed. Man was successful in making this crossing, but other placental mammals — except for bats and rats — were not.

The earliest tentative figure for human presence in New Guinea, based by inference on Australian paleoanthropological evidence,

Right: *Asmat stone war axes. Photograph courtesy the American Museum of Natural History.*

is 60,000 years ago. But there is in fact little hard evidence arguing for a date prior to 35,000 to 40,000 years ago, the more widely accepted figures. This is nevertheless very early — fossils of modern man are found throughout the Old World only from about this time.

Even for the later dates, however, linguistic comparisons are unable to relate the distribution of contemporary languages to the earliest migrations, and we have no way of knowing if there were one or many. And the archaeological evidence is meager. A dig has recovered 39,000-year-old stone tools from the Huon Peninsula, but little else from this earliest period.

A later Papuan migration may have coincided with the last glacial peak, which occurred some 16,000 to 18,000 years ago. After that, as the earth's atmosphere warmed, the seas rose as much as 6 meters (20 ft.) above their present level.

The Papuan inhabitants of 18,000 years ago lived in a New Guinea radically different from the one we find today. Ice sheets covered 2,000 square kilometers (800 sq. mi.) of the island and the snow line stood a mere 1,100 meters (3,600 ft.) above sea level. (Today there are only 8 square kilometers of glacier left.) The tree line lay 1,600 meters (5,200 ft.) below the present one and temperatures averaged some 7° Centigrade (12.5° F.) lower.

For many millennia after reaching the island, the Papuans expanded within New Guinea and to neighboring islands, while their aboriginal Australian cousins adapted themselves to a radically different ecology. The two gene pools have been isolated from one another for at least 10,000 years and probably longer.

A linguistic Babel

Linguistic studies show, moreover, that the various Papuan groups have evolved in relative isolation from one another for many millennia, partly because of the island's rugged geography but also because each tribal group is typically in a perpetual state of warfare with its neighbors. As a result, New Guinea, with only .01 percent of the earth's population, now contains 15 percent of its known languages.

Estimates of the number of distinct languages spoken by the 2.7 million natives of New Guinea vary from a whopping 800 down to about 80, depending on one's definition of what constitutes a distinct language. Some languages in Irian Jaya today are spoken by just a handful of people, and at least 80 different languages are spoken by just over a million people in Irian Jaya alone.

In trying to bring order to this linguistic chaos, experts have been forced to divide Irian's many tongues into at least four distinct phyla or families. (Languages in a phylum

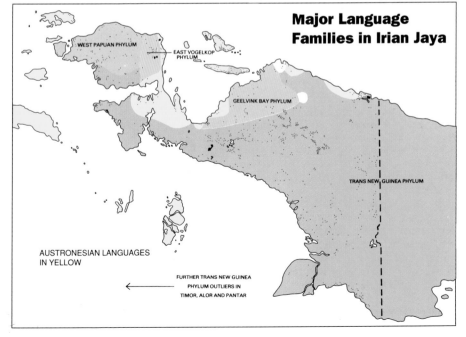

Major Language Families in Irian Jaya

WEST PAPUAN PHYLUM

EAST VOGELKOP PHYLUM

GEELVINK BAY PHYLUM

TRANS NEW GUINEA PHYLUM

AUSTRONESIAN LANGUAGES IN YELLOW

FURTHER TRANS NEW GUINEA PHYLUM OUTLIERS IN TIMOR, ALOR AND PANTAR share less than 5 percent of their basic vocabulary with the languages in another — and by way of comparison, most of the languages of Europe fall into a single family, the Indo-European phylum.) These are the East Bird's Head phylum, the Cenderawasih Bay phylum, the West Irian phylum (which includes north Halmahera) and the Trans-New Guinea phylum. The last is the most widespread on the island, comprising 84 percent of Papuan speakers and 67 percent of the languages.

As the climate of New Guinea warmed, more ecological zones became suitable for human habitation. Horticulture may have begun more than 20,000 years ago, but hunting and gathering remained the basic source of food for many thousands of years later. A lack of systematic archaeological work leaves us with hypotheses and conjectures for the next stages of human development, but it is likely that agriculture, based on taro as the staple, was already in progress 6,000 years ago. There is evidence of irrigation ditches in the highlands by 4,000 B.C.

The seafaring Austronesians

The peoples who are known today as Malays, Indonesians, Filipinos and Polynesians all have a common and glorious ancestry that can be traced back to a handful of hardy seafarers who left the coasts of southern China some 6,000-7,000 years ago. Collectively they are known today as Austronesians (formerly referred to as "Malayo-Polynesians"). Although the accepted wisdom has been that the original Austronesians moved down through mainland Southeast Asia and hence to the islands, contemporary linguistic evidence suggests that this group underwent a gradual expansion as a result of advancements in agriculture and sailing techniques, with Taiwan as the jumping-off point, whence they voyaged through the Philippines to Indonesia and out across the vast reaches of the Pacific and Indian Oceans.

Physically of Mongoloid stock, the Austronesians brought with them a social organization distinguished by what are called bilateral, or non-unilineal, descent — wherein both biological parents are recognized for purposes of affiliation. This contrasts with the unilineal societies of New Guinea and Melanesia which are mostly patrilineal — wherein descent, as in European societies, is recognized through the father — or sometimes the mother, but rarely both.

Austronesian speakers appeared in the islands of Indonesia by about 3,000 B.C. and over the next two millennia, through superior technology and sheer weight of numbers, they gradually displaced the aboriginal negrito and Papuan populations who then lived here. This seemingly inexorable displacement process never took place in New Guinea. The reason for this seems to be a combination of ecological factors and the existence of stable, sufficiently established groups of agriculturally sophisticated Papuans.

The two peoples intermingle

Although the Austronesians never penetrated to the interior of Irian, they settled and intermixed with Papuans along the coasts as well as on the nearby islands, mingling their genes, but imposing their languages. At about this same time — 2,000 B.C. — a major expansion of the Trans-New Guinea phylum of Papuan language speakers also occurred, west from New Guinea to the islands of Timor, Alor and Pantar, where they replaced earlier West Papuan language speakers. These islands had already been settled by Papuan speakers long before the Austronesian arrival, and there were probably two phases of Papuan settlement here: a first taking place many thousands of years earlier, and a second contemporaneous with the Austronesian arrival.

The second Papuan expansion was perhaps due to an agricultural "revolution" that included the domestication of pigs and tubers in New Guinea by at least 4,000 B.C. The Trans-New Guinea languages, strongly influenced by Austronesian loan words, also expanded into the island's central highlands by about 1500 B.C., wiping out traces of earlier diversity there.

A sweet potato revolution

The introduction of the sweet potato, *Ipomoea batatas,* ranks among the most crucial factors in New Guinea's evolution. It was once thought to have been introduced from the New World a few centuries ago by early Portuguese and Spanish navigators. But recently some plant geneticists have arrived at a much earlier date — about A.D. 500. Whenever it started, the *Ipomoea* revolution brought high yields at healthy elevations. Unlike taro, the sweet potato grows well up

Opposite: *Women tend their sweet potatoes in the Baliem Valley. The nutritious sweet potato offers a high yield and grows at high elevations. Its introduction around A.D. 500 was a revolution.*

to 1,600 meters (5,200 ft.) above sea level, allowing its cultivators to settle out of the range of the malarial *Anopheles* mosquito.

The sweet potato allowed for much more intensive agriculture, which together with healthier conditions, resulted in relatively higher population densities in the highlands. Crucial also was the development of a technically brilliant system of parallel or gridiron irrigation ditches allowing for fallow times equal to that of the cropping cycle. More primitive slash-and-burn techniques used elsewhere require 10-20 years of fallow time between crops, resulting in much lower population densities.

In another part of the island, the Marind-Anim of the south coast had their own agricultural revolution. Beds of earth, surrounded by drainage ditches, were here raised in the swamps and planted with yam and taro alternating with bananas, areca and sugar palms — providing food for similarly dense population settlements.

Prehistoric trade

Trade in the eastern islands of the archipelago began long before the common era. Fragrant Timorese sandalwood and Moluccan cloves are mentioned in early Han Chinese texts, and the latter have also been found in ancient Egyptian mummies. In early times this trade was undoubtedly accomplished through many intermediaries, with east Indonesian products ending up in China and Rome only very indirectly via the powerful maritime kingdoms of western and central Indonesia. It is unlikely that ocean-going sailing ships from China, India and the Middle East, which relied upon the seasonal monsoon winds, made regular voyages to eastern Indonesian waters much before about A.D. 1000.

Large, elegant bronze kettledrums provide the earliest concrete evidence of contact between mainland Asia and the New Guinea area. A fragment of one of these drums, cast by the lost wax process, has been found in western Irian. These drums — or more properly, idiophones, since they are more gongs than drums — were produced between about 400 B.C. and A.D. 100 in the area of Dongson, in what is now North Vietnam. Although metals were widely worked in Southeast Asia by 1500 B.C., no earlier metal artifacts have been discovered in Irian, and it is thought that these drums, which have been discovered elsewhere in the archipelago, were trade items brought from other areas of Southeast Asia.

Wet-rice agriculture, another import from the Asian mainland, was introduced in the archipelago between about 1000 B.C. and 500 B.C., albeit on a small scale. Due to ecological factors and the local preference for tubers, rice culture never developed on any large scale in Irian.

PEOPLES OF IRIAN

Cannibals, Cultivators and 'Big Men'

Even today, members of tribes unknown to the outside world occasionally pop out of the jungles of Irian Jaya. The major highland and coastal groups have been identified and catalogued, but a vast area between the coasts and the mountains remains concealed by a canopy of thick vegetation. As recently as 1987, members of two unknown groups surfaced. Representatives of the one tribe immediately disappeared again into the bush; those of the other took the first tentative steps into the outside world of modern medicine and steel axes. These latter tribesmen, distinguished by long, quill-like ornaments jutting straight up from holes in their nostrils, spoke an unknown language.

The many ethnic groups of Irian, speaking some 80-800 distinct languages and at least again as many dialects, are impossible to describe fully. Many, perhaps most, are barely known outside their own ranks, and only a handfull have been studied by Western ethnographers. The best known are the Asmat of the south coast near Agats and the Dani of the Baliem Valley, and the economy and customs of several others have been systematically recorded. Although impossible to neatly classify, for the purposes our discussion we have fit the major groups into rough divisions, chiefly according to ecology and agricultural techniques.

Coastal swamp dwellers

Nature has blessed Irian's malarial lowland swamps with an abundance of sago palms and fish. The trunk of the sago palm provides abundant starch, and fish provide necessary protein. In areas where stands of sago palm are widely dispersed, the populations lead a semi-nomadic life, living in "portable" villages. Coastal tribes near large stands of sago and major rivers have settled in villages averaging 300 up to 1,000 inhabitants.

The broad lowland plains of southern Irian, a band along the north coast, and the southern fringe of the Bird's Head are all inhabited by swamp dwelling tribes. The best known of these are the Marind-Anim and the Asmat, infamous for their (former) head-hunting and ritual cannibalism. The Asmat have also achieved world renown for their superb wood sculptures.

Asmat head-hunting formed the core of a complex belief system essential to their survival. Asmat leaders possessed charismatic power, dominating through force of personality and ruthlessness. These men were feared and obeyed because they displayed an unpredictable predilection for violence and seemed to possess magical powers. Whereas Dani ritual warfare (a rather less serious variety than that practiced by the fierce Asmat)

continues, albeit on a much smaller scale than in the past, Asmat head-hunting has been stopped by the government. (See "The Asmat," page 132.)

The Austronesians

In other coastal areas, garden and tree crops replace the sago palm, though fishing retains its importance. Many tribes on the northern coasts of Irian and neighboring islands speak Austronesian languages that are very different from the Papuan languages found throughout the rest of the island. Historically, these groups have been involved in trade with the sultanate of Tidore, the Chinese, the Bugis and other groups from islands to the west. Bird of paradise skins and slaves were the principal exports, along with whatever nutmeg could be taken from the Fakfak area.

Austronesian influences can be seen in the "raja" leadership system practiced among these groups, perhaps adopted from the sultanates of Ternate, Tidore and Jailolo. With their political power cemented by control of trade, some rajas controlled wide areas embracing several ethnic groups, from seats of power in the Raja Empat Islands, in the Sorong area, around Fakfak or in the Kaimana region.

A somewhat different system was found in the Austronesian areas around Biak, Yapen, Wandaman Bay and east of Manokwari. Here some villagers practiced a system of hereditary rule while the leaders of others were self-made, charismatic leaders or great war leaders.

Forest dwellers

Inland from the coastal areas, in the foothills and valleys of Irian, various tribes practice primitive gardening and pig husbandry supplemented by hunting and gathering. Swidden agriculture yields taro and yams, with sweet potatoes being of secondary importance. For some groups in this zone, a trade in pigs and cowrie shells was extremely important. In the interior of the Bird's Head, the Maibrat (or Aymara) ethnic group and surrounding tribes carried on a complex ritual trade involving *kain timur* — antique cloths from eastern Indonesia — which were obtained from coastal peoples in exchange for pigs and foodstuffs from the interior.

Every two years the Maibrat "Big Men" organized a huge feast involving payments to relatives and economic transactions between groups. The Maibrat believed that death and illness were the work of ancestral spirits. Good relations among the living, achieved through gift-giving, were essential lest the ancestral spirits be angered.

Some unacculturated ethnic groups live in the jungles upriver from Senggo on the south coast, and in several areas below and south of the central mountain wall. Cannibalism is frequently reported and surely practiced here. In some areas, it is believed that deaths are the result of witchcraft and a deceased's relatives must find the culprit and eat him (or her). One group believes that a sleeping deity will be awakened if the tribe receives foreign influences, with disasterous results. So they systematically reject — with arrows and spears if necessary — missionaries, government workers, airplanes, steel axes, nylon fishnets, nails and even tiny metal fishhooks.

Highland 'phallocrypts'

The well-known Dani are but one of many highland groups living in the rugged cordillera that stretches 1,200 kilometers (750 mi.) along the spine of Irian. Linguists tell us that Papua New Guinea's highland languages form a single phylum and Irian's another, although the division is not as arrow-straight as the border suggests. Irian's highland phylum comprises four language groups: Greater Dani; Dem; Uhundini (Damal) and Amung; Egaki (Kemandonga) and Moni. These families are split further into some 12 major sub-groups, each with several distinct dialects which are sometimes

mutually unintelligible. The Greater Dani, for example, are split into Western, Southern and Central groups. The Western Dani alone number some 70,000 while the two groups found in the Baliem Valley — the Southern Dani and Central Dani — together number another 50,000 people.

One sartorial trait distinguishes all of Irian's highlanders — they are "phallocrypts" (penis sheath wearers). Or at least all *were* until this eye-catching wardrobe

Opposite: *A Biak islander wearing a cassowary feather mantle. The peoples of Biak are of Austronesian descent.* **Above:** *An older Dani woman, dressed in marriage finery. The Dani, like most of Irian's highlanders, are Papuan.*

caught the attention of some puritanical missionaries. However, there is less pressure on the highlanders to wear clothes today than in the past, as both the Christians and the government have toned down their campaigns.

Highlanders practice pig husbandry and sweet potato farming. *Ipomoea* cultivation, featuring crop rotation, short fallow periods, raised mounds and irrigation canals, attains a peak of sophistication in the Baliem Valley. The first highland settlers here some 25,000 years ago relied on taro and yams as staples, adapting to the subsequent introduction of sugar cane, bananas, and much later, the sweet potato.

To the west of the Baliem, around Enarotali, live 10,000 Moni tribesman.

Neighboring the Moni are the Amungne, also numbering about 10,000. In recent years, the Amungne have had a tough time — their proximity to the Freeport copper mine forced a relocation, and malaria claimed many of the migrants. In the late '70s, some fell victim to dissident political activity.

The Western Dani

The Western Dani inhabit the highlands between Enarotali and the Grand Baliem Valley. The introduction of the Irish potato, which can withstand frost and cold, has allowed some of them to settle in ecological zones up to an elevation of 3,000 meters (10,000 ft.). The Western Dani have been responsive to the efforts of missionaries and the government, and have historically been far less warlike than their neighbors in the Baliem, as they farm far less fertile soil and consequently have less excess population and time to expend on warfare. The Baliem Dani's proclivity for warfare is considered to be a product of the spare time resulting from good soil and sophisticated agricultural techniques. (For more on the Baliem Valley Dani, see "The Dani," page 102.)

The Jale

The Yali tribe, numbering some 20,000, inhabit the isolated Silimo Valley, some 30 kilometers (19 mi.) southwest of Wamena. The group is distinguished by outfits consisting of numerous rattan hoops with a long penis-sheath sticking out from underneath. They maintain separate men's and ritual houses which are intricately painted. Their agricultural practices are marked by elaborate, walled gardens.

The Jale speak a language related to Dani. Their name comes from the Dani word *jale-mo,* meaning "the lands to the west." The Jale live in formidable terrain, and the rugged mountains delayed the arrival of both missionaries and the government. Though contacted in the late 1950s by the Brongersma Expedition, the first permanent outside presence was a Protestant mission established in the Jale-mo Valley in 1961.

When the first airstrip was built at the mission, one or two cowrie shells was still an acceptable daily wage and most of the Jale had only heard rumors of steel axes. The missionaries traded axes to acquire land and pigs, introducing the metal tool's widespread use. The Protestants began a school and offered medical aid including a cure for the festering skin ulcers called gramboisea (yaws) that plagued the highlands. Yaws, was eradicated in 1964.

Also in 1964, anthropologist Klaus Friedrich Koch arrived in Jale-mo, where he learned the language and did research for a book entitled *War and Peace in Jalemo.* Like the Dani, the Jale are farmer-warriors, but they live in a much more hostile environment. They responded well to the mission-sponsored introduction of new plants such as peanuts, cabbage and maize, as well as to animal husbandry — placing great demands on the first imported stud hog. By the time Koch left the field in 1966, there were already six landing strips in Jale-mo, opening this area to the outside world.

But the next year, the mission maintained

by the Dutch Protestant Gerrit Kruijt and his Biak preacher encountered a serious public relations problem. It seems that the preacher and his minister were dallying with the local women and, as Robert Mitton writes in *The Lost World of Irian Jaya,* "the locals decided that they had had enough of the Good Word, burned down the missionary's house and ate his Biak preacher and twelve of his assistants. Fortunately for them, the missionaries were on leave."

And in 1968, two Protestant missionaries, Australian Stan Dale and American Phil Masters, were killed and eaten while hiking from Koruppun to Nimia (see "Missionaries," page 44). Mitton refers to this area as "true cannibal country." While anxiously waiting for their helicopter amidst hostile natives, Mitton writes, "we could have been eaten and defecated by the time it got to us." When they were finally rescued, the natives shot farewell arrows at the helicopter.

The Kim Yal

The Kim Yal (sometimes called Eipomek or Mek) were one of the last major groups to take their place on the ethnographic map.

A pygmy group, the Kim Yal are peaceful folk. Like the Jale, they also dress in rattan hoops, resembling electric dynamos, but are not nearly as aggressive as the Jale. This in spite of their appearance — many of the men still wear bones in their noses, a cannibal cliché. Added color is provided by headdresses fashioned from bird of paradise feathers, or those taken from cockatoos and cassowaries. The Kim Yal's long, thin drums are painted black with red and white motifs.

Their isolation was ended by construction of a missionary air strip and the arrival of Summer Linguistic Institute researchers. The mission settlement of Kosorik is now either an exhausting 5-day trek or a 20-minute flight from Wamena.

The Ekari: stone age capitalists

Furthest to the west of Irian's highlands, in the fertile Paniai Lakes and Kamu Valley region, live 80,000 Ekari (also known as Kapauku) tribesmen. One anthropologist, Leopold Pospisil, has called them "primitive capitalists" for their acquisitiveness and desire to make money.

Of all highland groups, the Ekari have proved the most responsive to government programs such as improved animal husbandry and agricultural techniques. The first contact with the West came in 1938. One sub-

division of the group came under strong Roman Catholic influence after 1948 while others hosted Protestant missionaries.

Many groups in Melanesia are led by non-hereditary chiefs called "Big Men" who achieve their status through personal initiative. In Irian, such Big Men rise to their position through skills in war, oratory and trade, in varying combinations. The Ekari chiefs (*tonowi*) are an extreme example of wealth accumulating Big Men, depending on successful pig breeding, which in turn requires a large, polygamous household. This enables the leader to extend credit by lending pigs and to show his generosity to his followers.

The Ekari see life in thoroughly economic terms. They have no concept of a gift —

everything is leased, rented or loaned with elaborate calculations of credit and interest. Just about everything can be settled with suitable payments, including crimes such as rape, adultery and murder. A fee was even charged for raising a child.

After Dr. Pospisil gave the tribe a lecture on agriculture, he was given several chickens — the Ekari remembered what he had told them earlier about being paid to lecture to students in the United States.

Opposite: *An older Dani warrior wearing grease and a cuscus fur hat.* **Above:** *Moni tribesman. The 10,000 Moni, who make their home near Enarotali in the Sudirman range, are one of the lesser known of Irian's highlands peoples.*

The Ekari, who keep all accounts in their heads, work with a highly developed decimal system, which repeats at 60. Numbers are crucial. When Pospisil showed them a photo of a pretty smiling girl, the Ekari counted teeth. In a photo of a skyscraper, it was the number of windows. Boys considered it a special favor to be allowed to count the white man's "money," a collection of various shells and beads. The anthropologist was kept well advised, ahead of time, when his cash flow was getting behind. Not surprisingly, the Ekari became experts at mathematics when schools opened in their homeland.

Most unusual for a traditional culture, the Ekari have no communal property. Everything is owned, including each section of an irrigation ditch, a part of a road or footpath, even a wood-and-liana suspension bridge, wherein each participant in the construction project "owns" the trunks and lianas he brings to the project.

Conspicuous consumption is taboo: the most valuable shell necklaces are loaned or rented for ceremonies. Persistent stinginess can lead to capital punishment — execution by a kinsman's arrow.

The Paniai Lakes region is fertile when properly cultivated. In addition to the three existing lakes, Paniai, Tage and Tigi, there is another that began to dry out some 15 centuries ago, leaving behind the swampy Kamu Valley. Lake products are harvested exclusively by women, who collect crayfish, dragonfly larvae, tadpoles, waterbugs, frogs, lizards, birds' eggs, vegetables and fruits. The Ekari women know how to extract the maximum protein from these resources.

Ekari women: prized possessions

Women also play a key role in the slash and burn agriculture practiced along the slopes and in the irrigated cultivation of sweet potatoes in raised beds along the valley bottom. The men do the heavy work of clearing, fencing and laying out the irrigation works, then the women take over the planting, weeding and harvesting. Pigs, the principal source of wealth, are also in the care of women.

Wives are thus a great source of wealth, prestige and power. Pigs and shells serve as the currency for loans, bride prices, fines, and for purchasing land or trade goods. There are frequent pig markets, and animals and goods are required for small ceremonies. Every six years or so, an elaborate communal event called a *juwo* draws up to 2,000 participants. Aside from the business of buying,

selling and trading pigs, the *juwo* includes dances where young people woo each other with ornaments and clever phrases.

Women obviously do not come cheap here. In the old days, a bride would cost an average of some 120 old cowrie shells and 120 new ones, 300 glass beads, three shell necklaces and one large female pig. After inflation hit and trade goods became common (around 1975), a girl's price skyrocketed to 300 heirloom cowries, five large pigs (worth US$1,000), a dozen shirts, five blankets, five pots, a machete or two, a steel ax and, for an unusually pretty worker, a sewing machine or typewriter. No one wanted glass beads or shell necklaces any more.

Traditional Ekari religion

The Ekari creator was omnipotent, omniscient, omnipresent and… nonexistent. Only after missionaries arrived did the Ekari name their creator, Ugatame. They believed that since all good and evil came from this being, man had no free will — a most Calvinist philosophy. But religion occupied little of the natives' attention. Of the 121 tenets of Ekari belief compiled by Pospisil, only 14 dealt with the supernatural.

Christian missionary efforts ran into some problems. The Ekari refused to come to church after one of the missionaries stopped giving out free tobacco upon attendance. "No tobacco, no heleluju," said the men. And because natives in the highlands suffer from the cold, the Christian hell seemed like a nice place — warm and without the need to gather fuel for fires. (See "Missionaries," page 43.)

Historically, the Ekari had little contact with the outside world. They made periodic trips to the salt springs in Moni country just to the east, and participated irregularly in shell trade with tribes bordering the Arafura Sea. This last was irregular because it was dangerous — one could lose both one's head and one's trade goods at the hands of coastal cannibals.

First contacts with the West

In 1937, the Ekari saw an airplane fly overhead for the first time. The pilot, a certain Lieutenant Wissel, was credited with discovering the area and the lakes were named after him. (In 1962, the name was changed to Paniai.) Even many years after the event, the

Opposite: *A Moni woman and her child. The Moni live in the Irian highlands near Enarotali.*

Ekari clearly remembered exactly what they were doing when the plane came. In 1939, a Dutch government post was established at Enarotali and missionaries soon followed. World War II interrupted the process of modernization. The Japanese soldiers forced the tribesmen to participate in labor gangs and to feed them, leading to resistance and deaths on both sides.

After the war, the Dutch returned and the pace of change picked up. Thanks to the good advice of Roman Catholic priests, the Ekari radically improved the utilization of their lands by building large-scale irrigation ditches to prevent flooding. New crops and livestock caught on quickly, including coffee, chickens (for meat and feathers but not for eggs), ducks, geese and rabbits. For some reason, tomatoes never caught on as food but became wildly popular when boys realized their tremendous potential for play fights.

The construction in 1958 of an airstrip at the western edge of the Kamu Valley, which brought in cash wages, ended the Ekari youths' dependence on loans from their rich elders, leading to a loss of influence and prestige for the older generation.

The Ekari became long-distance traders. They even began to rent missionary airplanes to take pigs and other trade items to outlying areas. Dr. Pospisil, who wanted a ride on one of these flights, was told he could — for a fee. He was directed to sit in back with the pigs. When he objected because he wanted to take photos, he was allowed to sit next to the pilot — for an added charge.

The ending of warfare and the speedy acceptance of Western medicine led to a population increase which Dr. Pospisil termed "catastrophic" in some areas. Many Ekari left to seek a livelihood outside their homeland, especially after a road connected the Kamu Valley with the district capital of Nabire. By 1975, over 2,000 Ekari had settled there. In Nabire, the traditional Ekari pragmatism and economic philosophy has served them well. Ekari couples are famous for their thrift, hard work, and purposeful accumulation of capital. No other highland tribe has entered Indonesia's modern economy with nearly as much vigor.

Need for further study

As one author put it, Irian's "ethnographic blanks" are many. The largest remains the Fakfak Peninsula and the lowlands of the southern Bird's Head. Other areas needing work include the regions south and east of Jayapura, the whole of the lakes region of the Mamberamo River and its tributaries, the Etna Bay region, and the southern Casuarina Coast, including the great stretches of swampland spreading inland to the mountains. Difficult access and political problems have kept many areas of Irian off-limits for ethnographers.

EUROPEANS IN IRIAN

Rumors of Gold and Exotic Trade

Within a few months of the conquest of Malacca in 1511 by the Portuguese, an expedition was dispatched to locate the fabled spice islands. Some sources state that Antonio D'Abreu, the captain of this pioneer expedition, sighted Irian's coast in 1512. We doubt this claim. But soon thereafter, references to New Guinea begin to appear in the western literature.

In 1521, 27 months out of Spain, Antonio Pigafetta, the chronicler of Magellan's epic world circumnavigation, received a first whiff of (false) information about Irian while loading cloves in Ternate: "...the king of these heathens, called Raja Papua, is exceedingly rich in gold and lives in the interior of the island."

In 1526, the first Portuguese "governor" of the Moluccas, Jorge de Meneses, landed on Waigeo Island. Meneses was sailing on the northwest monsoon to take up a new post at Ternate, when he was driven eastward by adverse winds. Meneses baptized the island Ilhas dos Papuas from the Malay word *papuwah,* meaning "frizzy haired."

Search for the 'Isla de Oro'

After this initial forced landing, the more dynamic Spaniards made contact with Irian as a result of their colonization of the Philippines. In Mexico, on the other side of the Pacific, Hernan Cortez, that prince of the conquistadores, heard also reports of this island of gold. Already in Mexico, and soon in Peru, the Spaniards had plundered a vast store of gold from the Aztecs and Incas. But this had been accumulated over generations, and after their initial euphoria, the Spaniards had to settle for the more mundane mining of silver. But if the Americas held no El Dorado, why not seek one on the other side of the Pacific?

In 1528 Cortez equipped and sent one of his lieutenants, Alvaro de Saavreda, to relieve a Spanish outpost under siege at Tidore by the Portuguese — and, not so incidentally, to discover and conquer the "Isla de Oro." While trying to return to Mexico from the Moluccas, Saavreda reached a large island, probably Biak, which he thought was the island of gold. Spending one month among "naked black people," Saavreda made plans for further discovery and settlement even

though not a trace of gold was found. He tried twice to return to Mexico along the equator but was turned back both times by contrary winds. Later, the Spaniards discovered that the only way to reach the Americas from Asia was to sail north to the latitude of Japan before catching the winds that would carry them east.

In 1537, the ever-optimistic Cortez directed Hernan Grijalva to discover the island of gold. The expedition ended in disaster — not only did they find no gold, but the crew mutinied and murdered their captain. The disintegrating ship was abandoned in Cenderawasih Bay, and the seven survivors were then captured and enslaved by the natives, becoming Irian's first white "settlers." Years later they were ransomed by the Portuguese governor of Ternate.

Ynigo Ortiz de Retes, another Mexican-based Spanish captain, took the honor of giving New Guinea its name while claiming it for the King of Spain in 1545. He chose the name, Nueva Guinea, either because of the natives' resemblance to Africans or because of the island's location on the other side of the globe from the "dark continent." New Guinea thereafter appeared on Mercator's 1569 world map.

Retes' explorations dispelled the illusion of easy gold for the taking, so Spain soon lost interest. (There in fact was plenty of gold in New Guinea, but the first gold rush, in Laloki, near Port Moresby, did not take place until 1878.) The last Spanish exploration of New Guinea occurred in 1606. Torres, a Portuguese in the service of Spain (as had been Magellan), sailed the length of New Guinea's south coast and, in two places, landed and claimed possession for Spain. The annexation was ephemeral, but the strait Torres discovered still bears his name. He was first to prove that Australia was separate from New Guinea. Spain maintained the fiction of its claim to New Guinea, based on Torres' voyage, until the treaty of Utrecht in 1714 formally "relinquished" the island to Holland and England.

In an era of conflicting claims, might made right. In her push for a monopoly on the spice trade in the Moluccas, Holland muscled aside the Spaniards, the Portuguese and, for good measure, her own English allies. Nor did the Dutch neglect explorations to the east. In 1606, the same year that Torres made his discovery, Dutch navigator Willem Jansz sailed along New Guinea's west and south coasts. Also looking for gold, he touched land at various points, including the mouth of what has since been called the

Opposite: *Early explorers steam up Irian's jungle rivers.* **Below:** *Early colonial explorers found Irian's natives, particularly the coastal tribes, to be quite hostile. Much of this ill will was due to the slave trade that flourished in the archipelago.*

Digul River. Ten years later, two more Dutchmen, Le Maire and Schouten, surveyed New Guinea's north coast, including the islands of Cenderawasih Bay. Then, in 1623, Jan Carstensz sighted snow-capped peaks while sailing along Irian's southern coast. His reports were ridiculed in Europe, as no one believed that there could be snow so near the equator (4° S). None of the doubters bothered to check with the Spaniards about the Andes, and 200 years would pass before whites saw the snows of Kilimanjaro.

Birds of paradise and slaves

Although Irian harbored no gold, there were nevertheless valuable trade items emanating from the island, as the Dutch belatedly discovered. Javanese, Bugis, Bandanese and Seramese traders were conducting highly profitable forays to the west coast of Irian. In exchange for Javanese brass gongs, Chinese porcelain, cloth and metal implements, the traders received massoi bark (a medicinal prized by the Javanese, taken orally or as an oil smeared on the body to cure various illnesses, including venereal disease), an inferior quality of nutmeg (whose export irked the Dutch monopolists), trepang (dried sea cucumbers, a Chinese delicacy), tortoiseshell, pearls, bird of paradise skins and very valuable slaves.

From their bases in the nutmeg islands of Banda and clove-producing Ambon, the Dutch sent out their own trading ships but soon ran afoul of the "treachery" of the Irianese. Not without justification, the Dutch blamed the hostile attitude of the Irianese on the forcible capture of slaves by other traders. Muslims from Seram Laut practiced the most effective means of control of Irian's trade. A contemporary Dutch account states that the Seram Muslims married Irianese wives ("in which they are not very choice") and then instructed the children of these unions in the Muslim faith. Through these relatives, the Seram Laut men controlled Irian's trade.

In 1660 the Dutch East India Company recognized the Sultan of Tidore's sovereignty over "the Papuan Islands in general" while signing an "internal alliance" with the sultan. The treaty stipulated that all Europeans, except the Dutch, were forbidden in the area. The Dutch also reinforced the brutal Tidorese tribute-collecting flotillas to increase the sultan's authority and wealth.

While the Dutch were quite successful in maintaining a spice monopoly in the Moluccas, Irian was too far away for effective control. The great French explorer Bougainville initiated a round of expeditions to New Guinea in 1768. The prince of navigators, James Cook, having made a series of historic discoveries in the Pacific, rediscovered the Torres Strait in 1770, then had a run-in with Irianese natives who apparently attacked him with an incendiary mixture which behaved like exploding, but noiseless, gunpowder. Other early sailor-geographers to visit New Guinea included Dampier, Dumont d'Urville and two particularly bothersome (to the Dutch) Britons.

In 1775, Thomas Forrest of the British East India Company landed at Doreri Bay, near present-day Manokwari, on Cenderawasih Bay. He was looking for a source of spices outside the Dutch sphere. Forrest was told that no Dutch "burghers" traded there — only Chinese, who easily obtained passes from the Sultan of Tidore and flew Dutch colors. They were trusted not to deal in spices. Forrest learned that these traders brought steel tools, weapons and Chinaware to exchange for massoi, ambergris, trepang, tortoise shell, bird of paradise skins and slaves.

Another Briton, John McCluer, stopped on the southwest coast of Irian in 1791. His name then stuck to the gulf which he correctly mapped as almost cutting off the Bird's Head from the body. After Irian's integration into Indonesia, the name of the bay was changed to Berau. McCluer found some nutmeg in Irian, but of the inferior elongated variety, not the prized round type.

European outposts established

Irian's first European settlement was a disaster. Without adequate knowledge of local conditions, the British Captain John Hayes chose a spot on Doreri Bay based on an account of Forrest's brief stopover. He named the settlement New Albion and claimed the area for an unwilling Britain. Acting on McCluer's hunch that Irian might be a good base from which to launch a British spice trade, Hayes was elated to find nutmeg trees, dyewood and teak, and dreamed of great economic potential. On his own account and without official backing, the captain brought a group of 11 European settlers and an equal number of Indian *sepoys* to plant missory and nutmeg trees.

The settlers built Fort Coronation to defend themselves against native hostility and an expected Dutch attack. But the Dutch did not need to bother — after 20 months native arrows, a lack of supplies and disease forced the evacuation of the colony. All the men who had not been killed or taken as slaves by the natives were by this time ill. To add insult to injury, the quality of spices gathered was very disappointing, and the British East India Company declined to even recognize the settlement. The survivors spent six months on Seram as guests of Prince Nuku, a bitter enemy of the Dutch. After that, the sorry settlers were repatriated to Calcutta.

The next European colony did not fare much better. Stung into action by false rumors of a British trading post somewhere in southwest Irian, Pieter Mercus, the Dutch governor of the Moluccas, sent an official expedition in 1826 to claim New Guinea's south coast up to the 141st parallel. Expedition leader Lieutenant Kolff published a most interesting account of the effort.

Based on Kolff's report, a government post and colony named Merkussoord was established on Triton Bay. The beautiful but malarial harbor, on the underside of the Bird's Head, hosted the colony for 10 years, until 1838. Fort du Bus, built of stone, was named for the Belgian Viscount du Bus de Ghisignies, governor-general of the Dutch East Indies. The fort's garrison consisted of a lieutenant, a military doctor, 11 unhappy Europeans and 20 despondent Javanese soldiers and their families. A scowling group of 10 Javanese convict laborers were stuck with all the dirty work. Some Malay Muslims voluntarily joined the colony and Seramese trading boats called regularly. Malaria finally forced the abandonment of the colony.

Prompted again by British activities, in 1848 the Dutch reinforced the Sultan of Tidore's nominal control of Irian's north coast. An 1850 report of the sultan's yearly tribute-gathering *hongi* expeditions describes them as unabashed excercises in pillage, rape and abduction.

Around this time, official accounts indicate that Irian's most important exports to Ternate were trepang, tortoiseshell and massoi, with lesser quantities of cedar, ebony, sandalwood, rubber, pearls and copra leaving the island. An indeterminate number of slaves and highly prized bird of paradise skins round out the list.

The plumes were traded to Persia, Surat and the Indies, where the rich wore them in their turbans and used them to decorate their horses. Europeans who ridiculed the Orientals' penchant for these feathers were soon obliged to buy their wives French-

designed hats made from them.

The Dutch early claimed sovereignty in New Guinea but were a long time in following up with direct administrative control, were finally prodded into action by developments on the other side of the border. In 1884, a British protectorate was proclaimed at Port Moresby in eastern New Guinea and, in the same year, the German Imperial flag was raised on the Island's northeastern coast. Fifteen years later, the Dutch finally established two permanent posts in the west, at Fakfak and Manokwari. The boundary with the British was settled in 1895 and with the Germans in 1910. It followed the 141st parallel with the exception of a slight westward blip at the Fly River.

In 1902 a post was founded at Merauke as an embarrassed response to complaints that the theoretically Dutch-controlled subjects regularly crossed the "border" to bring back British-administered trophy heads. The habits of the tribes of southeast Irian, in this case the fierce Marind-Anim, were responsible for the Dutch names given to two rivers in the area: Moordenaar (Murderer) and Doodslager (Slaughterer).

Above: *Father Tillemans poses in the Irian highlands with a Tapiro dwarf. The first modern Western explorers in Irian were naturalists and traders; later, these were replaced by missionaries and anthropologists.*

EXPLORATION OF IRIAN

Naturalists, Mountaineers Map the Island

For a long time after the Dutch took formal control of Netherlands New Guinea, their administration amounted to little more than a name on a map. One observer of the situation described Netherlands New Guinea as: "the stepchild of the Indies, neglected backwater against foreign intrusions, a place for tours of punishment duty by delinquent civil servants and of exile for nationalist leaders." But if Dutch administrators ignored Irian, a small but hardy group of explorers — Dutch, English, and American — boldly charting the island's wildlife, geography and peoples.

Englishman Sir Alfred Russel Wallace was the first in a line of distinguished biologists to visit the island. Wallace spent eight years in the archipelago collecting specimens and theorizing about patterns of speciation. Bursting with initiative and energy, he sent back to Britain an incredible number of specimens —

mammals, reptiles, birds, shells and insects. He also postulated the existence of a biogeographical boundary dividing Asian and Australian species — now called the Wallace Line — where glaciation never lowered the seas sufficiently to allow for an overland spread of wildlife species. (See "Flora and Fauna," page 16.)

Wallace spent three months on the shores of Doreri Bay, two months in the Aru islands and three months on Waigeo. In addition to a description of his biological work, his famous work, *The Malay Archipelago,* includes accounts of the lives and habits of the natives in the areas he visited as well as an account of an early Dutch expedition along Irian's north coast. Wallace also reported on trading patterns in Irian, describing the yearly monsoon-borne sailing fleets that left south Sulawesi and spent several months at Dobo in the Aru Islands.

Biologist-explorers who followed in Wallace's footsteps included Italians L. M. d'Albertis and Odoardo Beccari, who trekked in the Arfak Mountains of the Bird's Head trading Venetian beads for birds and insects; and Nicolai Miklucho Maclay, who spent four months at Triton Bay, making his way a short distance inland seeking exotic local species.

The Dutch explore Irian's interior

After a late start, Holland unleashed a veritable flood of exploration at the beginning of

FRANK HURLEY

this century: 140 expeditions to the interior between 1900 and 1930. The most important of these were military-sponsored missions that began in 1907. At times the parties included over 800 men and had budgets totaling millions of guilders. Blanks on the map were quickly filled in and the newly discovered peaks took the names of Dutch royalty.

The Dutch were first-rate explorers but terrible storytellers. One laconic example: "Today was very difficult. We advanced only 750 meters." In spite of themselves, circumstances sometimes forced a sense of humor on the normally dour Dutch. When Mt. Goliath, which had already been named, was finally climbed by a team under Van der Ven, a tribe of short-statured locals was baptized the "Goliath pygmies."

In 1905, the Dutch steamer *Valk* chugged 560 kilometers (350 mi.) up the Digul River's winding course from the south coast, a distance of only 227 kilometers (140 mi.) as the crow flies. A new snow-crested peak was sighted and dubbed Wilhelmina Top in honor of the Dutch queen. Other expeditions steamed up the Mappi River to a lake of the same name, then onto the Eilanden (Islands) River — now Pulau Pulau — and its tributaries, the Vriendschaps (Friendship) and Wildeman.

While the upriver jaunts were relatively comfortable, overland treks to the central highlands tested the mettle of the toughest explorers, and the logistics of keeping such teams supplied were mind-boggling. The high glacier fields and snow-capped peaks were the most challenging sites to explore, not so much because of the mountaineering skills required (the Himalayas, Andes and even the Alps require greater technical proficiency), but because of the effort required simply to arrive at the base of the mountains. As was the case earlier, it was the British who spurred the Dutch into action. Competition with the British Ornithologists' Union led to a race to the untrodden equatorial snows of the Lorentz Range in south-central Irian.

A race to the peaks

Both the British and Dutch teams found that the best porters were muscular Dayaks from Kalimantan (Borneo). Quite a few were made available — mostly convicts serving time for head-hunting. The Dayaks from the mountainous interior of Kalimantan were accustomed to the cold climate of the highlands. But if Dayak porters were equally available to all comers, fair play stopped there. Taking advantage of their bureaucracy, the Dutch held up the British teams with stacks of paperwork.

Left: *Captain Frank Hurley's seaplane in New Guinea.* **Below:** *Hurley was an explorer and early photographer of East New Guinea. Photographs courtesy American Museum of Natural History.*

The Dutch left the competition filling out forms and set out from Irian's south coast in 1909. Led by Dr. Lorentz, they eventually reached the base of Mt. Wilhelmina (now Puncak Trikora), then the snow line. Each Dayak porter was rewarded by a tattoo showing a snow-capped mountain and a dragon, to symbolize the hardships. Keeping their upper lips stiff, the British finally obtained their permits and gave chase, reaching an elevation of 4,532 meters (14,866 ft.) before turning back. Neither team made the summit.

Four years later, in 1913, a group led by Dutch Captain Franssen Herderschee scaled Wilhelmina Top's 4,743 meters (15,562 ft.). The Dayaks, who had never seen snow, celebrated with a snowball fight.

Mt. Carstensz (now Puncak Jaya), Irian's highest peak, remained for some time the most obvious challenge. In 1913, Wollaston had reached the snows of the Sudirman Range but no one had yet climbed the higher peaks. Prodded by rumors of yet another British expedition in 1937, national Dutch pride was aroused and an expedition was launched.

By the time an attempt was finally made on the Carstensz, logistics had improved considerably. The first airplane had flown out of Port Moresby in 1922. In 1926, a Dutch-American team became the first expedition to rely on air transport, the seaplane *Ern*. And in 1936, the Dutch pilot Lieutenant Wissel discovered, from his plane, the Paniai Lakes which for a while bore his name.

The Dutch were now ready for Carstensz Top, named after the first white man to sight it and report snows in the tropics in 1623. After Wissel's aerial reconnaissance in an amphibian Sikorski, the expedition, led by Dr. Colijn, plotted a course from the south coast. Once the party was underway, Wissel made two supply drops by parachute then paddled upriver himself to catch up with the group. On December 5th, after a four-hour climb from the base camp, they reached the peak called Ngga Pulu. The mountaineers celebrated by devouring a tin of marzipan.

Nearby Carstensz Peak, the island's highest peak (4,884 meters [16,020 ft.]), was not scaled until 1962 by Austrian Heinrich Harrer.

The Meervlakte

While the explorations of the highlands proceeded apace, other teams made their way inland from Irian's north coast. The only logical route was up the Mamberamo River, navigable for over 150 kilometers (93 mi.).

In 1907, Captain Franssen Herderschee (who later climbed Wilhelmina) shot the rapids on the Mamberamo to reach a large crescent-shaped basin that he dubbed the Meervlakte — the "Lake Plains." The basin is formed by the Taritau River (Idenburg), which flows from the Jayawijaya Range (Oranje) in the east, and the Tariku River

(Rouffaer), coming from the Sudirman Range (Nassau) in the west. The two rivers unite to form the Mamberamo.

After Herderschee, several more expeditions motored up the Mamberamo, but the upper reaches of the Taritau remained uncharted until the 1950s. By the 1920s, monstrously large teams of up to 800 men (mostly porters) headed inland, supplied by flying boats. They did not always meet with a warm welcome from the natives. Aviators told of arrows bouncing off their fuselage. One pilot writes that as he and his crew were flying over the sea off Irian's coast "our engine developed a miss, so did our hearts…we saw millions of sharks in our minds, the engine took delight in missing more frequently."

The Baliem Valley discovered

The discovery of the Baliem Valley in 1938 by American explorer Richard Archbold was the grand prize of New Guinea's exploration. Peering from a giant seaplane dubbed the *Guba,* Archbold was the first white man to lay eyes on the fabulous 60 by 15 kilometer (37 by 9 mi.) wide valley.

The 50,000 Stone Age Dani living in the valley had at this time had no previous contact with the outside world. A couple of Dutch expeditions had passed close, but missed this pocket of flat, arable land — the highlands' largest and most fertile. Surveying the scene from his plane, Archbold described the valley's neat geometric gardens and irrigation ditches as being "like the farming country of central Europe." He later ferried in 30 tons of supplies and a team of 195 men, mostly Irianese porters backed up by 72 hardy Dayaks.

Dutch captain Teerink, one of Archbold's team, was the first to reach the valley with a few porters. When a fuel drop floated off on the river the captain sacrificed his only bottle of gin to the generator to maintain communications with the base camp. (See "The Archbold Expedition," page 98.)

The post-war Dutch era saw two major explorations. The Wisnumurti (Star) Range was reached from the Sibyl Valley at the headwaters of the Digul River. The second major trip, a joint French-Dutch effort, was led by Pierre Dominique Gaissau. The record of this harrowing trek from the southern Asmat coast to Hollandia became a spectacular film, *The Sky Above and The Mud Below,* and *Paris Match* photographer Tony Saulnier produced a first class book of still photographs.

Opposite: *Explorers of the Paniai Lakes region, posing with Ekari tribesmen. The explorers, left to right: Lieutenant Wissel, Jean-Jacques Dozy (he discovered "Copper Mountain") and Dr. de Hartog.*
Above: *Irian's peaks were not technically difficult, but their remoteness made them challenging. Just reaching the base required huge expeditions.*

WORLD WAR II

MacArthur's New Guinea Campaign

For many, the Second World War put New Guinea on the map. Though the Japanese at first swept quickly through the East Indies into Irian and on to east New Guinea, their seemingly inexorable advance was finally stopped 50 kilometers (30 mi.) from Port Moresby — from which Australia was but a short hop away.

Vicious jungle fighting by tough Australian troops slowly pushed the Japanese back. As the war progressed and American might came into play — churning out airplanes, ships, weapons and fighting men — the Allies slowly acquired the means to sweep back the Japanese invaders. After the reconquest of east New Guinea, the pace quickened.

By the time the Allies were prepared to mount an assault on the area, the northern coast of Irian was defended by some 55,000 Japanese troops, considerable air power and substantial naval forces based in the secure waters of the Moluccas, to the west. Thanks to intercepted Japanese communications and broken codes, General Douglas MacArthur learned about the defensive weakness of Hollandia (now Jayapura) — although 11,000 Japanese troops were stationed there, only about one-fifth were combat soldiers.

Risking an attack on his exposed flank, MacArthur then bypassed Japanese troop concentrations at Wewak and Hansa Bay and launched a daring assault on Hollandia itself. Control of the skies made a landing possible. The U.S. Air Force, with its 1,200 planes, wiped out the Japanese air fleet at Sentani, destroying over 300 craft. Only 25 serviceable planes were left by the American pilots.

The Hollandia campaign

For the Hollandia landing, at the time the largest operation in the Pacific, MacArthur employed 217 ships and 80,000 men, led by 50,000 combat troops. The initial objective was to seize a coastal strip some 40 kilometers (25 mi.) wide, between the landing points at Hollandia and Tanah Merah Bay. The lack of Japanese resistance was a godsend, as a chaotic debarkation took place amidst heavy rain and over difficult terrain. When the beachheads were secured on April 22, 1944, MacArthur and his staff celebrated by quaffing ice cream sodas. The next day, as a landing craft ferried the commander-in-chief to the beach at Tanah Merah, a lone Japanese plane appeared and gave everyone a thorough scare. But the pilot, unaware of the landing craft's passenger, flew on to seek a more sizeable target.

The Hollandia campaign, considered by war historians as a model strategic maneuver, cost the Allies only 159 lives. More than 4,000 Japanese were killed and 650 prisoners were taken. About 7,000 Japanese tried to escape to Sarmi, a stronghold over 200 kilometers (125 mi.) down the coast, but disease, starvation and wounds claimed all but 1,000 men.

Meanwhile, Allied engineers reinforced and enlarged the roads and airstrips at Sentani, as the Japanese-built runways were neither sturdy nor long enough for the U.S. B-29 Superfortress bombers. A total of 240 kilometers (150 mi.) of roads and airstrips were laid. Sides of mountains were carved away, bridges and culverts were built across rivers and creeks, gravel and stone was poured into sago swamps to support highways "as tall as Mississippi levees."

Building a command post

Almost overnight, Hollandia mushroomed into a city of 250,000 — with 140,000 Australian and American troops and support personnel. The area became one of the war's great military bases, with most of the southwest Pacific command operating from here during the summer of 1944. MacArthur chose the best spot for his sprawling headquarters complex — a 250-meter (820 ft.) hill overlooking Lake Sentani. Rugs and furniture from the general's Brisbane, Australia office filled prefab army buildings. One of MacArthur's staff described the view thus: "deep green hills of central New Guinea formed a backdrop of peaks, ravines and jungle growth that was almost unreal. Little cone-shaped islands, with native houses on stilts clinging to their shores, dotted the lake."

War correspondents, not always in awe of the quick-tempered MacArthur, filed a story about the general's million-dollar mansion with lavish furnishings and a custom-built drive. MacArthur was furious. After the Philippines had been secured, the missus decided to stop at Hollandia on her way to Manila to be reunited with her husband. She wired him, "I want to see that mansion you built — the one where I'm supposed to have been living in luxury!" Those present did not dare record even a censored version of MacArthur's reply. Another wartime story, probably apocryphal, recounts that it was while gazing out on island-dotted Lake Sentani that General MacArthur conceived his famous island-hopping strategy.

The huge airfield complex at Lake Sentani was to eventually house 1,000 planes. An almost equal number of ships ferried in countless tons of supplies and equipment. Humboldt Bay, with hundreds of ships linked by catwalks and lit up at night, was described by war correspondents as "a city at sea."

The north coast falls

Because soil conditions at Sentani precluded the speedy completion of a bomber base, the Allies set their sights on the Japanese airfield on Wakde Island. After two days of bitter fighting, with 760 Japanese deaths as against 40 on the Allies side, the strip fell. More tough fighting was needed to secure the shores of Maffin Bay on the mainland near Wakde, essential as a forward staging area. The final toll here was 4,000 Japanese killed and 75 taken prisoner, with 415 U.S. casual-

ties. The Tornado Task Force secured all important positions, but at the end of the war there were still some Japanese soldiers holed up in nearby Sarmi.

Despite increasing Allied control of the air and sea lanes, the Japanese tried to send 20,000 troops to Irian from China. The reinforcements never made it. Allied submarines sank four transport ships, drowning 10,000, and the rest of the convoy fled.

The next Allied objective, Biak Island off the north coast of Irian, stopped the U.S.-led blitzkrieg cold. The 10,000 Japanese troops on Biak were well-organized and well-prepared. (See "Introducing Biak," page 54.)

The last Allied offensive in Irian occurred on the northern shore of the Bird's Head. Amphibious landings at Sansapor and Mar here went unopposed. These beachheads were only 150 kilometers (93 mi.) west of Manokwari, the headquarters of the Japanese 2d Army. Quick work by engineers soon yielded operational airfields from which the next objective, Morotai Island off northern Halmahera, could easily be reached. In just four short months, from April to July of 1944, the whole north coast of Irian had fallen to the Allies.

Below: *Allied bombing and shelling prior to the Hollandia invasion destroyed all Japanese shipping to and from the area, including this unfortunate craft, now rusting in Yotefa Bay.*

IRIAN TODAY

Dutch New Guinea to Irian 'Victorious'

After World War II, the Dutch returned to an Indonesia unwilling to revert to its former colonial status. As the Japanese saw their fortunes slipping toward the end of the second world war, they openly encouraged anti-colonialist movements and, in a last-ditch effort to maintain eroding Indonesian support, promised independence after the war. Nationalist conferences were held and the political infrastructure for an independence movement was in place by the time Japan surrendered on August 15, 1945.

On August 17, nationalist leaders Sukarno and Mohammed Hatta declared *merdeka,* "independence." But it took four years of fighting on Java and the threat of a cut-off of Marshall Plan funds to Holland to make the declaration stick. The Dutch formally ceded sovereignty on December 27, 1949, and on August 17, 1950 — five years after the original proclamation — the Republic of Indonesia was born. Indonesia was now independent — all of Indonesia, that is, except New Guinea.

Colonial holdover

The 1946 Linggadjati Agreement, signed by Dutch and Indonesian representatives, states that the Dutch were to relinquish the "whole territory of Netherlands India." But as fighting flared anew before the agreement could be implemented, the Dutch considered it null and void. For their part, Indonesian nationalists always believed that Irian was an integral part of their country. In the final document ceding control of Indonesia, the status of Irian was purposely left vague. The Indonesians were anxious to get on with building their country, certain that the Irian question would eventually be resolved in their favor. They took to heart Dutch negotiator Dr. Van Mook's assurances that "it is absolutely not the government's intention to shut West New Guinea out of Indonesia."

Holland soon found an excuse to withhold her half of New Guinea, however, when Indonesia turned its agreed-upon federal structure into a unitary republic with power concentrated in the capital and the president. The Dutch regarded this as a breach of the Round Table Agreements that had led to Indonesia's independence. But it was the internal politics of Holland, more than any other factor, that led to the retention of

Netherlands New Guinea.

Right-wing parties at home insisted that the Dutch flag remain planted in at least one portion of the former colony, and the presence of oil around Sorong was most certainly a factor as well. By portraying Irian as an anti-communist bastion in the Pacific, the Dutch also sought and received U.S. backing.

Dutch conservatives wrung support from the Labor Party to obtain the two-thirds parliamentary majority needed to exclude Irian from the Transfer of Sovereignty. Australia, also headed at this time by a coalition of conservatives, supported Holland. In 1952, the Dutch parliament even amended the constitution to incorporate West New Guinea (as well as Surinam and the Antilles) into the Kingdom of the Netherlands.

While the young Indonesian nation struggled to consolidate its scattered islands and peoples, the Dutch tried to make up for their years of neglect of Irian. In the 1930s, 200 Europeans lived in Irian. In 1949, following Indonesian independence, this figure leaped to 8,500 — including thousands of Eurasians who fled here, worried about retribution in the young and still volatile Republic. A Dutch exodus from the rest of the archipelago also swelled Irian's expatriate population. Newcomers settled in areas around Manokwari, Sorong and, particularly, Hollandia.

Before the war, Dutch posts along the coast were widely scattered and controlled little beyond their immediate vicinity, and the only inland post was one at the Wissel (Paniai) Lakes, established in 1938. This situation quickly changed after 1949. During the 1950s the Dutch set up a number of new centers in the highlands, and began to take oil out of the Sorong area, nutmeg and mace from Fakfak, crocodile skins and copra from Merauke, and copal and copra from the Raja Empat Islands and the Bird's Head. A new sawmill at Manokwari began to exploit Irian's huge forest reserves. The lion's share of exports headed to Holland and Singapore.

But the cash inflow from exports was dwarfed by Holland's massive subsidies to Irian. While as late as 1957 less than a quarter of Irian's population fell under any sort of administrative control, by 1961 the total had risen to two thirds, with 52 percent of government positions (mainly at the lower levels, of course) filled by Papuans and Melanesians.

President Sukarno and the Indonesian nation viewed these Dutch activities with dismay but at first could do little but make vociferous demands that Holland leave. To make matters worse, Dutch elections held in May

Opposite: The monument to Irian's Independence in Jakarta. The young nation strongly supported President Sukarno's efforts to bring Irian into the Republic of Indonesia. **Below:** *Regular air service is an important part of a modernization program for Irian's rugged and inaccessible interior.*

of 1959 put into power the most conservative and uncompromising coalition since the war.

Early 1960s: the Irian 'problem'

It has often been written that Sukarno focused on the Irian "problem" to rally his nation behind him and draw attention away from pressing domestic problems. Sukarno's economic policies were indeed nothing short of disastrous, and it was only on the strength of his personal charisma and oratory that he was able to maintain the delicate balancing act that kept the Army, the Muslims and the Communists in check. But regardless of his motives, Indonesians were very much behind him on the Irian issue.

Sukarno at first tried to work within the United Nations to resolve the Irian question by diplomatic means. His appeal failed, in part because Indonesia was receiving Soviet military aid and the growing strength of the Indonesian communist party scared off potential Western allies. When the United Nations rejected Sukarno's demands, he pulled out of the body and nationalized all remaining Dutch-owned businesses.

Failed diplomacy left only one option — the military. Organized by General Suharto, who was given widespread powers as major-general early in 1962, Indonesia began a campaign to infiltrate 1,500 troops into Irian in order to spur the villagers to rebellion. The campaign was less than a resounding success, but it showed Indonesia's determination.

While sporadic fighting continued, Indonesia kept up the diplomatic pressure. The key to her eventual success was the United States. Fearing that a protracted military action against the Dutch would draw Indonesia even further into the Soviet fold, the Americans finally decided to support Indonesia in its claim to Irian.

The 'Act of Free Choice'

Soon, Holland saw her only alternatives as an escalating war without U.S. or European support, or relinquishment of Irian. Following mediation talks in the United States, the so-called New York Agreement of 1962 provided for a U.N. transition team to administer West New Guinea in preparation for an eventual plebiscite, the "Act of Free Choice." In 1963 the U.N. handed over Irian to Indonesian control, and in 1969 the Act of Free Choice took place.

Instead of a referendum, the Indonesian government chose some 1,000 representatives who eventually voted unanimously to join the republic, and in August of 1969, West New Guinea formally joined Indonesia. The territory was later renamed Irian Jaya, "Victorious Irian." The methods chosen by the Indonesian government came under fire, but considering the state of affairs in Irian at the time, it is impossible to imagine that a true plebiscite could have been administered.

The Indonesianization of West New Guinea was not free of incident. In 1967, aircraft were used against Arfak tribesmen near Manokwari and rebellions broke out on Biak and around Enarotali, near the Paniai Lakes. And a number of early Indonesian government policies were misguided — such as *operasi koteka,* designed to get the highlanders to quit wearing their penis sheaths — and led to unrest among the Irianese. In some areas this crystalized into guerrilla movements opposed to Indonesian rule — best known is the Organisasi Papua Merdeka ("Free Papua Movement"). The OPM was formed as the result of graceless actions by the government and unrealistic expectations of self-rule, fanned by the Dutch. When the Dutch saw the tenability of their position in Irian fading, they quickly set up elected councils and other trappings of self-rule — with the full knowledge that Indonesian rule was inevitable, and perhaps even desireable. Today, military commanders are still reluctant to open certain areas of Irian to tourism because of the OPM, which has degenerated into groups of bandits.

One of the most controversial of Indonesia's Irian policies has been its *transmigrasi* program, begun in the 1960s, wherein the government has been relocating people from overpopulated Java to Sumatra, Kalimantan (Borneo), Sulawesi (Celebes) and Irian. Initially this program encountered some problems, such as relocating Javanese rice farmers on land that was used as a hunting and gathering ground for the local population. Moreover, the land was often not even fertile enough to grow rice. The government now takes traditional land rights into account when settling transmigrants, and the sites are chosen with greater care.

Although there have been problems in the past, today Indonesia's Irian policy seems to be following an enlightened and successful course in bringing the Irianese into the modern world. Roads are being built, an extremely difficult job considering Irian's rough terrain, schools have been built, and an increasing number of native Irianese are participating in government bureaus.

MISSIONARIES

'Mandate' to Save a God-Forsaken Land

Missionaries have been active in Irian for well over a century. When Sir Alfred Russel Wallace arrived on the shores of Doreri Bay (near present-day Manokwari) in 1858, he met two German pastors who had been sent there three years earlier by the Dutch Reformed Church's Utrecht Missionary Society. Though these Protestants learned the native language and eventually established four stations in the vicinity, during the next 25 years more of them died in New Guinea than natives were "saved." One account refers to these deaths as "rather prosaic martyrdoms of malaria".

Protestants and Catholics

During the 1890s and the first part of this century, as Dutch administrative control spread through West New Guinea, many more missionaries arrived. The missionary administration, creating a duplicate of Holland herself, decreed that Protestants should work the north and Catholics the south.

The results of this division are still visible today, with more Catholic converts found in the south and more Protestants in the north. Since 1928, however, the various faiths have been free to proselytize anywhere and consequently have made inroads into each other's "territories." Most recently, American fundamentalists have made great progress in the highlands.

Protestant Christianity is the religion of over 200,000 Irianese highlanders as well as most inhabitants of the coastal areas, except for the cities, where many of the recent arrivals are Muslims from other parts of Indonesia. The Mission Fellowship, an umbrella organization which coordinates the activities of nine separate Protestant groups

in Irian, comprises 182 individuals or couples. Most Protestant missionaries are married, and the majority are Americans. Many Protestant churches are also now run by Indonesian pastors.

The Catholic missions, staffed by 90 priests, 26 brothers and 95 sisters, are divided into four dioceses. The diocese of Merauke claims more than 100,000 Catholics, Agats 20,000 plus, Sorong 20,000 and the Jayapura diocese some 70,000 converts, with about half of them living in the Paniai Lakes region. The Catholics claim that 220,000 Irianese — about 20 percent of Irian's total population — practice their faith.

Converting the highland tribes

In 1938, a year after the highland Paniai Lakes of western Irian were discovered, the Dutch opened their first post at Enarotali. This same year, the first Roman Catholic missionary arrived at the western-most extremity of the highlands. Shortly thereafter, the first American Protestant missionaries arrived, following an 18-day, 100 kilometers (62 mi.) hike through torrential rains from the coast. As the result of a "gentlemen's agreement," the western highlands were divided into two spheres of influence — the Catholics took the area around Lakes Tigi and Tage (as well as in the Moni enclave of Kugapa in the east) and the Protestants the Ekari territory on the shore of Lake Paniai.

Right: *A missionary nurse administers antibiotics to a native family in East New Guinea. Photograph courtesy the American Museum of Natural History.*

One of the immediate results was hyper-inflation in the native currency of cowry shells, as the missionaries brought with them huge supplies of shells to finance their operations with native labor. Gone were the days when one cowrie shell would buy a 5-gallon tin of sweet potatoes and 50 of them fetched a wife or a fat pig. It soon took 2 steel axes and 240 blue porcelain beads to convince a porter to carry a pack on the 13-day trek from Enarotali to Ilaga.

Life was not easy for these early missionaries in Irian. Hob-nailed boots were essential for hiking across moss-covered logs, slippery trunk bridges and frequent mud. Four pairs of these tough boots could be worn out in a month. Exhausting treks were necessary to scout out locations for new missions. Months of hard work by natives paid with steel axes were required to carve airstrips out of the steep slopes. Small planes first dropped in supplies and then, when the strips were complete, transported missionary wives and children and a plethora of goodies with which to tempt the natives.

Cargo cults

Irian's highlanders, for their part, often confused these strange foreigners with powerful ancestral spirits who were believed to help their descendants if proper rituals were performed. Thus when the whites arrived with their enviable material possessions, the natives assumed that rituals performed by missionaries, such as eating at tables, writing letters and worshipping in church, were responsible for the arrival of such goods. One can imagine how it appeared when spoken appeals to a metal box led to a seemingly endless supply of steel ax heads, metal knives and food being dropped from the sky.

This led to the development of "cargo cults" — mystical millenarian movements (the highlanders also believed in a "second coming" — a golden age of immortality and bliss. See "Cargo Cults on Biak," page 56.) In the Papua New Guinea highlands (where there has been more research), these cults led to the construction of model airplanes and mini-airstrips in hope the spirits would send plane-loads to the Papuans as well as to the whites.

The cargo cult mentality definitively gave a boost to the missionaries' message. In Irian, many of the locals at first thought of the whites as demi-gods, both for their incredible material possessions and for their "magic" in curing disease. This belief was heightened because the whites murmured mysterious

incantations over their patients as they cured them (with a quick shot of penicillin) from the huge, disfiguring skin ulcers, called yaws, that plagued the highlands.

Cargo cultism no doubt contributed to the American fundamentalists' success in the highlands, but great energy and sacrifice also contributed to the evangelical drive. Particularly convincing were the native preachers, first from a Bible school on Sulawesi and then from among the highlanders themselves.

Success among the Damal

Following the Allied victory in World War II, the Christian and Missionary Alliance (CMA) established its headquarters in Enarotali on the Paniai shore. Following up on their pre-World War II work, Protestants trekked east from the Paniai to their former post in the Kemandora Valley. From here, a station was built in Homey, among the Moni tribemen controlling the highlands' best brine pools.

By 1954, the missionaries reached the Ilaga Valley, about halfway along the 500 kilometer (310 mi.) path between Paniai and the Baliem Valley. The Ilaga region is the hub of a wheel of valleys where fertile soils provide abundant harvests of corn, beans and peas, in addition to the staple sweet potato. The abundance of raspberries here led to the practice of using raspberry juice, along with chunks of sweet potato, for communion. The first converts were 1,200 Damal tribesmen living here as a minority in a Dani area.

While victories were being won for Christ in the Ilaga, back at CMA headquarters serious difficulties had arisen. A widespread pig epidemic was blamed on the spirits' displea-

Above: *The mission station at Pyramid, run by American fundamentalist Protestants, is the largest in the highlands.* **Opposite:** *John Cutts, the son of missionaries, grew up with the Moni tribe near Enarotali. His ultralight airplane allows him to land at even the tiniest of bush airstrips.*

sure with the foreigners. The Ekari at Enarotali revolted, killing their Christian tribesmen as well as an Indonesian preacher and his family. They also destroyed the mission's airplane, which was crucial for ferrying supplies to the highland stations. The trouble-makers were finally subdued — not by Dutch rifles and mortars — but by well-aimed Christian arrows.

On to the Baliem Valley

In 1955, under pressure from the influential Roman Catholic political party, the Dutch parliament finally passed a bill allowing unrestricted activities on the part of all mission societies in Irian. After some brief explorations and the establishment of a station at Hetegima at the southern end of the valley, Protestants began expanding into the previously off-limits Baliem Valley at a rapid pace.

The mission at Pyramid, at the northwestern end of the valley was the first to be established. A major trade route already led here from the Western Dani centers of Bokondini, Karubaga and Mulia. Because of its strategic location, more missionaries were sent to Pyramid than anywhere else and the mission retains its importance today as a regional center.

The mid-valley station at Tiom and one at Seinma in the Baliem Gorge area south of Hetegima were both opened in 1956, one year before the Dutch government estab-lished its first outpost in the valley, at Wamena. In 1958, a year after Wamena was established, Catholics entered the valley.

When Dutch control came to the Valley, the various Protestant sects — CMA, the Australian Baptist Missionary Society, the Regions Beyond Missions Union, and the United Field Missions — joined forces for financial and logistical reasons as well as counteract the Roman Catholic presence. The Catholics' more flexible policy toward native beliefs was a sore point with more fundamentalist Protestants. Said one polemicist, "the Catholics' attempts at accommodation have at times produced hybrid creeds scarcely recognizable as the continuation of historic, Biblical Christianity."

With the competition for souls heating up, gone were the "gentlemen's agreements" of old. But old-fashioned Protestant missionaries who, for example, insisted on clothing being worn in church, were also fading. Younger, more open-minded Americans who had taken university courses in anthropology and linguistics after their years of Bible college were now joining the ranks. This new breed of missionaries enjoined only against those practices that were in direct conflict with the Bible — killing twin siblings, spirit worship and the execution of women accused of witchcraft.

Fearing a Catholic monopoly on education, the Protestants also agreed to partici-

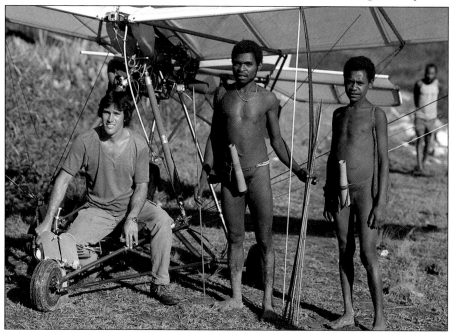

pate in secular educational programs sponsored by the Dutch government. And, albeit reluctantly, the Americans also participated in setting up a government-subsidized public hospital at Pyramid.

Pockets of heathenism

In the early 1960s, the pace of missionary activities slowed. The country was undergoing a difficult transition from Dutch to Indonesian rule, and the frenetic pace of evangelical advances had left pockets of heathens untouched as well as pockets of heathenism in the minds of the recent converts. It was time to consolidate gains.

Preachers found that even well-behaved flocks were sometimes operating with pretty strange notions of Christianity. Natives held such beliefs as that sitting in church would result in immunity from sickness and that forgetting to shut one's eyes during prayers would lead to blindness. Missionaries responded to these setbacks and superstitions by swearing to persevere against this "black magic," which they called "Satan's counteraction to God's perfect will for man."

The Protestants, resolving their internal difficulties, at this time planned a two-pronged strategy to conquer the remaining Western Dani — moving eastward from the Ilaga Valley and northwest from Pyramid. Setting aside jealousies and theological differences, the Australian Baptist Missionary Society joined forces with Regions Beyond Missions Union to help the United Field Missions build an airstrip at Bokondini. Areas thus opened up were divided into exclusive spheres of influence.

From Bokondini, missionaries trekked to Mulia to spread the gospel to the "crazy people" — Danis suffering from huge goiters and giving birth to cretins. Disease in this tragic place, the "most concentrated goiter pocket in the world," was soon cleared up with iodine injections and prayers. By 1963, a conference in Bokondini attracted 51 Dani church leaders. In the same year, Bokondini became the site of a teacher-training school.

While the Gospels swept into Western Dani areas, the Baliem Valley offered surprisingly stubborn resistance. Powerful war chiefs here resisted the new creeds, correctly viewing them as as a threat to their authority. A man who has more than 20 confirmed kills to his credit isn't going to give up his hard-won prestige to a religion that proposes that "the meek shall inherit the earth." Many leaders also objected to the secrets of salvation being revealed to women — religious lore had always been a male preserve.

There were other reasons for a slowing of proselytization here, too. With the civil government providing medical care and newly arrived merchants offering essential material goods, Bible preachers lost some of their punch. In fact, the greatest concentration of Dani who today refuse Christianity live in and around the administrative center of Wamena.

Life among the cannibals

The hardships and tragic incidents suffered by missionaries in Irian could fill volumes. One story involves a two-man evangelical team — Bruno de Leeuw, a gentle Hollander, and Stanley Dale, an abrasive former Australian commando — who were dispatched to convert a group of Yali villagers in the highlands southeast of the Baliem.

For a while, the Yali believed that the two newcomers were reincarnations of two of their deceased leaders, turned white after passing through the land of the dead. But they soon realized that the missionaries were ordinary humans, and following several misguided attempts at "reform" — including mass fetish-burning — the bodies of the two men were found riddled with arrow shafts "as thick as reeds in a swamp."

Another tale involves Dutch Reverend Gert van Enk, 31, a tall, tropics-cured veteran of five year's service, who has been working among the Korowai tribe in what he calls the "hell of the south." The Dutch Reformed Church has been trying to proselytize the Korowai for ten years and so far has not celebrated one baptism among the 3,000 Korowai. Van Enk is not allowed into most of the tribal territory, and if caught there would be pin-cushioned with arrows. But he has no thoughts of giving up. His countrymen, he says, took centuries to become Christians.

Confirming other sources, Van Enk says that cannibalism is still common among the Korowai. A death is believed to be caused by witchcraft, and a culprit (or scapegoat) must be found, killed and eaten by the relatives in revenge. This leads to a never-ending cycle of cannibalism. Infanticide by mothers is also common. Sexual intercourse starts when girls are eight or nine years old and the first pregnancy usually occurs around 13. Infanticide, the missionary says, is the result of the girls just not being ready for children.

Opposite: *American missionary John Wilson poses with a Dani tribesman at Pyramid.*

PART II

The North and West Coasts

The northern and western coasts of Irian Jaya, including the Bird's Head region, Biak Island and Jayapura, are the easiest parts of the island to visit, with a well developed communications and transportation network.

Biak Island is the first Indonesian stop for travelers flying Garuda from the United States, and while most visitors who disembark here are in a rush to get to Jayapura and the highlands, Biak offers a number of attractions, including war relics, coral-filled waters and fine sand beaches. The snorkeling off the beautiful islands close to Biak's coast is spectacular. Better yet, make the short trip to nearby **Numfor** or **Yapen**, which offer beautiful and secluded diving spots and, in the inland forests of Yapen, the spectacular birds of paradise.

Jayapura, Irian's capital and largest city, began its life as a Dutch port and administrative center — just a stone's throw from the border with a German colony to the east. For many years a small, back-water town, Hollandia leaped suddenly onto the world stage during World War II as a staging point for General MacArthur's Pacific campaign. Today, it is a thriving city of 100,000 with, in addition to Irianese, a mixed population of Javanese, Makassarese and Bugis Muslims, as well as many Ambonese and Menadonese Christians. Jayapura is of the few places in Irian with paved roads and public transportation (and private taxis), travel around the area is easy.

From here, a short hop to **Yotefa Bay** offers the spectacle of scattered World War II relics — half-sunken ships, beached tanks and landing craft. Or your pilot can take you to nearby fishing villages that consist of huts mounted on a forest of stilts. At high tide, the water reaches a meter and a half beneath the village; at low tide, a wide expanse of mud flats is revealed, which, in at least one area, the locals turn into a makeshift soccer field.

Nearby **Lake Sentani**, dotted with islands offers a stunning panorama of velvet-green hills easing their way into the lake. A meal of crispy lakefish and even water-skiing is possible here.

The Bird's Head Peninsula, so-called because on the map it looks like the head of a huge westward-flying creature, is a rather more remote area with three major coastal towns: Manokwari, Sorong and Fakfak. A working knowledge of Indonesian and plenty of initiative are essential to move around the area, though the towns are all served by scheduled flights and occasional steamers.

Manokwari is one of the main missionary centers for American evangelical sects on Irian, and the hub of a rapidly-growing network of transmigration settlements, logging concerns and plantations. The nearby islands of Cenderawasih Bay and the inland Anggi Lakes are noted for their scenery.

The oil-town of **Sorong** at the western tip of Irian is the jumping-off point for visits to the Raja Empat Islands to the west — reportedly the best place to witness the birds of paradise in their natural habitat.

The district capital of **Fakfak**, which controls the lower coast of the peninsula, may be reached by air from Sorong and Manokwari. The scenery around here is spectacular, and there are rock paintings similar to those produced by ancient Australian aborigines in the vicinity, as well as in Kaimana to the east.

A visit to any of these out-of-the-way coastal areas is an exciting adventure, and particularly rewarding for marine enthusiasts (be sure to bring along your mask and fins). Scuba diving tours to **Cenderawasih Bay** are just now beginning — and this is an area that is said to have some of the best diving in the world.

Overleaf: *The popular "Base G" beach, on the outskirts of Jayapura, takes its name from a World War II Allied base.* **Opposite:** *A dancer on the island of Numfor, a short hop from Biak.*

INTRODUCING BIAK

Strategic Island to Irian's North

Biak's beautiful, palm-fringed shores and unspoilt neighboring islands combine to create a seldom-visited tropical idyll — second to none in the world. The Melanesian inhabitants, moreover, are open, hospitable and friendly. Although most of their traditional culture has been wiped out by missionaries and everyone today dresses in western clothes, elements of the old lifestyle remain. Traditional dances in loincloths and fire-walking rituals can still be arranged. Many of the more remote villages, unable to afford those awful corrugated metal roofs, still consist of thatch-roofed huts with palm-ribbed walls raised a meter above the sand or over the sea.

The bride price, still widely used on Biak, consists of antique porcelain plates, silver bracelets made from old Dutch or American coins, along with cold cash. The average value is currently $350. Aside from wedding feasts, there are ceremonies connected with childbirth such as the first haircut, and others timed to the Christian calendar. The use of magic has not been lost, especially in seeking abundant catches of fish.

Despite the island's newfound status as a major air stopover, most passengers don't even bother to disembark here, which is a shame because the island is rich in history and natural beauty. During World War II, in fact, tiny Biak loomed large on the world map. After the war, the Dutch took over the American airfields and docks and, during the 1960s, the Indonesian government followed suit. Today Biak is the first Indonesian stop on Garuda Indonesia's direct flights from the United States.

Geography and economy

Boot-shaped with a crooked toe, Biak Island extends 50 kilometers (31 mi.) northwest to southeast, with an average width of only 18 kilometers (11 mi.). The island covers some 1,800 square kilometers (700 sq. mi.). The northernmost shore reaches within 60 kilo-

meters (37 mi.) of the equator and the central part of the island lies at 1° S latitude.

Just northwest of Biak, across a narrow, coral-filled strait, lies Supiori Island; about 100 kilometers (62 mi.) due west is Numfor Island. Geologically, all three consist of limestone, with coastlines often ending in impressive cliffs that rise 60 meters (200 ft.) or more straight up from the sea. Raised coral outcroppings are also much in evidence. Inland, the terrain is generally flat, except in the northern part of Biak where elevations reach 700 meters (2,300 ft.).

Biak, together with Supiori, Numfor, and 41 smaller islands, forms one of nine *kabupaten* or administrative districts in Irian Jaya. The total population of the district is a bit over 81,000. Half of these live in Biak town and the immediate vicinity. Recent transmigrants have swelled the population of the town — most are Muslims from Java or Sulawesi and Christians from Ambon or Menado. The island of Biak has 65,000 inhabitants; Supiori has 8,500 and Numfor 7,000. Eighty-five percent are Protestant Christians. Catholics and Muslims, found mainly in Biak town, number 1,600 and 8,700 respectively.

Biak's economy looks to both the land and the sea. Taro is the staple crop. Also grown are sweet potatoes, cassava, soybeans, vegetables and a variety of fruits. Dried coconut meat or copra has long been the principal cash crop. Still being developed are cocoa, cloves and coffee.

Most gardens and plantations are located inland, behind the narrow coastal range. Recently, chickens, a few head of cattle and goats have been introduced to supplement the native pigs. Despite this diversity of livestock, most Biak islanders get their protein from the seas. Fishermen bring a bewildering variety of fish to the local markets.

A large fishing operation, run by Bretons, exports enough skipjack and yellowfin tuna to be Biak's leading exporter. The fish is shipped mainly to Japan and Thailand. Over 200 fishermen are employed on seven modern French trawling boats. Several hundred more work on land, making this $30 million a year enterprise one of Biak's two biggest employers (the other is a lumber mill). Over 2,500 tons of tuna are canned monthly. In one convoluted transaction, a shipment of canned tuna from Biak was sold to Italy and re-labelled there for sale to the U.S. market.

Opposite: *Boys paddle their small outrigger in one of Biak Island's many coastal lagoons.*

Other sea products exported from Biak include trepang (sea cucumber) and sharks' fins — both prized by the Chinese — along with mother-of-pearl and agar-agar, a gelatin extracted from seaweed. The recent introduction of seaweed cultivation is giving the economy of several islands a welcome boost. Products from this versatile plant, including agar-agar and carrageenan, have many uses: in cosmetics, toothpaste, pie filling, ice cream and cheese as a thickener and emulsifier; as an additive to paint on supersonic planes to prevent peeling at twice the speed of sound; to clarify beer; to prevent shrinking in textiles; as an additive to jumbo jet brake fluid and as a culture medium. The raw seaweed, *Eucheuma* sp., fetches $500 a ton in Surabaya.

The power of the ancestors

Biak islanders are a seafaring people, and even a few decades ago the men's houses in Biak were topped by boat-shaped roofs, and the bones of the dead were stored in boat-shaped coffins. Languages related to that spoken here are found as far away as Halmahera, and the name 'Irian' is in fact a Biak word meaning something like "hot land rising from the sea."

Biak's ancient animist religion emphasized the spiritual importance of ancestors, who were considered mediators of the wishes of *nanggi,* the central power of the universe. In times of scarcity, a ritual called *fan nanggi* ("feeding the sky") was performed with offerings that the ancestral spirits carried upward to the heavens, there interceding on behalf of their descendants. Some villages still maintain formal committees that keep track of family genealogies.

Evidence of traditional beliefs can be found in strikingly beautiful ancestral sculptures. These small figures, called *kowar,* are vessels containing the spiritual power of the deceased. Before any important occasion, such as a war expedition or a fishing trip, a shaman/oracle would go into trance to consult the *kowar.* The figures were asked to keep away storms, bring favorable winds and protect the warriors or sailors against illness and evil spirits. *Kowar* from Biak became prized items in the collections of French surrealists André Breton and Paul Éluard.

Unfortunately, few of these sculptures escaped missionary burnings. Although missionaries enjoyed some success in Biak in the early 1910s, shortly before the establishment of a Dutch outpost here, an outbreak of smallpox later wiped out their achievement. The disease was blamed on the ancestors' wrath at the people of Biak for abandoning their traditions. Despite this setback, the missionaries returned in 1929 and succeeded in destroying most (but not all) of the physical manifestations of Biak's animist religion. (See "Cargo Cults on Biak," page 56.)

The people of Biak, excellent sailors and

traders, have long maintained contacts with Irian and other Indonesian islands to the west. A war-loving people, they staged raids far into the Moluccas, even reaching Sulawesi and Java in their search for women, slaves and goods for ceremonial exchanges. These exchanges, the most important of which was the bride price, required goods of foreign origin, which could only be acquired by trading or raids. Today, as a result, the people of Biak share bloodlines with the peoples of Seram, Ambon, the Sanghir Islands, the Kei Islands and Alor.

The Sultan of Tidore

The closest "foreign relations" were with the spice island of Tidore. Gurabesi, a culture hero from Biak, was supposed to have won the hand of a princess of Tidore, the daughter of Sultan Jamaludin. As part of the bride price, a light tribute had to be taken yearly from Biak to Tidore. In return, the aristocrats of Biak received prestigious titles from the rulers of Tidore. The nobles who bore the tribute each year were also granted the privilege of touching the Sultan's big toe — which charged the supplicants with magic power, most useful in impressing the less fortunate classes back in Biak. Gurabesi and his Tidorese wife were the (mythical) progenitors of Biak's leading clan, as well as the forebears of the rulers of the Raja Empat Islands west of Irian's Bird's Head.

Tidore's domination of Biak — as well as of other areas of Irian — was reinforced by periodic *hongi* expeditions of war canoes. The purpose of these raids was the collection of tribute, but they included thievery, pillage and rape as a matter of course, all made possible by firearms that the Sultan had obtained from Europeans. But internal strife and predatory expeditions between Biak and Irian were far worse than the Tidorese *hongi*. In the late 18th century, Prince Nuku, dispossessed pretender to the Tidorese throne, recruited Biak warriors, who fought under his banner for 25 years. By 1861, the power of Tidore had waned, and the *hongi* ended.

In the course of their many wide-ranging trade and raiding expeditions, the men of Biak acquired techniques for forging metal. With iron from Halmahera and Gebe (which have myths and languages similar to those of Biak), metal implements were forged by shaman-smiths, who labored under an aura of supernatural power and knowledge. Metal work, as well as trade, was under the control of the noble caste, the *manseren*, who sat on top of a social pyramid composed of commoners and slaves. Biak traders also picked up more sophisticated technologies for canoe construction, learning to bulwark their canoes with boards and to use more efficiently shaped outriggers.

Men of the cloth

Missionaries began their labors on Biak after a Dutch government post was established in Manokwari in 1898. The first Protestant mission, on Supiori Island, was followed by a second at Bosnik, on Biak Island, in 1912. The Biak mission lasted just two years before a smallpox epidemic allowed the ancestral spirits to reestablish their spiritual authority.

This victory was, alas, temporary. The indigenous traditions of Biak, of which warfare was an essential element, were dealt a death blow in 1915. In that year Dutch forces under Lieutenant Feuilletau de Bruyn, "pacified" Biak and the other islands of Cenderawasih Bay. Fighting and head-hunting were banned, and the old system was left impotent, laying the groundwork for conversion to Christianity. Missionaries began proselytizing in earnest during the 1920s, picking up where they had left off in Bosnik.

As in other areas of Indonesia where the Protestants followed pacification programs, Christianity brought with it a program of Western education. The schools of Biak have furnished many of Irian's civil servants and their numbers are disproportionate to their population — a product of the educational head start they receive in their overcrowded and not particularly fertile island.

World War II on Biak

The Japanese defense of Biak was, in the words of Lieutenant General Eichelberger, "based on brilliant appreciation and use of the terrain." The commander of the Allied Hurricane Task Force describes the defenses of his enemy thusly:

"A few aerial vertical photographs failed to show the terrain features dictating the enemy defenses: the network of caves. Within the terraces and cliffs are countless caves, many of which are connected and interconnected by fissures and tunnels. Stalactites and stalagmites add to the near impregnability of the caves as defensive posi-

Opposite: *Dancers on the island of Biak. The drums, with elaborately carved handles, are unique to the island. The mantles worn by most of the men are made of cassowary feathers.*

tions, making the battlefields of Biak a military nightmare.

"The Japanese were free to chose the location of their position at will. During the night the enemy came out of their cave positions and made a series of harassing attacks. Mountain guns and mortars were brought out from the caves. Before morning they were returned to the caves, which caves, the infantrymen did not know. A form of warfare was encountered that required experimentation, trial and error, and all of our available weapons before the mission could be accomplished."

Initial Japanese opposition at the landing site of Bosnik, 16 kilometers (10 mi.) from the airfields, was slight — but this, it turned out, was a ploy. Japanese Colonel Naoyuki Kuzume had purposely withheld his main forces until the U.S. troops had advanced to the rugged terrain beyond the beaches. Then, from the dominating cliffs and caves overlooking the moving Allied columns, the Japanese launched a savage counter-attack and succeeded in driving a wedge between the beachhead and the invading forces. That night, the Japanese brought in an additional 1,000 men from Manokwari.

The situation was critical until Allied reinforcements arrived. Even then, the fighting was tough. U.S. infantry units were bogged down in the heavy fighting, suffering from extremely unfriendly terrain, intense heat and a scarcity of water. A new form of warfare was encountered that required novel tactics and all available weapons, including flame-throwers. One product of American ingenuity was eventually employed with deadly effectiveness: a cocktail of TNT and aviation fuel poured into the caves.

The immediate Allied objectives were the three airfields at Mokmer (one of which was later to become today's Frans Kaisiepo commercial airport), Borokoe and Sorida. The aerodrome of Mokmer was seized on June 7 but the struggle continued unabated as the Japanese poured heavy fire into the newly established field positions. It was another week before the airstrip could be used. Effective resistance on Biak was overcome by June 21, 1944. The final toll was 400 U.S. soldiers killed and 7,400 Japanese, many of whom committed ritual suicide when they realized their situation was hopeless. Only 220 Japanese surrendered or were captured.

The Allies quickly developed the captured airfields for their own use. An important heavy bomber base was constructed on Biak, and fighters and medium-sized bombers were stationed in Wakde, Numfor and at Sansapor on the northwestern tip of Irian. From these bases, the Far Eastern Air Force was to strike for the next weeks at Japanese positions in Seram, Sulawesi, Halmahera, Kalimantan, Java and the Palaus, in preparation for the assault against the Philippines.

CARGO CULTS ON BIAK

The Island's Odd *Koreri* Movements

A messianic *koreri* cult of Biak was one of the largest "cargo cults" the world has ever seen, and also one of the bloodiest — because it ran afoul of the Japanese war machine. The movement peaked in the years 1938-1943, during which cult leaders had the charismatic authority to raise an army of thousands.

Cargo cults are cultural/religious movements that developed throughout Melanesia and New Guinea following the arrival of Europeans.* Sometimes characterized as "messianic movements," they were strange combinations of beliefs produced when indigenous traditions concerning the ancestral spirits mixed with the observed habits of European traders and missionaries.

Most traditional cultures in Melanesia believe in the supernatural powers of the ancestors. If proper rites are performed, these ancestors bestow good health, food and material goods. The first whites, who looked like they performed many strange rituals, seemed to obtain — without working — huge quantities of highly desireable goods.

Imagine how a tribesman, used to performing rituals in honor of his ancestors to procure good fortune, good sailing weather and material goods, would interpret the behavior of the Europeans. They scrawled occult symbols on a flat piece of bark (later spoke into a steel box) and with no more effort than that, 100 steel axes and a plethora of other goods would arrive.

In some areas, the natives set up tables and chairs and ate with knives and forks, hoping that this was the proper "ritual" to obtain the goods. Many of the local people thought of the whites as gods, because of their incredible material possessions and their "magic" ability to cure diseases such as the disfiguring yaws. (See "Missionaries," page 43.)

The cults that developed on Biak are

* Much of the information in this section is taken from F.C. Kamma's excellent book Korei.

known as *koreri* or *manseren* movements. *Manseren* means "noble," or "lord." *Koreri* is a more complex term, meaning something like an ideal state or eternal order, and implying immortality.

There was an old belief in Biak that a hero named Manarmakeri, rejuvenated in a baptism of fire, had the power to usher in a time of eternal, utopian life. Manarmakeri himself was recognized as Manggundi, or Manseren Koreri — the "Lord of Utopia." After spending some time on Biak, he departed westward, promising to return. When he came back, he said, the dead would be resurrected and there would be plenty of food and material treasures. (There is a similar belief heard throughout the archipelago concerning Ratu Adil, the righteous king, whose appearance will usher in an era of just rule and prosperity.)

First signs of *koreri* cults

Upon initial contacts with Europeans, the natives of Biak thought that the whites were their returned ancestors. But the foreigners' all too human nature soon became apparent, although the people of Biak still had no way of fathoming how so many ships and treasures were brought by the Europeans. Some decided these abundant cargoes had been sent by their ancestors, and that the whites had usurped consignments rightfully belonging to them. As a result they raided the Dutch ships.

The first reports of a cargo cult-like movement in the area date from 1854. In 1855, as part of certain messianic expectations, the people of Numfor Island refused to pay tribute to the Sultan of Tidore. This turned out to not be a wise move, as a punitive *hongi* expedition soon brought devastation and a return to submission and tribute payments. On Halmahera, from 1875 to 1876, the "Prophet of Kau" led a movement that attracted over 30,000 followers. This cult adopted a strong anti-foreign stance, directed specifically against the rulers of Ternate and Tidore. Kau fancied himself the messiah, and with his "chosen" was said to be ushering in a utopia.

Once the Dutch government became established enough on Biak to enforce its policies, head-hunting and warfare were banned. Missionaries wiped out other practices to which the Western sensibility objects, such as the Biak tradition of reinforcing the brother-sister bond by mixing blood from the brother's prepuce into the sister's food. The

Opposite: *A kowar ancestral sculpture from Biak.*

loss of these and other traditions created a vacuum that Christianity couldn't fill. Imperfectly assimilated Christian teachings produced one cult that considered the penis to be the entrance to Paradise, with a woman's nipples serving as the keys. During a "spiritual" marriage, to win the right to enter Paradise, the partners held each other's genitals.

'Mary' and the Biak cult

The most important *koreri* movement on Biak — indeed one of the most widespread cargo-type cults found anywhere — occurred between 1938 and 1943. It eventually spread from Biak to Numfor and Yapen as well as to parts of Irian's north coast.

The cult started when an elderly woman, Angganitha, was abandoned by her relatives on Supiori Island. She was "miraculously" cured, however, and is said to have become endowed with magical healing powers. People believed that she would usher in the awaited utopia.

The cult started to spread, and Dutch authorities arrested the woman. She was tried but acquitted on Yapen Island. Upon her return she became fiercely anti-Dutch and began to accuse missionaries of having ripped out the page in the Bible that showed that Jesus was Manggundi. She took the Biblical name of Mary and some of her followers began to worship her as a goddess. When her mass meetings began to attract 6,000 people, the authorities re-arrested her.

After the arrest of "Mary," a new leader, Stephanus, took charge of the *koreri* cult. Stephanus, a convicted murderer, began to amass a small army, but by this time the Japanese had taken Biak, and they had little patience for such things. They beheaded both Stephanus and Mary, thinking that would end the foolishness. It didn't.

Stephen Wanda, self-proclaimed Raja of Supiori, became the new leader of the cult. He had his men dig for oil and build a house in the shape of a huge airplane, and he planned on manufacturing guns, radios and telephones. Wanda's most ill-advised move was to rebuild the *koreri* army and attack the Japanese. It resulted in a massacre. The cult lost between 600 and 2,000 men, and all the leaders, including Wanda, were beheaded.

Still the cult did not die. Survivors of the *koreri* army skirmished with the Japanese for the remainder of the war, with many casualties on both sides. When the U.S. Army finally landed on Biak, the defeat of the Japanese was hailed as a vindication of the *koreri* cult. Immediately, the members took to killing as many Japanese as they could find.

On Biak, the *koreri* cult faded after the war. But elsewhere in the archipelago, the material goods brought in by American G.I.s contributed to renewed cargo cultism. And in Biak, the minds and hearts of the older generation are still susceptible to this thinking.

SIGHTS OF BIAK

White Beaches and Sparkling Blue Seas

White sand beaches, crystal-clear waters and sea gardens of brightly colored fish are Biak's prime attraction. Most beaches can be reached by paved road, and sturdy motorized outrigger canoes will whisk you to the offshore islands. Limestone caves, the cornerstone of the Japanese defense of Biak during the war, are just 15 minutes by taxi. Nearby shore batteries and a rusting anti-aircraft gun are poignant reminders of the war.

With a day or two advance notice, visitors can arrange to see traditional dances or firewalking. The island's handicrafts include models of local canoes, with carved decoration. Craftsmen also offer larger ancestral sculptures, carved in the traditional manner.

Touring the island: to the east

Paved roads radiate out from Biak Town toward the north, east and west. Most are relatively short, with the 50 kilometer stretch to the Wardo market and bay to the west being the longest. On crowded public minibuses, it can take up to two hours (after waiting for departure) to arrive at any of the end points. Better to charter a minibus if you can afford it.

To the east, it's 18 kilometers and a half-hour ride to **Bosnik** and its white sand, coral-reefed beaches. On the way, you pass Panai Parai beach, sheer limestone cliffs and a lovely brook fringed with sago palms. From Bosnik, occasional motor boats run to the small, paradisiacal Padaido Islands — some uninhabited, others with a hospitable village.

On the way to Bosnik, some five kilometers from Biak Town, you can stop at **Swapodibo Village** to see the work of Micha Ronsumbre. He carves drums, canoes, ancestral figures and panels, all featuring ancient motifs and designs. A roadside sign outside his house says "Sanggar Kerajinan." Made mostly from local ironwood, items for sale include drums ($25-30), model canoes ($40-

Right: A young fisherman displays his catch.

45) and stylized human figures ($18-30). A bit further along the road, a short but steep path leads down to a grotto with clear blue waters.

About two kilometers beyond Bosnik and its market (Wed. and Sat.), there's a white sand beach cum picnic area abutting on a sweep of raised coral bordering transparent, shallow seas. Rusting remains of American built World War II piers lie off the beach. Coconut palms everywhere.

The paved road continues to **Opiaref Village**. In back of the elementary school, there are some large grottos dripping into blue water ponds. Opiaref is also noted for its woodcarvers. With sufficient notice (a day or two), you can see a dance performed here. Ask for the older dancers, not schoolchildren.

The paved road beyond Opiaref peters out just before reaching the next village, **Saba**. Plans call for extending the road all the way to Biak's southeast extremity, Cape Barari. Saba village, just beyond a creek, nestles into a bay with several raised coral reefs — now miniature islands.

The road to Saba rises occasionally to give a panorama of villages and some of the Padaido Islands. But the shoreline is monotonous and the houses are nondescript huts with rusting tin roofs, nary a thatch in sight. Occasionally a hut perches on stilts over the water, next to its outhouse offspring.

If you arrive on market days, it's possible to hop on a motorized outrigger to **Owi**

Island, the closest of the Padaidos, for less than 30¢. Owi Island has a wide sand beach on its north shore, facing Biak. The best blacksmiths are said to live here, forging excellent machete blades and capable of making functional firearms. You might also ask around to see if any of the motorized canoes are heading for islands beyond Owi. Hop on and return on the next market day, or a week later. On non-market days, you can ask to be paddled across to Owi, about $1.50 each way.

The Padaido Islands

Biak Town is the usual jumping-off point for a jaunt to the Padaido Islands, scattered to the southeast. The ride reveals a wonderland of tropical islands, multi-hued seas and coral formations with kaleidescopic schools of fish. The islands is divided into two groups: Padaido Atas (Higher or Further Padaido) to the east and closer Padaido Bawah (Lower or Nearer Padaido), with Pakreki Island smack in the middle.

If time and finances permit, we suggest an overnight excursion to **Padaido Atas** — way off the incipient tourist circuit. An expert working for Jacques Cousteau has checked out several spots here, giving it high marks for sport diving. For those interested, the easternmost isles of Padaido Atas — Runi, Wamsori, Nukori and Workbondi — are fringed by seas with an abundant shark population. Some divers actually look for sharks:

they almost never attack unless you are bleeding or carrying speared fish, and it's a rush to see them gliding around, in complete control of their environment.

For ordinary mortals, **Padaido Bawah** will do just fine. These islands were of crucial importance during World War II. Five landing strips were laid down on Owi and a submarine base built off Nusi. The various islands are all low-lying, with shores of white sand or raised coral. Huts line the bigger islands. Men in tiny outrigger canoes, with patched-up sails, fish with hook and line.

There is quite decent snorkeling and diving off uninhabited **Ruebas Island**, with several underwater caves. Two tiny islands, **Urip** and **Masurbabo** off eastern Nusi Island, are but sandbars with a few trees rising out of the shallow seas. Just east of these, a 15 to 20 meter drop next to a wide stretch of shallow coral in 1-3 meters of water offers excellent snorkeling — we saw lobsters, a couple of small reef sharks, blue-spotted rays, a moray eel and a meter-and-a-half-long black and white banded seasnake slithering in and out of the coral.

While you are swimming and snorkeling, your boatman will probably be fishing. With a bit of luck, a delicious grilled fish dinner will await you. If your boatman was unsuccessful, you can always buy fish from one of the little outriggers.

Most of the boats taking tourists to the

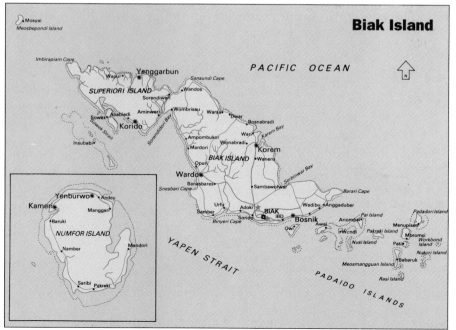

Padaidos have a cabin amidship. We still recommend a hat, sunscreen, long-sleeved shirt and long pants. And, unless an agency has set up the trip, bring plenty of drinking water, fruit and snacks for the day.

World War II caves

From Biak town heading north, there is a turnoff just outside the urban area to the "Japanese" cave, **Goa Binsari**. Before reaching the cave proper, one signs the guest book. A small building nearby houses a couple of Japanese skeletons and a few vintage World War II rifles, quietly rusting alongside disintegrating army-issue footwear. Further on, a stairway, festooned with moss and lined with fern-covered stalagmites, leads into the cave's mouth. A short passage, dripping water from its high ceiling, leads to a large, circular opening with sky above. An American bomb collapsed the cave's roof here, creating a circular sinkhole with sheer vertical walls some 15 meters (50 ft.) high and about 25 meters (80 ft.) in diameter. The earth accumulated on the cave floor, now open to the rains and the sun, nourishes a profusion of vegetation. Further exploration here or in any of the many other cave-labyrinths of Biak requires a trustworthy flashlight, a good guide and a bit of bravery.

Other than a few bits of rusting metal, nothing remains in these caves. The useable metal has been carted away as scrap, and the

bodies of the dead have been laid to rest. The Americans took away their dead during and after the war, and the Japanese came in the late 1960s to cremate the remains of their dead according to Shinto ritual. A simple monument has been erected on top of the cave to the Japanese soldiers who died here. Some of the soldiers' relatives come once a year, to pray at the cave's entrance and at the statue of the Goddess of Mercy, which stands in front of Hotel Irian.

Quite near the Goa Binsari cave is a strategic promontory that overlooks the airport. The Japanese bunkers, which blend into the landscape, and heavy shore batteries — made in Germany — attest to the tactical importance of this location. On a clear day, one can see as far as the island of Yapen, about 60 kilometers (37 mi.) away. Before leaving the area, ask to see the anti-aircraft gun which, still in good shape, stands mute in back of a nearby house.

Fire-walking

This ancient custom, forbidden by the Dutch, was associated with traditional events such as weddings and feast given by powerful leaders. Men accused of adultery or corrupting unmarried girls could prove their innocence by walking over the red hot stones with feet intact. Fire-walking is now allowed once more, and some north coast villages occasionally perform it, but it is much easier to

see in **Adoki**, a village at the end of a paved road some 11 kilometers from Biak Town. There is also excellent swimming at a beach just before the entrance to this village, reached by a concrete staircase.

While the four families whose members can walk on the burning stones had not tried it since the early 1930s, a couple of men recently gave it a go, just to show that their art has not been lost. Although not essential for the performance, the two men wore red loincloths — one over his shorts, the other on bare flesh.

Kindling and logs were laid down and coral rocks piled on top. The pyre burned for about an hour, until the coral rocks were red hot. Men and women removed any remaining smoldering wood and with long sticks pushed and pulled the heated stones to shape a more or less flat bed of glowing rocks. Waves of heat furiously rose from the surface. The two men stood at the edge, prayed, then rubbed a bit of saliva on their soles. The oldest man started first, a bent-over octogenarian with a sense of humor. Full of confidence, he strode over the stones but about half way across he started hopping and covered the remaining distance in record time, shouting that there was danger in fire walking. Someone cracked a joke: the old man must have been messing around with a girl. Everyone laughed except the chap with the singed feet, who was rubbing betel juice on

his soles to relieve the pain. His partner, evidently a more moral man, walked across the scorching stones several times and experienced no problems.

In spite of the burned feet, the people of Adoki village stated that they would repeat the fire-walking with more participants, including women and children of ten years of age. Perhaps next time they may follow the old ritual with a feast of pork, cassava and other local delicacies.

Korem and the north coast

On the main road heading north out of Biak Town, villages and gardens set among low hills alternate with scrub vegetation. It is said that at certain times of the year, clouds of butterflies drift back and forth across the road. The asphalt greets the north coast at Korem, a nondescript little town on a wide, curving bay. Heavy breakers crash ashore during the west monsoon. At the eastern edge of the bay, an incredibly clear creek provides swimming and fishing for happy little boys. The western end of the bay receives a wide, sluggish river which can be crossed by canoe.

On the other side, work is proceeding on a paved road that will eventually reach

Opposite: *The cave at Goa Binsari, used by the Japanese in their World War II defenses.* **Below:** *Fire-walking, a Biak tradition that had been banned by the Dutch, is now enjoying a resurgence.*

Supiori Island. A bridge once spanned the narrow channel separating Biak from Supiori, but it collapsed and another is in the works. Once completed, the road will reach **Wapur Village** on Supiori, reputed to be the best in the area for swimming and snorkeling.

It's well worth the effort to travel to the west beyond Korem. Starting on the other side of the river, the paved road follows the palm-fringed shoreline past bays, coves, inlets, stretches of white sand beach and raised coral. Bridges cross clear streams where locals bathe or wash laundry. About five kilometers before the village of Warsa, a waterfall cascades down a mountainside several kilometers away. At Warsa, another waterfall tumbles some 15 meters, just by the main road. Children gleefully jump or dive off the top to entertain visitors. Although there are some corrugated metal roofs and sawn timber walls, most of the beachside huts and houses remain traditional: thatch roof, walls of *gaba-gaba* (the central spine of the sago palm leaf) with open porch, all raised on wooden piles a meter or so above the sand. And best of all, the people are handsome and friendly. On request, coconuts are brought down for thirsty travelers.

The economy and subsistence of this stretch of the coast, as with much of the rest of Biak, centers around fishing and small-scale agriculture. Garden plots in generally poor soils, prepared by the slash-and-burn technique, yield tubers and vegetables. Coconuts are home-processed into copra and oil. Sago tree trunks provide edible starch paste. Occasional hunting of wild pigs with dogs and spears provides entertainment and protein. (Domestic pigs are killed only for festivals.) Pigs and other game are also caught in traps set in the jungle. A variety of fish provides both a daily staple as well as cash. Tiny fish are hunted in tidal pools with mini-bows and arrows while hook and lines from outriggers land sharks up to 1.5 meters. Dried shark's fin, eventually ending up in Chinese stomachs, fetches up to $18 a kilo. If you are traveling along this stretch in December, ask about a special rite performed prior to setting out to catch flying fish. Magic formulas are also used for other species.

Wednesdays and Saturdays — market days in Korem — are best for travel along Biak's northwest coast. Public minibuses between Biak Town and Korem are more frequent then. Korem functions as one of the district's three secondary markets (the other two are Wardo and Bosnik) and transportation hubs. All villagers on Biak's and Supiori's north coasts trade at Korem unless they are willing to make the longer journey to Biak Town. From Korem, you can also catch a boat to nearby villages, accessible only from the sea. If you have time and a bit of luck there's an occasional boat from Korem to the far-off, paradisical island of Meosbepondi.

To the west: Wardo

The bay-side market of Wardo lies at the western end of a 50 kilometer paved road from Biak Town. This road branches off to the left (west) from the main road to Korem. The 1.5 hour ride is somewhat monotonous once you have taken in the roadside gardens and an occasional village popping out of the jungle backdrop, with waving kids and adults. Much of the area is uninhabited. A couple of kilometers before reaching the market, a paved strip to the right leads to the Wapsdori waterfall.

From the end of the road, there is a steep downhill path to the top of the falls. But you can't see the falls very well from this position. For a good view, you have to somehow descend to the river at the bottom — difficult even for mountain goats. Not for the faint-hearted. Instead of trying it this way, we recommend hiring a little outrigger canoe ($3 and perhaps 1.5 hours) from the bay next to Wardo market, and gliding up the river through lush tropical vegetation for the several kilometers to the falls. This real-life jungle river-boat ride is worth the trip. Those in a hurry could take a motorized outrigger, much faster but noisy, thus losing much of the ride's quiet charm.

A narrow, palm-fringed inlet reaches several hundred meters inland from the west coast of Biak at the Wardo market. Outriggered canoes and precariously balanced boats glide across the mirror-smooth waters. Large outriggers with an open cabin amidships and powered by 40 Hp outboards insure communications with Korido and other villages on Supiori's south coast. On market days, several of these boats make round-trips to Supiori, 2 to 3 hours each way, charging $3-5 per head. If you arrive early enough, it may be possible (but this is not guaranteed) to head out and back to somewhere on Supiori.

Korido Village, not very attractive, should not be your primary goal. If you want to visit a largish, accessible-only-by-boat village on the coast of Supiori, head for **Sowek Village** instead. The high hills of Supiori are often shrouded in grey and black clouds, forming an impressive backdrop to the sunny coast. The shallow reef apporach to Sowek spreads long and wide, jutting a long ways into the

sea before dropping off. The transparent waters provide ample work for local fishermen in tiny outriggers.

As you approach the entrance to Sowek through the open reef, a tree-crowned island with a spit of white sand beach could be a good spot for swimming and a picnic. Most of Sowek's houses are perched on stilts, lining the bay's inner shore. Very seldom visited by outsiders, the people are friendly and helpful.

The *camat* (head) of the south Supiori subdistrict lives in Sowek. **Insubabi**, a couple of inhabited islands and several "wedding cakes" of raised, vegetation-covered coral heads, lie a short ride away. Here again, the people are very friendly. The recent introduction of commercial seaweed production (for agar-agar), provides needed cash income to the inhabitants of Insubabi.

A wide coral bed lies in front of the village, with steep drop-off edges for good snorkeling. Turtles are common, along with harmless reef sharks and all the usual colorful reef fishes. To the south of Insubabi, shallow, sand-bottomed waters surround **Rani Island**. A long spit of white sand extends from the island's north side, another delightful swimming and picnic site. If you did not make plans to spend the night in this area, you will wish you had. You could also motor up to **Meosbepondi Island**, surrounded by beautiful waters full of fish and holding a nicely laid out, friendly village.

Opposite: *A coconut is deposited by the waves on the deserted beach at Korem on Biak Island.*
Right: *A stunning waterfall in western Biak.*

NUMFOR ISLAND

A Tropical Island Paradise

A stupendous, magical lagoon awaits lucky visitors to the west coast of Numfor. Coral outcrops and clear, tepid waters host brightly colored fish. The occasional outrigger squeezes under narrow, jagged coral overhangs. A tasty meal rewards every skillful throw. Palms and mangroves ring the lovely lagoon with bright red parrots squawking overhead. A dream-like setting — yet another tropical paradise.

Laid-back Numfor Island remains largely undisturbed except for the occasional group of Japanese war veterans. Villages lie scattered all along the island's 70-odd kilometer circumference, where mangrove swamps alternate with white sand beaches. But paradise has its price: there are no hotels or English speakers.

A 50-kilometer (30 mi.) road, built by the Americans during World War II, runs roughly parallel to the coast, encircling about two thirds of Numfor. With a bit of notice, you can hop on the back of a motorcycle to get around. Or better yet, hire a 40 Hp motorized outrigger, stopping along the way to snorkel or visit villages. This can be a bit expensive, as fuel costs are high, but is definitely worthwhile for at least several hours. Land travel is cheaper but roads seldom run within sight of the coast. Riding or hiking through the jungle can become tedious as only the occasional plumage bird enlivens the scenery.

For the purposes of administration, Numfor is divided into two subdistricts, east and west. These are further split into village areas, each of which includes a primary school and several scattered hamlets. East Numfor has six villages with a total population of just over 4,100 while West Numfor has five villages with some 3,800 inhabitants.

All households fish and farm for a living, which provides the basic necessities without a great deal of effort. Bits of metal left over from the war are forged and shaped into machetes, canoe-making adzes and other implements.

The island does have several exports: delicious smoke-dried fish, seashells, green beans, coconuts and trepang (a sea cucumber prized by Chinese epicures). There are small stores stocking basics such as soap and batteries, but nothing requiring sizeable amounts of cash.

Small local motorboats, which shuttle passengers and goods between Biak and Manokwari, levy high charges, discouraging exports and doubling the cost of imported fuel. Plans are afoot to build a pier at Manggari to accommodate larger and more cost-efficient boats. The government hopes that this will encourage people to produce more for export. But with plentiful fish and

fertile soil, it is unlikely that the Numforese will jump on the consumer bandwagon.

Around the island by boat

During most of the year, motorcycles can take you around two thirds of the island, but boats are the only convenient way to reach picturesque coastal villages such as Bawei and Mandori, unless you are prepared for several hours of hiking. **Bawei Village**, less than an hour's canoe ride from Yemburwo, has a church built on a pile of raised coral.

Boat travel also allows for lots of snorkeling off the reefs which fringe Numfor, often too far from shore for easy access. Many of the coral formations are under one to ten meters of water, with a fair variety of colorful pelagic fish. On the edge of the reef between Andei and Manggari villages, the remains of a U.S. fighter plane from World War II lies partially exposed to the waves.

On arrival in **Yemburwo**, by the airstrip, check out the simple Japanese Shinto war memorial with a cross just in back of an enclosed space next to the main road. A local pastor helped to dedicate the monument, hence the cross. Near the memorial, the fuselage of a U.S. bomber served for many years as a home for a family. Today, it is used for storage. The plane's serial number and seal can still be clearly seen on a sheet of metal. Another part of the fuselage, where the letters "U.S.A." are clearly visible, encloses a privy perched on stilts over the water.

Just two kilometers from Yemburwo, the village of **Andei** is home to a couple of small boats that make runs to Biak and Manokwari. From Andei, the road cuts inland through the jungle, with paths leading to small seaside settlements or inland gardens.

Manggari Village contains the crumbling remains of a U.S. built dock area, a small Japanese ship partially submerged in the sand and the wrecks of a dozen amphibious landing vehicles. A bell, formerly used to call GIs to chow, has been hung in front of the church to call the faithful to prayer.

A shorter jaunt out of Yemburwo leads west some 5 kilometers to a beautiful long white sand beach at **Asaibori**, near a small village. A bridge, built over a wide creek during World War II, has now collapsed. As this was on the main road to the west, the currently used road, which cuts inland, misses this nice beach, favored by the local population for Sunday picnics.

The road along the western shore of Numfor reaches the village of **Saribi**, then peters out in the jungle before **Pakreki**. This last village remains accessible for motorcycles but to travel to Mandori, on the east central coast, you must go by boat or on foot.

Heading west from Yemburwo, you cross the boundary between Numfor Timor (East Numfor subdistrict) and Numfor Barat (West Numfor). Report to the West Numfor police, in the subdistrict capital of **Kameri**, just off the main road at the entrance to the village.

Offshore from Kameri, an American plane crash-landed in ten meters of water. South of Kameri, there are inland caves occupied by the Japanese during World War II. **Baruki**, the first village south of Kameri, lies at the end of a deep bay, fringed with white sand and protected by an island at the entrance.

With sufficient notice, rousing song-and-dance performances can be arranged here for visitors.

Namber, the next village down the coast, should figure on your agenda as an overnight stop. The scenery, especially the fish-filled bays, will easily occupy any spare time on your schedule. The village is split into two settlements, Namber Lama (Old Namber) and Namber Baru (New Namber). A short walk from the main road brings you to an exquisite spring-fed cove whose waters flow through a narrow channel into a mangrove-lined bay. A few huts perched on stilts form part of the village, most of which is located at a slight elevation. Here you can easily hop into a small outriggered canoe to explore the

bay, the uninhabited island of Pulau Manem and a delightful lagoon-bay called Kasyom a short way down the coast to the south.

Manem Island, a Japanese oupost during World War II, now hosts birds which flock to the mainland at dawn and return at dusk. Just south of Namber, at Rumboi, you can see the remains of a jetty built by the Americans. Another jetty was built near Saribi village. People at both Saribi and Pakreki say that there are weapons and other war artifacts inland. If you are willing to trek with them, they will be happy to show you the relics.

Opposite: *A young Numforese boy.* **Above:** *A spring and lagoon on the west coast of Numfor — a deserted little corner of paradise.*

YAPEN ISLAND

Coral Gardens and Birds of Paradise

Yapen island is a convenient distance from Biak and offers clear waters with excellent swimming, snorkeling and diving. Curious stilt-perched villages jut into the island's many small bays. A permit, necessary for a stay in Yapen, can be easily obtained at the Biak police station.

The island is shaped like a cigar — 150 kilometers (93 mi.) long and about 30 kilometers (19 mi.) wide in the middle. The interior is steeply mountainous with a blanket of multi-hued vegetation. Two small villages, located some 1,000 meters up in the tangle of forests and crags, grow some of the world's best coffee. Their problem is in marketing it — hiking the difficult route with 10 kilo bags of coffee beans. Local trekkers say it takes two to three days to cross Yapen from Serui on the north coast. The only dangerous animals are snakes, with one small species,

called *ular bisa,* reputed to sting with its tail.

Together with a chunk of the mainland of Irian, Yapen forms the *kabupaten,* or district, of Yapen-Waropen, with a total population of 60,000. About 10,000 of these live in Yapen, one-fifth in Serui town. The district's 700 Muslims live in town. Everyone else on the island is Protestant.

Cacao and timber lead Yapen's cash economy, followed by fish, coffee, trepang and massoi bark (this last used in Javanese folk medicines). Oil from the massoi bark, mixed with water, served in rites of purification, necessary after one had slain an enemy. After the oil-and-water bath, the deceased's spirit could not molest its conqueror.

Serui, a nondescript town if ever there was one, nestles at the bottom of a wide bay. The landing field spreads out at the edge of town. Merpati Airlines flies the 40 kilometers (25 mi.) from Biak every day except Saturday for $28 round trip. Passengers, riding in 18-seat Twin Otters, spend 25 minutes in the air over the sea, as Yapen's steep, vegetation clad mountains rise into view. The plane banks over a turquoise bay dotted with stilted huts before landing at the town.

The best accommodations, at Losmen Merpati on Jalan Yos Sudarso, cost $9 a day for a fan-cooled room with attached ladle-type bath, sit-down toilet and three complete meals and snacks. Free rides to and from the airport are included. Two bare-bones accom-

modations, the Losmen Bersaudara and the Marena, run $3 a day without food.

Serui hosts a bustling early-morning market with vegetables and fish brought in by canoe. A paved road on the west side of the bay leads to two villages perched over the water: **Pasir Hitam**, a half hour's stroll, and **Pasir Putih**, which takes about an hour. If you prefer, entrepreneurs will paddle you there from Serui in a canoe for a pittance.

Serui is heaven for serious bird watchers. A day's walk into the uninhabited mountainous interior reportedly affords glimpses of several species of birds of paradise and other shy and exotic forest denizens. The locals set noose traps for wild pigs and snare birds. Unfortunately, they also hunt the protected birds of paradise, the skin and feathers of which fetch some $30 (or more) in Jakarta. As most of the hunting takes place near the more heavily inhabited southern coast, it is said that the birds have fled to Yapen's north shore — easily accessible by boat from Biak.

Shallow seas and bays, replete with coral gardens and fishing villages, are Yapen's main attraction. Sturdy bamboo outriggers can be hired for $20 to $30 a day, plus fuel. Petrol runs about $3-4 an hour at 10-12 knots. The canoes have a little cabin across the hull, and are powered by 40 hp Yamaha outboards. The pilot will stop at villages and diving spots, according to your mood and interest. A mini-yacht in paradise — but not advisable during the season of heavy seas, September through December. If your Indonesian is up to it, bargain and charter one of these canoes. Otherwise, arrangements can be made through the Losmen Merpati or the Reverend Mesak Dawir, tel. 67.

Ambai Village makes the perfect destination for a half-day outrigger trip. It is less than an hour from Serui, and on the way there are plenty of sheltered bays with clear water and coral. Fish are more abundant outside the bays. Be careful of the red-and-white striped lionfish. Although this beautiful creature won't attack, contact with its dorsal fins will prove excruciatingly painful. More mundane, though more likely, is stepping on a sea urchin. The imbedded spines are prone to infection and can take a long time to heal.

Ambai, perched on stilts on a small island facing Yapen, is huge by local standards — 3,000 people, including the "suburbs." Every Tuesday and Wednesday on a tiny island in the bay, people from Ambai bring fish to barter for vegetables brought from the facing "mainland" village. Long-established practices keep bargaining to a minimum. This picturesque market is strictly for early birds — 5:30 a.m. to 6:30 a.m.

Opposite: *A brightly colored traditional canoe slices through the water off Yapen Island.* **Below:** *The beauty of the lionfish,* Pterois volitans, *can be deceptive — its dorsal spines are poisonous.*

Biak Practicalities

All prices in U.S. $; Biak city code: 961

With an increasing number of Garuda flights from Los Angeles landing here on the way to Bali, with other airlines (JAL, Qantas, Air Niuguini) requesting landing rights, and a new diving boat (the *Tropical Princess*) calling it home, Biak has the potential to become a full-fledged tourist destination. But before hordes of tourists descend from the jets, the place needs much better infrastructure.

Although rumors raise five-star hotels all over the place, ground has yet to be broken for any international standard accommodation. The road network, a slowly expanding strip of asphalt leading to remote villages previously accessible only by sea, will remain inadequate for years. Boats available for charter — outboard powered, twin hulled catamarans with a little roofed cabin midship — are neither cheap nor comfortable. But we highly recommend visiting Biak before it becomes another Bali, because it has all the necessary attractions.

ARRIVAL

If arriving directly from the United States, immigration and customs formalities are taken care of at Biak airport. Since the flights (which continue on to Bali) come in quite early in the morning, you may have to wait a while until the officials show up. On the outward-bound flights, passengers boarding in Jakarta or Bali go through immigration and customs before they reach Biak. Only those boarding here have to be cleared at Biak.

Inside the airport or just outside, minibus and taxi drivers compete for your business. Town is about 2 kilometers away. There is no fixed price, and the going rate is US$2-4, depending on your bargaining skills, command of Indonesian, and the current demand. On the main road to town just outside the airport, you can catch a public minibus to town for Rp200. The three Titawaka hotels usually have a bus waiting at the airport for their guests. The Irian Hotel is about 100 meters from the terminal. If you stay there, an airport porter will take your luggage to the lobby for US$1, more or less.

ACCOMMODATIONS

Adequate creature comforts are available in Biak, from quite nice air-conditioned hotels at varying prices to some very cheap digs for $3-4 a night. Hotel Irian, just across the road from the airport, retains a leisurely, colonial feel in its combined lobby and dining area. The bar, the only decent one in town, often hosts Frenchmen working in the sawmill or the fishery. The dining room provides quite passable, filling meals. Nice view over a wide lawn to the sea, but watch out for the sea urchins if you go swimming. There is lots of shallow coral before the deeper waters.

For a very pleasant small hotel in town, try the Wisma Titawaka. A bit expensive, but it has

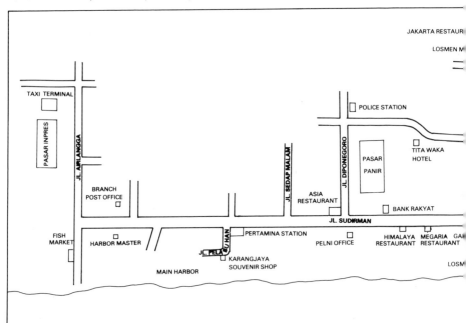

a pretty view and a fair amount of art on display. The nearby Titawaka Home also shows lots of art, along with birds and crocodiles. **Wisma Titawaka.** Jl. Selat Makassar 3, P.O. Box 536, Tel: 21658. 12 rooms. Overlooks the harbor, and has a display of traditional carvings with some items for sale. $26 S, AC w/ meals. **Titawaka Home.** Jl. Monginsidi 14, P.O. Box 536, Tel: 21891. 10 rooms. Located right on the sea; crocodiles and birds, tasteful decorations. $26 S, AC w/ meals. **Hotel Irian.** Across from the airport on Jl. Ahmad Yani, P.O. Box 546, Tel: 21139 and 21839. 65 rooms, 43 w/ AC. Spacious lobby and dining area. Dutch-built, scheduled for upgrading, but okay as is. Two kilometers out of town, but frequent public transportation. Shrine for Japanese war dead on front lawn. $16 S, $21 D, w/ AC; $10 S fan-cooled. Prices include three meals. **Hotel Mapia.** Jl. A. Yani, Tel: 21303. 23 rooms. Owned by Natur. All rooms with ladle bath. Large traditional canoe in front. AC $15 S, w/ meals, $18 S. Fan-cooled $9 S, w/ meals, $15 S. **Losmen Maju.** Jl. Imam Bonjol 45, Tel: 21841. 12 rooms. No meals but rooms have basic attached toilets. $5 S. **Sinar Kayu.** Jl. Selayar, Tel: 21613, at the edge of town. 24 rooms. Fan-cooled only, toilets outside rooms. $3. **Losmen Solo.** Jl. Monginsidi 4, Tel: 21397. 17 rooms. Next to night market stalls, just off the harbor. Fan-cooled with shared toilets, $3 S.

LOCAL TRANSPORTATION

Taxis. Within Biak itself, minibus/taxis are abundant and make frequent runs to the ends of the paved roads. But first they wait at the terminal, next to the Inpres Market, until they overflow with passengers. The public minibuses charge Rp250 in town and the immediate vicinity. Chartered taxis in town are $3/hr. To Bosnik by public transportation is Rp200-300. Round-trip charter to Bosnik, including waiting time, about $10. Public transportation to Koram, Rp500; round-trip charter, including waiting time, $20.

Local boat travel

The double outriggered, outboard powered canoes, are locally called "Johnson" — though the engines are all Yamahas today. Cheapest if you go as one of many paying passengers. Most frequent on market days. To the Padaido Islands from Bosnik, to north Biak and north Supiori from Korem, to south Supiori from Wardo. Motorized canoes from various villages arrive either the afternoon before or on the morning of market days to return home that day or the following morning. Prices, depending on distance, vary from $2 to $6. Some boats have a little roofed cabin, others don't, so be prepared for hot sun or rain. You can probably return on the next market day.

Some of these boats can also be chartered, with prices depending on distance and your bargaining skills in Indonesian. Anywhere from $30 to $175 for a round trip. Plan on staying overnight to take full advantage of your trip and not to have to hurry back.

Minibuses run much less frequently after dark, so unless you return to Bosnik, Korem or

Biak Town

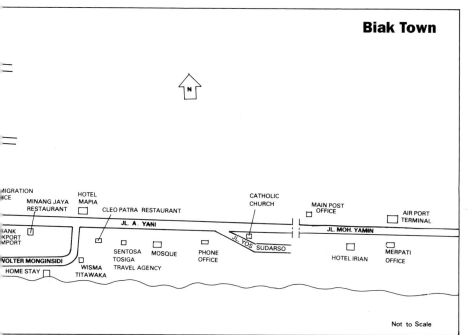

Wardo before 6 pm, you might have a 2-3 hour wait — or sleep there.

Outrigger canoes can also be rented from the fishermen's cooperative in Biak town. Ask someone with some English to take you there and arrange things. Chartering to visitors is new, so it could take a bit of time — a day or two — to arrange. Of course, travel agencies can set up everything, albeit at a higher cost. They usually run tours only to the Padaido Islands.

Sea travel can be uncomfortable during the *musim ombak*, the season of waves or heavy seas. This starts between late September and early December, lasting through March or April.

DINING

The restaurants in Biak serve basic Indonesian and Chinese dishes, all quite tasty and moderately priced. All the better hotels serve meals.

Jakarta. Jl. Imam Bonjol 58, tel. 21969. Simple Indonesian dishes $1-$1.25; crab $3; squid $2.50; beef $2.50; large fish $4; shrimp $3. The only place in town serving trepang, $3.

Minang Jaya. Jl. A. Yani, tel. 21591. Typical Pandang-style. Eat your fill for $2-$5.

Megaria. Jl. Sudirman. Asparagus and goodies soup, $3.50-$9; chicken or crab $2.50-$3; beef $4; pigeon (imported frozen) $5; big fish $3-$4.50; squid or pork $2.50-$3.

Himalaya. Jl. Sudirman. Hard liquor $10 a bottle or $1.50 a shot. Chicken, pigeon, shrimp, beef, pork, soups, crab, frog or squid, fish $2-$6. Frequented by some expat Frenchmen.

Asia. Jl. Sudirman. Varied menu, cheaper than other restaurants. More spacious, but darker and less business-like than the others.

Cleopatra. Jl. A. Yani. Pleasant in good weather, with outdoor tables under umbrellas. Inexpensive chicken dishes, $3; shrimp $3.50; fish $3. Less varied menu than other restaurants.

BANKS AND MONEY-CHANGING

The Expor-Impor Bank, on Jl. Sudirman, and **Bank Rakyat** will change American Express travelers checks. They will sometimes change Bank of America travelers checks and U.S. currency — but only if the bills are in perfect condition.) Both banks are open 8 am -12:30 pm.

POST OFFICE

The main office is on Jl. A. Yani, towards the airport. There is a branch office on Jl. Sudirman, in town. Both are open 8 am to 5 pm.

MEDICAL

The hospital is **Rumah Sakit Umum**, on Jl. Sriwijaya Ridge 1, tel. 21294. Some of the doctors speak passable English Pharmacies include Apotik Cenderawasih, Jl. Imam Bonjol 34, Tel. 21754, and Apotik Gandawati. Jl. A. Yani.

BOOKSTORE

Pojok Buku. Jl. Mongonsidi 18, Tel: 21425 and 21498. Some English language books, including the best of the missionary literature on Irian. This store is run by American Jacob Hanas, who is quite helpful.

SHOPPING AND SOUVENIRS

At all the Titawaka Hotel locations; at the airport (mostly awful Asmat rip-offs and stone axes that fall apart); Karang Jaya on Jl. Pelabuhan (mostly seashells); and Kios Jaya at Pasar Panir (basically ceramics and crafts).

MARKETS

There is not much excitement in Biak town, but a walk through the markets can always reveal strange produce, new smells and surprises. There is an early morning and (sometimes) afternoon open air fish market just off Jl. Sudirman, past the branch post office, toward the sea. There are two other markets: Pasar Inpres on Jalan Teuku Umar, next to the "terminal" or central taxi station. Here you can find fresh food and some dry goods. The Pasar Panir market, on Jl. Selat Makassar, sells (illegal) bird of paradise skins, Chinese ceramics, dry goods, clothes and household items.

AGENCY TOURS

Sentosa Tosiga. Jl A. Yani 36, Tel: 21398 and 21956. Sentosa Tosiga is the only travel agency to organize tours out of town. As elsewhere, tours are expensive for just one or two clients, and the per-person price drops dramatically for a large group. City tours, including the caves and beach, run $17-30 for two — if a dance is included, $52-80. A tour to Korem beach costs $22; to the Padaido Islands — Ureb, Mansubabo and Nusi — $90. Tour to Padaido Bawah, Auki and Owi, $85. Ask also at the Titawaka hotels about their tours.

AREA TRANSPORTATION

Biak is well served by both Garuda Indonesia and Merpati Airlines. Merpati serves 14 towns in Irian from its base in Biak, but Garuda has fewer delays and plane changes. The schedules below were accurate at the time of this writing, but they change constantly. Always check with the airlines for current schedules and prices.

Garuda Indonesia. Jl. Sudirman 3, Tel. 21416.

Ambon, Ujung Pandang	SuTuWF
Ambon, Ujung Pandang, Denpasar	M
Denpasar, Jakarta	SuTu
Jayapura	Daily
Jayapura	M
Jayapura	WS
Sorong, Menado	WS
Timika, Jayapura	SuTu
Ujung Pandang, Surabaya, Jakarta	Daily

Prices: Ambon $59; Denpasar $147; Jakarta $187; Jayapura $36; Menado $97; Surabaya $167; Timika $36; Ujung Pandang $114.

Merpati. Jl. M. Yamin, opposite the airport, Tel: 21213.

Nabire	Daily
Kaimana	MWTh
Fakfak	MW
Manokwari	Daily
Bituni	MWThF
Serui	MTuWThFSu
Jayapura	MTuThSSu
Tanah Merah	M
Wamena	TuThSSu
Sorong	Su
Taminabun	Su
Ambon, Ujung Pandang,	
Surabaya, Jakarta	FSu

Prices: Ambon $54; Fakfak $80; Jakarta $159; Jayapura $31; Kaimana $47; Manokwari $26; Merauke $84; Nabire $27; Numfor $26; Serui $15; Sorong $37; Surabaya $143; Ujung Pandang $97.

Pelni. Jl. Sudirman 27, Tel: 21056 or 21593. Pelni boats (deck passage only) run to Jayapura and Sorong every 10 days or so. They have two ships doing circle routes, Jayapura-Sorong, calling at Sarmi, Serui, Biak, Nabire and Manokwari. Four days to Jayapura and 3 days to Sorong, deck passage, no food provided, $10. Other boats have various runs, some taking 20 days and calling at dozens of small Conradesque places. Forget schedules. Bring at least a mat to sleep on and survival food.

EXCURSIONS

Birding. Possible on Biak or Supiori with a fair number of species. It is said that birds of paradise are quite easy to see with a local guide on the north coast of Yapen Island during the early morning hours. Count on about $200 for an overnight round-trip by motorized outrigger from Biak.
Fire-walking. In Adoki village, with a day or two's notice required. For groups of five, $50. If you want a native style pig barbecue feast also, it's $85 for the package, including dances while the food is cooking. Additional fee for groups over five. At the time of this writing, fire-walking on Biak had not yet been performed for tourists.
Roofed graves. All over Biak. The metal roofs covering the graves are to keep the ancestors in good shape for the day of final judgement.

WEATHER

Yearly rainfall is a bit under 3,000 millimeters (118 in.) on Biak during some 170 days. Unlike Western Indonesia, the rainy season here is unpredictable. The wet season is December to March, during the westerly monsoon, but it seldoms rains more than a few days at a time. The dry season is July to September, during which time the notorious *wambraw*, a desiccating southeast wind blows, sometimes makes canoeing tough going.

Numfor Island

Visits to the island begin at the landing strip at Yemburwo, unless you arrive by boat. If you can afford it, hire a motorized canoe and spend two or three days motoring around the island, sleeping in villages along the way. While actual travel time is only some 10 hours, stopping at various villages and exploring the deep inlet at Bawei will make this journey much more memorable than a quick zip around. As several sides of Numfor are fronted by wide tidal flats, you can travel close to shore only at high tide. Plan on spending one night at Namber Village, as the best scenery lies in the vicinity.

GETTING THERE

By air. Flights to and from Biak and Manokwari on Tuesdays and Fridays. From Biak $20, from Manokwari $15.

As the plane from Biak usually arrives quite early in the morning, once you have settled in at the *camat* and taken your passport and *surat jalan* to the police, there's still a good half-day left to explore a part of the island. Head east and make a round trip from Yemburwo to Manggari, some 11 km away.
By sea. Boats once or twice a week from Biak, 8 to 9 hours — $6. Same frequency to and from Manokwari, 5 hours — $4.50.

ACCOMMODATIONS

The *camat* (government head) at Yemburwo, whose house is next to the landing strip, has spare bedrooms and his wife prepares very passable meals. Elsewhere, you could stay with the island's other *camat* at Kameri, one of the village heads (*kepala desa*), a schoolteacher (*guru*) or anyone willing to give you a bit of space. An air mattress and sheet are handy. Meals can be prepared on request.

At the *camats'* houses the cost is $4.50 a day. Elsewhere, $3. Motorcycle rental (with driver) is $4.50 half day; $7.50 full day. Guide/porter costs $6 a day.

LOCAL TRANSPORTATION

Boat rental costs $12 per hour of actual motoring time. Takes about 10 hours to circle Numfor. Reasonable waiting time is free, but negotiate this beforehand. Hiring or riding on the back of a motorcycle is an alternate way to explore the island.

MISCELLANEOUS

Market days at Yemburwo are Wednesday and Saturday (5:30 to 7 am). Song and dance performances cost $6 to $30 depending on the number of participants and the number of different dances.

Electricity is found only in Yemburwo, from 6 pm to midnight. Scheduled in Kameri for sometime in the future.

JAYAPURA

Irian's Bustling Provincial Capital City

Jayapura began its life as Hollandia in 1910, became Kota Baru after Irian's integration into Indonesia, and again changed briefly to Sukarnopura before assuming its current name. The bustling city of almost 100,000, spreads in back of what used to be known as Humboldt Bay, now Teluk Yos Sudarso.

The best view of the town and harbor sweeps out from the base of the tall red-and-white communications tower. A paved road leads to the top of the steep hill but no public transportation climbs up there. Still, locals occasionally find a way up to take in the panorama, especially on those evenings — every two weeks — when the huge *Umsini* passenger ship is expected to call.

Founding the city

In 1858, the Dutch war-steamer *Etna* cruised Irian's north coast on its journey of colonial exploration. The *Etna* visited Humboldt Bay and a landing party scouted the immediate surroundings. On its way back to Ternate, the Dutch team called at Doreri (near present day Manokwari) where the ship's officers gave Sir Alfred Wallace, the great British naturalist, an account of their findings. Wallace writes: "They had stayed at Humboldt Bay several days, and found it a much more beautiful and interesting place than Dorey [Doreri], as well as a better harbour."

The Dutch were finally prodded into founding Hollandia by German claims on the northern coast of New Guinea. The 141° E longitude line had been settled upon as a border, and by positioning their capital just 22 kilometers (14 mi.) from the line, the Dutch figured on making it easier for the Germans to respect the border. Civil servants formed the nucleus of Hollandia's tiny community until World War II broke out. The Japanese quickly swept aside the Dutch defenders and built Hollandia into an important base.

Allied units under General Douglas MacArthur captured Hollandia after an amphibious landing and made it into a gigantic forward staging area from which to wage the Pacific campaign. The Japanese-built airfield at Sentani, enlarged and improved, became the home base for a wing of Superfortress bombers and swarms of fighters. At the height of the Allied push, Hollandia's population reached a quarter mil-

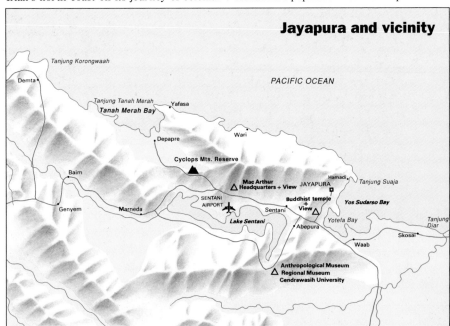

Jayapura and vicinity

lion. (See "World War II," page 38.)

After the war and Indonesian independence, the Dutch hung on to Irian as their last remaining possession in the East Indies. In 1955, Hollandia's population of 16,700 was made up chiefly of those fleeing from the Sukarno regime. But during the 1960s, Irian and Hollandia were integrated into Indonesia. In 1971, the capital's population reached 35,000 and thereafter increased steadily to today's 100,000. Many Javanese, Makassarese and Bugis Muslims, as well as Ambonese and Menadonese Christians, have migrated to Jayapura — where, in a "frontier" economy heavily subsidized by Jakarta, jobs are more readily available.

Hamadi: beachside suburb

The beachside suburb of Hamadi, located off the main road to Sentani about 4 kilometers (2.5 mi.) out of town, has the only souvenir stalls in the area. Don't expect any real antiques or masterpieces — only souvenirs, reasonably priced, consisting of crude Asmat and local carvings, penis gourds and other goods from the highlands. On the outskirts of Hamadi, a couple of World War II vintage tanks and landing craft rust peacefully, sinking slowly into the sand along the beach. Swimming is possible here, but is no great joy. Better go to the opposite end of Jayapura, about 7 kilometers (4.5 mi.) west , to old Base G for clearer water and a cleaner beach.

Locals go there in hordes on Sundays, the only day public transportation makes the run.

Short jaunts out of town

The stilt-perched village of **Engros** on Yotefa Bay — in front of Hamadi — might be fun to visit, even for an overnight stay in a losmen over the water. There are no luxuries here, but Engros offers a good look at the coastal lifestyle. At low tide, the bay bottom next to the village turns into an animated soccer field. Probably the only place in the world where the tides interrupt the matches.

There are several beaches a bit out of town yet still within striking distance. About 60 kilometers (37 mi.) from Jayapura, an hour or so past Sentani town, a paved road reaches **Tanah Merah Bay**. The snorkeling here is quite good, and for those who somehow can get hold of scuba equipment, there are World War II wrecks at reachable depths. **Holtekang Bay**, in another direction, has a good sandy beach, and is quiet even on weekends. There is no coral here, so forget snorkeling, but several interesting species of birds are known to inhabit the vicinity. Another good birding spot, the lighthouse a half hour's climb from Base G, also offers spectacular dawn views of Jayapura. Below the lighthouse, big waves crash around the

Overleaf: *Beautiful Jayapura Bay on Irian's North Coast.* **Below:** *An island village in Jayapura Bay.*

rock formations. Another superb little bay, locally called **Pasir Enam**, can be reached either by boat from Jayapura or by an hour's stroll along a footpath beginning at the expat enclave of Angkasa II. There is an isolated beach there, and the reefs offer good diving.

A half-day excursion out of Jayapura (or Sentani) covers several points of interest between the airport and the capital. The **University of Cenderawasih Museum** in Abepura boasts quite a good collection of Irianese artifacts and a souvenir stand offering recent carvings and craft items. A few kilometers further out of town, the **Museum Negeri** offers exhibits on the natural history and material culture of several Irianese ethnic groups. Both museums are open from 8 am to 1 pm Mon - Fri.

There are two floors to the Museum Negeri's main building, housing a variety of artifacts from all districts of Irian. Some are labelled in English and there are plans for more thorough descriptions. For those whose interests are strictly aesthetic, the collection of the University of Cenderawasih is preferable. At the Museum Negeri, however, you get a better idea of the material culture of several Irianese groups. There are miniature huts showing regional variations in living quarters, including a 1:4 scale front of an Asmat men's house and a Dani *honai,* also a men's hut. Lots of bone tools, including some made from human bones. Particularly fasci-

nating are two Asmat trophy or ancestral skulls, skillfully decorated. One display is of traditional bride price items, another has musical instruments. Upstairs, the Summer Institute of Linguistics has listed 245 languages and dialects of Irian, keyed to a large map. Historical trade contacts with the island are documented with Chinese, Japanese and Dutch porcelain and other exchange items.

Lake Sentani

Just out of Sentani, a paved road winds upward for 6 kilometers (4 mi.) and climbs to Mount Ifar in the Cyclops Mountains. At Ifar stands a monument to General MacArthur, whose headquarters were here. The site overlooks the humid lowlands and offers a splendid view of the lake. Local lore states that while gazing out over island-strewn Lake Sentani, MacArthur conceived his famous island-hopping strategy in the Pacific.

At several places on the shores of **Lake Sentani**, you can arrange to rent an outboard-powered dugout ($10 to $15/hour) to visit the island villages or just ride around the lake. While there are regular services, it's better to charter one of these outboard-powered canoes, if you can afford it. Some are magnificent craft, hollowed out from a single, huge trunk. Many have painted or carved motifs in the old Sentani style, formerly one of Irian's great art centers. One of the canoes, with a raised human figure in a styl-

ized background, should belong to a museum. But it looks as if there are still years of service left in its beautiful old body.

If you rent a boat, ask to be taken to **Apayo Island** where craftsmen churn out bark cloth paintings and sculptures of the traditional style. Or just ride around for an hour or two and take pictures of the hills disappearing into the water at the foot of the Cyclops Mountains. It is safe to swim in the lake. If there are any crocodiles left, they are concentrated around the more remote shores where there are no buzzing motors.

The locals fish the lake from tiny canoes. Women do most of the fishing, and the men work the sago palm and fish only occasionally. The men's canoes are more rounded than the ladies' and more difficult to balance in. Don't take your camera if you want to try out one of the little canoes by yourself.

Occasionally one of the boys from the **Yugga Restaurant** on the shores of the lake uses scuba equipment to spear fish here. The lake said to reach to depths of over 100 meters (300 ft.). Our diver says that visibility is so bad that you have to be almost touching the fish before spearing them. He also tells of some men with *ilmu,* or "knowledge," who dive without any equipment, stay underwater for three days and bring back a huge catch.

Crocodile farms

Four crocodile farms raise the critters in the vicinity of Jayapura. If you want to visit one, we suggest c.v. Bintang Mas. There is no road sign for the croc farm, but it is about halfway between the 6 and 7 kilometer markers on the road from Jayapura to Sentani. Watch on the right-hand side for Klinik Pantai Nirmala. A dirt road to Bintang Mas runs right next to the clinic. In about a half kilometer you will see the roadside pens.

At the farm, crocodiles of different sizes are carefully segregated to prevent the smaller ones from getting gobbled up by their elder siblings. Feeding time — fish and shrimp — is around 3 p.m.

Thanks to the farms, you can buy crocodile meat around Jayapura for $3 per kilo, less than one third of the price in Hong Kong or Singapore — where much of the frozen meat ends up. The Chinese believe crocodile meat cures asthma and other ills.

Of course, the crocs are not raised for their meat, but for the valuable skins. Most of the 15 farms in Irian raise the animals for 3-4 years, when their length reaches 1.5 meters (5 ft.). At this size, a croc produces 15 kilos of

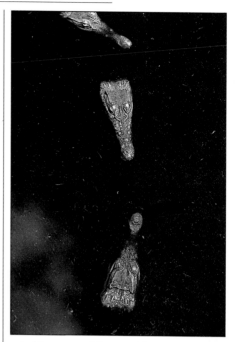

saleable meat and the crucial 30-40 centimeter (12-15 in.) width of belly skin. At this size, the skin is tough, yet still pliable. The belly skins end up in Paris or Tokyo, and the rest of the hides get worked into local souvenirs.

Breeding crocodiles in captivity is a very tricky affair. The eggs react to minute changes of temperature and humidity and unless conditions are perfect the embryos turn out to be all males — or all females, or they all even die. (In a natural setting the mother crocs pull together a heap of vegetation, and the heat of decomposition incubates the eggs.) Rather than trying to hatch eggs, the crocodile farms find it much easier to buy small, month-old crocodile babies. These are purchased from the natives who live near the animals' natural nesting grounds.

Conservationists approve of this method, because it involves the local community in the crocodile's welfare — the locals don't eat the eggs or kill the reptiles, and the economic motive gives them an incentive to keep out poachers. In addition, the egg collectors cash payment is sometimes supplemented by chicken eggs so that the old source of protein will not be missed.

Opposite: *Women fishing on Lake Sentani. The lake is rich in delicious fish.* **Above:** *Crocodiles in a pond near Jayapura. Crocodile skins, from 25 farms in the region, are a valuable export. The best hides wind up in Tokyo and Paris.*

Jayapura Practicalities

All prices in U.S. $; Jayapura city code: 967

All flights land at Sentani Airport, some 40 kilometers (25 mi.) from Jayapura. Outside the airport, minibuses wait to take you to town. $5-9 to Jayapura for the minibus/taxi — make sure you and your driver agree to a price before getting in. If you have little luggage and a tight budget, walk the 200 meters from the airport complex to the main road. The trip to town by public minibus consists of two legs: to Abepura, change buses and then to Jayapura (50¢).

If your visit to Jayapura is just a hurdle on the way to the Baliem valley, you may want to just drop your gear at one of the losmen near the airport and zip to town for your Merpati ticket (leaving at 7 am the next day) and police permit. Count on 3-5 hours for the trip including waiting for the *surat jalan* and ticket.

The bulk of Jayapura nestles in a short valley running straight inland and most government offices are along the shoreline. Commercial activity centers on Jalan Ahmad Yani, which slices through town with a constant flow of traffic unchecked by stoplights. The police station, needed for the essential *surat jalan*, and the Expor-Impor Bank, the only one in town that deals in international currency, are on Jl. A. Yani.

SURAT JALAN

The police station, next to the Hotel Matoa, issues the essential *surat jalan*, the travel permit required for the interior. Bring your passport and four photos — usually only two are enough, but you never know. A half-hour should do the trick, unless the man who controls the stamps is out. Merpati, the only scheduled airline flying to the Baliem, has its main office on the other side of the Matoa. (See "Travel Advisory" page 150 for more on the *surat jalan*.)

ACCOMMODATIONS

Jayapura is well provided with a number of air-conditioned hotels — none quite as illustrious as the Matoa — as well as with losmen catering to the budget traveler. But there are no accommodations as cheap as in Java and Sumatra, for example.

Hotels in Jayapura

Matoa. Jl. Ahmad Yani 14; Tel: (0967) 22336 or 22936; Telex: 76208 Matoa IA. Two stars; the only international standard hotel in town; with continental breakfast; all rooms with central AC; dining room/bar; helpful staff; elevator; taxis in front. All rooms with color TV/video, mini-bar. $25 S, $30 D, $45 Suite.

Triton. Jl. Ahmad Yani 52; P.O. Box 52, Tel: 21218 or 21171. 24 rooms. Free airport taxi; lounge with color TV/video, all rooms AC. Next to the Rasa Sayang Restaurant (steak, occasionally venison). $13 to $20 w/ breakfast.

Irian Plaza. Jl. Ahmad Yani 65; Tel: 21575 or 22539. 40 rooms with varying facilities divided

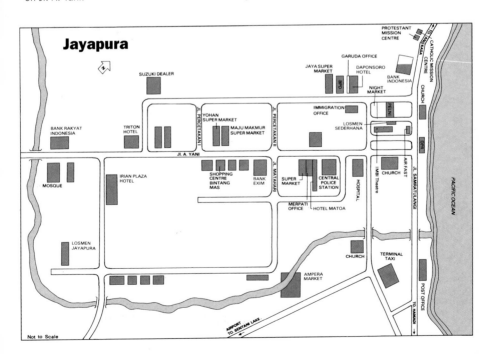

into three classes. Meeting room, phones in rooms. $13-$18 S; add 15% for D; w/ light breakfast.

Dafonsoro. *Jl.* Percetakan Negara 20/24; Tel: 21870 or 22285. 28 rooms, all AC. Restaurant; Garuda Office next door. $13 S, $15 D w/ simple breakfast.

Numbai. *Jl.* Trikora 1; Tel: 21394 or 22185 — about 5 km from downtown, close to the bemo route "Dock 5." AC $10 S, $13 D; $3 less if fan cooled. All w/ simple breakfast. Meals available ($2.50) if ordered ahead.

Losmen in Jayapura

Losmen Sederhana. *Jl.* Halmahera 2; Tel: 21292 or 22157. 15 rooms, some AC, some fan-cooled, some with attached bath. (try bargaining) with AC and attached bath $15; with fan, outside bath $8; add 30% for two in room; all prices include simple breakfast; warung-style meals brought in on request, $1 to $2.

Losmen Lawu. *Jl.* Sulawesi 22; Tel: 21937. About 4 km from downtown; 15 rooms, 4 with AC. AC $8 S, $14 D; Fan-cooled $4.50 S, $8 D; all w/ simple breakfast. Meals from food stalls, $1 to $3.

Losmen Kartini. *Jl.* Perintis 2; Tel: 22371. 12 rooms. With outside bath $5 S, $10 D. W/ attached bath, $6 S, $12 D. All w/ simple breakfast.

Losmen Agung. *Jl.* Argapura 37.

Losmen Hamadi. *Jl.* Amphibi 1 Hamadi.

Losmen Jayapura. *Jl.* Olahraga 4.

Losmen Rahayu. *Jl.* Argapura 37.

Mess GKI. *Jl.* Sam Ratulangi 6; Tel: 21574.

Losmen in Sentani
All include simple breakfast

Mansapur Rani Guest House. 200 meters from the terminal, *Jl.* Jaboso 113, 4 rooms $9 per person.

Minang Jaya. In the town of Sentani, just off the main road to Jayapura, past airport turnoff; 14 rooms, $6.50/ person.

Sentani Inn. 3 km from the airport on the main road to Jayapura. 15 rooms. breakfast and free taxi to air terminal. With AC $12 S, $15 D; Fan-cooled $7 S, $12 D.

LOCAL TRANSPORTATION

Jayapura is compact and you can walk around most of the town, but to reach Sentani and the beaches, you need transport. The hub of the public transport system (minibus) is the taxi terminal across the road from the post office. Drivers wait for at least a partial load before leaving and most swing through town before setting off, shouting to raise additional passengers. Prices are 15¢ to 30¢ to Abepura (whence the airport and Sentani), Base G beach, Dock 5, etc.

Taxi (minibus) hire runs $3 to $10 an hour, depending on distance and bargaining ability. Be sure you notify your hotel ahead of time if you will need a taxi. There may not be one available for spur of the moment excursions.

DINING

For a seafood orgy — sitting in comfort — try the Porasco, located near the harbor, next to the big church. The food is great, but not cheap — up to $15 per person, including cold beer. Jayapura also boasts numerous sit-down restaurants serving tasty Indonesian and Chinese dishes based on chicken, pork, shrimp, squid, beef and fish for a moderate $2 to $6. A few places serve Western food, not very good and pricey.

Hawaii. Next to the movie house, just off the park down-town—good box lunches (nasi bunkus istimewa); shrimp, chicken dishes; reasonably priced, good service, air conditioning.

Himalaya. *Jl.* Matahari, half block from the main drag, *Jl.* Ahmad Yani. Cold beer; chicken dishes $4 to $6; cuttlefish, pigeon, frog dishes $4; shrimp, beef $5 simple, filling Chinese dishes $1.50 to $2.

Jaya Grill. On the water, towards the main docks, enclosed and AC'd. *Jl.* Koti #5, Tel. 22783; hours 10:30 am to 2:30 pm and 6:30 pm to 10:30 pm. Shrimp, seafood cocktail $3.50, hamburgers $5 to $6, steaks (from Jakarta) $8-$10, abalone $15, crab, shrimp, squid, chicken, frog, pork — $5-$6; simple Chinese or Indonesian dishes $1.50 to $2.50; wide variety of booze; hard stuff, $1.50-$5, cold beer; horrible service but most frequented by local expats.

Matoa Restaurant. In the Matoa Hotel. Pleasant, modern dining room (at last check, still waiting for cook who can prepare European food); in the meanwhile, Bloody Mary, Singapore Sling $2.20, fish dishes $6-$15, squid $6, chicken $5-$10, paklay $5-$6, beef $4-$15, soups $8-$19, crab dishes $9, shrimp $6, abalone $32, pigeon $9, frog $6; also, a few cheaper Indonesian/ Chinese dishes; juices, canned drinks $1.10; beer $1.25; imported liquors $5.

Nirwana. *Jl.* Ahmad Yani 40, on the main drag. Good selection of Padang style food, AC; about $3-$4 for a meal; grilled goldfish available.

Padang Simpang Tiga. *Jl.* Percetakan 92. Large and clean; Padang style; what you eat is what you pay for from the choice of dishes on the table; reasonable prices.

Porasco. On the bay, next to the church; This open-sided restaurant is open only from 6:00 pm to 11:00 pm. Before you enter, you look over the variety of fish, squid, lobster and choose what you want (ask the price at this stage, as it can get quite expensive). Then the cook grills your choice; cold beer. Simple fish fillet $4-$6 depending on variety and size.

Queen. Behind the Expor-Impor Bank. Best for a big table with lots of people: steamboat or other large dishes for parties; whole pig $75; huge dishes for four people $15 simple

Chinese dishes $1.50-$2; private dining room available; soups, chicken, shrimp, crab, squid, much more in many varieties of preparation.
Rabina Coffee House. Jl. Angkasa/Trikora, 5 km from downtown; tel. 21490. Run by a very pleasant woman, mostly frequented at night by the younger set under the eye of Nyona Meles, the boss/owner/cook; *bakso* soup 75¢, soft ice cream 75¢, sundaes $1.50; other meals have to be ordered one day ahead, even the hamburgers ($1.30).
Rasa Sayang. Part of the Hotel Triton, Jl. Ahmad Yani 52, tel. 21171. Crab, pigeon, frog, shrimp, pork, fish, cuttlefish, sate $4-$5; abalone $10, steaks $6 to $10; venison (average availability: twice a month) $12; smaller dishes of all of the above about 40% less.
Yotefa. Jl. Percetakan 64; A new place, nicely decorated; European and Indonesian food, cold beer; chicken, shrimp, squid dishes — $2-$3, fish up to $5 depending on size, rice and noodle dishes $1-$2.

Warungs and food stalls

Lively night market, or *pasar malam,* in front of the Pelni office, serving *bakso,* soto Madura, bubur, and lots of fried bananas and other tasty snacks. Just a bit further, towards the harbor, on Jl. Halmahera, you can find delicious, inexpensive grilled fish and squid — big fish steaks 75¢, whole fish $2. In the area are fruit stands, cigarette stalls, and patent medicine hawkers. Good ambiance. There are more food stalls in back of the mosque on upper Jl. Ahmad Yani.

BANKS AND MONEY EXCHANGE

Money is exchanged only at the Expor-Impor Bank on Jl. Ahmad Yani. 8:00 am to 12:00 pm, except Friday, to 11:30 am. U.S. dollars, Australian dollars, Yen, Deutsche Marks, Pounds Sterling, and Swiss Francs exchanged.

Travelers' checks (in U.S. dollars) exchanged: American Express, Bank of America, Bank of Credit and Commerce, Barclays, Citicorp. Yen: Sumitomo; Cooks, in U.S. dollars, Pounds Sterling, and Swiss Francs, are also accepted.

MEDICAL

Puskesmas. (hospital) Jl. Ahmad Yani. Dr. Toni Pranato is the malaria and dengue specialist.
Dr. Oey. Jl. Kesehatan, just below the hospital, Tel. 21789. Dr. Oey speaks English and German. His advice, in the highlands, is to eat only well-cooked pork as there is danger of cysticercus.

NEWSPAPERS

Newsweek, Time and the English language newspapers from Jakarta are only available at a shop called Ayumas Irian Jaya, across the street from the movie house on Jl. Irian.

SHOPPING AND SOUVENIRS

Store hours in Jayapura generally run from 8 am to 12 m, and then again from 5 pm to 9 pm. Souvenirs can be found at the Hotel Matoa shop, at the shop attached to the museum at Cendrawasih University (and the Negeri Museum mentioned above) and at the Perindustrian office in Adipura. in Hamadi (a suburb of Jayapura, about 3 km from downtown) are several stalls: *horim* (penis sheaths) 75¢ to $1; new or imitation Asmat carvings — $15-20; grass skirts or net bags $2-3; bow and arrows sets $2-4; stone axes $2-3. Bargaining is expected.

EXCURSIONS

The folks at your hotel can help you design your own tour around the Jayapura-Sentani area. Some suggestions:
Boating in the harbor. Rent a catamaran — 40 hp motor, around $15/hr. — and cruise Teluk Yos Sudarso (Jayapura Harbor) and see Kayu Island with its church and Kosong Island with its mosque. There is a beached World War II amphibious assault tank on Debi Island in Yotefa Bay.
Visit Lake Sentani. Nearby Lake Sentani, dotted with islands and local fishermen landing tasty lake fish from little canoes, makes a pleasant day's diversion. Motorized dugout canoes rent for $10-$15/hour; paddled canoes, negotiable. There are only two certain places to rent, Jahim and the Yugga Restaurant.

Jahim, which is the "market harbor" or *pelabuhan pasar,* is at the end of a side road that runs by the Sentani town market, ending after a couple of kilometers at the lake. There are usually at least half a dozen dugout canoes stationed here, waiting for passengers to ferry to the islands of shoreside villages.

Yugga Restaurant, 22 kilometers (14 mi.) from Jayapura, is right next to the main road and Lake Sentani. The Yugga has outrigger sailboats (2-3 people, $6/hr.) and two motorboats — $16/hr. Plans are afoot for water-skiing and a bungalow-style, 6-room losmen. The restaurant's speciality is goldfish and a local variety called *mujahir,* served grilled or fried and priced according to size, $2 to $10. The place is quiet on weekdays and busy on weekends, especially when the governor comes by for a game of billiards or a ride on the lake to his home village.
Visit Engros village. Engros is a fishing village, perched on stilts off Abe beach. There is a losmen or sorts here, too. Get a permit at the Kanto Yayasan Pembangan Masyarakat Desa (YPMD — Rural People's Development Foundation). Their office is just across from the PISGA church on the main road to Sentani. When you get your permit you pay $3 a night for as many nights as you wish to stay in Engros village. Then you catch another bemo/taxi from Abepura to Abe beach (15¢) whence you can be paddled across to Engros for $1.

Once you get there, a nice old man will set up mattresses in the "losmen" for you and and fill the "bath"; if you want to eat fresh grilled fish, ask for it ahead of time; it will cost $1.50-$6 depending on size. For about $50, you can commission a dance. 20 to 30 men wearing old beads, traditional decorations, and loin cloths. At low tide, watch the soccer matches next to the village. At high tide, the village perches above some 1.5 meters of water. This is a typical fishing village, with friendly people and few tourists.

REGIONAL TRANSPORTATION

Jayapura is well connected by air to the rest of Indonesia. Within the province, Merpati connects the main towns while missionary planes and grass strips have opened much of the interior. Sea transportation, to Jakarta or less distant points, is also available. Garuda and Merpati have a disconcerting tendency to be overbooked. Check, double-check, and reconfirm your reservations — often. Below are some of the flights available at press time, but check with the airline offices for current schedules.

Garuda. Jl. Percetakan 2, Tel: 21220. Hours: 7:30 am to 4:30 pm.

Biak, Ujung Pandang,	
Surabaya, Jakarta	Daily
Sorong, Menado	WS
Merauke	SMTuTh
Biak, Ambon,	
Ujung Pandang, Denpasar	STuThF
Timika, Biak, Ambon,	
Ujung Pandang, Denpasar	STuThF

Prices: Ambon $96, Biak $36, Denpasar $183, Jakarta $208, Menado $114, Merauke $54, Sorong $78, Timika $65, Ujung Pandang $150.
Merpati. Jl. Ahmad Yani 15, next to the Hotel Matoa, Tel: 21111. Hours: Mon-Thurs, 8 am to 3 pm, Fri to 12 pm, Sat to 1:30 pm, Sun 10 am to 12 pm. The Merpati hub is Biak, so few flights leave out of Sentani; the most important is the daily 7 am to Wamena. Cost $25.

Monday: Nabire, Enarotali, Biak, Kaimana, Fakfak, Ewer, Manokwari and Serui.

Tuesday: Biak and Manokwari

Thursday: Biak, Ambon, Ujung Pandang, Surabaya and Jakarta (a horrible milk run, not worth what you save by not flying Garuda). 6:30 am departure.

MAF. The Missionary Aviation Fellowship (Protestant) office is next to the Sentani air terminal; no commercial flights to where either Garuda or Merpati flies. Officer: Wally Wiley, Tel: by day (Sentani) 171, evenings 178. For charters, they can be contacted through the Missionary Fellowship office in Jayapura, located a bit past the Bank of Indonesia on the harbor road; Tel: 21264, Telex: 76142 (sometimes the telex is down for a fortnight at a time), P.O. Box 38, Jayapura.

MAF's schedule is set according to the church's requirements, and they take into account the weights of passengers, including their luggage, with missionaries having first priority. For a special chartered flight, contact them several months ahead of time. Then confirm, 2 weeks prior. (See "Baliem Practicalities," page 124, for more information on the MAF.)

AMA. The American Missionary Alliance is the Roman Catholic equivalent of MAF. Officer: Bosco Fernandez, whose office is close to the Sentani airport, next to MAF. Tel: 26. The AMA flies to Agats at least once a week. About $120 one way with a maximum 4 passengers of 400 kg. total weight. Planes are Cessna 185s. To Enarotali, $90; to Ilaga, $110. Charters run $180/hour. AMA can be contacted through Airfast (a cargo outfit, but they also charter HS748s at $1,100 per hour) at telex 76122 AIRFAST. or Jl. Sam Ratulangi 3, P.O. Box 523, Jayapura. Tel: 21925.

Sea transportation

Pelni Lines. Jl. Halmahera 1, Tel: 21270. Their huge passenger ship, the *Umsini,* calls every 15 days; up to some 2,400 passengers can travel on this efficient, German-built ship from Jayapura to Jakarta and points between. There are five classes of cabins (the cheapest is dormitory style but still clean). Some prices:

Jakarta	1st class $170/dormitory	$60
Surabaya		$155/$50
Ujung Pandang		$110/$40
Bitung (near Menado)		$80/$30
Ternate		$70/$27
Sorong		$42/$19

The *Umsini* takes a week to Jakarta. It is not a cruise ship, but the food is good and it's an excellent alternative to flying if one has a bit of time to spare. Book your passage as early as possible. Pelni has other ships where deck passage is available, for example to Biak about twice a month for $5-$10, to Sorong for $10 (a week to get there with several calls on the way).

Yotefa shipping lines. Jl. Percetakan 90A, Tel: 21823, telex 76148 YAKJ. If Jack Saenen is around, he will be very helpful. They have 200-ton coasters that take up to 50 deck passengers from Jayapura to Sorong (and points between) about once a month; from Merauke to Fakfak and to Aru, about every six weeks.

Route No. 1: Jayapura-Sarmi-Serui-Biak-Nabire-Manokwari-Sorong-Manokwari-Biak-Nabire-Sarmi-Jayapura on the Jayapura-based *Dayala Nusantara.* 14-day cycle, 26 voyages a year, total distance: 1,826 nautical miles.

Route No. 2: Jayapura-Sarmi-Trimurus-Bagusa-Kasanaweja-Bagusa-Trimurus-Puwai-Kaipuri-Dawai-Ambai-Serui-Waren-Waipoga-Napan-Nabire-Biak-Korido-Jeggerbun-Ransiki-Windesi-Waior-Nabire-Biak-Ansus-Serui-Dawai-Waren-Serui-Kaipuri-Sarmi-Jayapura on the Jayapura-based *Nyala Perintis.* 28-days cycle, 13 voyages a year; 1,804 nautical miles.

MANOKWARI

Hub of the Bird's Head Peninsula

This small town on the Bird's Head's north-central coast takes pride in having hosted the first permanent Christian mission in New Guinea. On February 5, 1855, after sailing for 25 days out of Batavia (now Jakarta — then as now the capital of Indonesia), German missionaries C.W. Ottow and J.G. Geissler landed on Mansenam Island in Doreri Bay.

For many years, the mission achieved little success, but nevertheless laid the groundwork for the district's current Christian majority. The fact that the pale white missionaries bore an uncanny resemblance to the locals' conception of ghosts did not help to attract converts. The graves of these pioneer missionaries now lie under an elaborate monument — a traditional hut with lots of pop art, just outside of town.

Missionary efforts were renewed after World War II, mostly by well-organized and financed American fundamentalists. Two of them, Walter Erikson and Edward Tritt, were slain by their porters when they tried to penetrate the Kabar district to the west of the town.

A theological seminary, located in the suburb of Sowi (past the airport), has been named after the two martyrs. Currently, their are 48 students here. Missionary presence, as well as that of the Summer Institute of Linguistics, is strong in Manokwari. If you want to meet the missionaries, go to Pasir Putih beach on a Saturday afternoon. White skin and pale-blond hair no longer excite the curiosity of the locals.

Shortly after Ottow and Geisler established their Christian beachhead on Mansenam, the great naturalist, Alfred Wallace spent several months at Doreri (often spelled Dorei) Bay. A couple of decades later, the Italians, d'Albertis and Beccari landed here and trekked into the Arfak Mountains where they discovered many new bird and insect species and had a brush with native tribal warfare.

Because it has a well protected harbor, the Dutch set up the administrative post for Irian's north coast at Manokwari. The area later lost much of its importance when Hollandia became the capital of Dutch New Guinea. During World War II, the Japanese established a military base here, bombed and bypassed by the Allies. After the war, the Dutch returned to prepare Irian for independence. After Irian was handed over to Indonesia, some rebels in the hills resisted the new administration, but the fighting ended in the 1960s.

Diverse peoples

While linguists classify the peoples of the Manokwari region into over 30 separate language groups, the government has simply divided the district into three ethnic groupings: the Wamesa in the south, the Arfak in the Arfak mountains and the Doreri, belonging to the Biak language group, along the coast. The latter arrived from Numfor and settled around Manokwari as well as on Leman and Mansenam islands centuries before the arrival of the first Europeans. A majority of the district's 120,000 inhabitants — 67 percent — are Protestants, with 20 percent Muslims and 8 percent Catholics. The population density is very low — just under 3 per square kilometer.

The economy of the Manokwari district is richly diversified. The Bintuni subdistrict produces oil and Koreans are now logging the mangroves as well. Realizing the district's potential, with soils among the best in Irian, the Dutch established an agricultural station. This is now being followed up by a branch of the University of Cenderawasih.

Cash crops include cacao from a a British-run estate at Ransiki, palm oil from a processing plant in the Warmari district, cloves from around Manokwari and coconuts everywhere along the coast. Major exports also include sea products such as smoked and dried fish, shark's fins, seashells and turtle shells.

Sights of Manokwari

The town of Manokwari, stretching around Doreri Bay, lies in an attractive setting of low hills dominated by the Arfak Mountains to the south. Indonesian-Chinese owned shops are well stocked with all the essentials and a fair number of luxuries. The main shopping area is **Jalan Merdeka**, near the Hotel Mokwam. A newer shopping complex has gone up near the Hotel Mutiara.

Opposite: A palm-lined beach near Manokwari.

For the best overview of town, hike up to the **Japanese War Memorial**, about 2 km from the Hotel Arfak. You start off on a paved road, then a wide earthed path climbs up a sweat-inducing slope before leveling off for a pleasant jungle stroll in the **Gunung Meja Park**. The simple, enclosed monument is complemented by a concrete and wood repica of a traditional native hut set on piles. The panorama, a bit hemmed in by trees, looks over much of the town, Doreri Bay and a chunk of the Arfak Mountains. Continuing on the same path for some 4 kilometers brings you to a branch of Cenderawasih University.

Heading out of town past the hospital and the police station towards Pasir Putih, you soon reach **Gereja Koawi**. The monument to the first missionaries, built over some of their graves, is located just in back of the church. Two angels trumpet away over the entrance. A large traditional native house sits on piles over the graves with local warrior statues guarding the sides. A long panel in the back, colorful if not of high artistic value, shows life in the region before and after the arrival of Christianity. The same bayside road continues on to **Pasir Putih**, "White Sand" beach. Good swimming here and a shallow coral bank with decent snorkeling and a fair variety of reef fishes. Continuing on the seaside road, you reach a lighthouse where several species of birds flock.

Manokwari's central market spreads out along the west side of Doreri harbor. A series of high-roofed buildings shelter mini-stores, the occasional butcher and scattered piles of fresh vegetables. Try not to walk on the harbor side at low tide as the market's accumulated garbage takes the charm out of any stroll. The taxi terminal is next to the market. While the central market operates all day, the fish market just to the south starts at dawn and lasts until about 9 am. There might be a huge spotted grouper for sale, or a batch of barracuda, red snappers and many other species. Motorized outriggers depart from here later in the day in various directions, pulling up next to the fish market to wait for passengers.

If the weather is clear, take a boat out to Leman and Mansenam Islands. Motorized outrigger canoes can occasionally be found at the main dock but your chances of finding one are better next to the fish market, by the central market. The right light brings out shades of the sea ranging from clear white to turquoise to deep blue, depending on the depths. The waters of Doreri Bay, lined with wooden houses perched on stilts and fronted by a variety of boats, remain surprisingly clean — but don't look too close to the shoreline, especially near the market at low tide.

After a tour of the harbor, head to small **Leman Island**, its few huts and white sand beaches standing out against the backdrop of the Arfak Mountains. Just offshore to the

north of **Mansenam Island**, facing Manokwari, a large white cross commemorates the pioneering work of missionaries. This was where Ottow and Geisler landed to set up the first mission outpost in Irian. Just inland from the cross, there's an old church and well.

The eastern side of Mansenam presents stretches of coral raised to the tree line, alternating with short stetches of white sand beach, inviting for a secluded dip. A tangle of jungle reaches the sea here. As you approach the island's southern shore, look for birds and trees full of flying foxes who often take off and circle by the hundreds. A semi-circular bay on the far south side of the island faces coral formations making up the area's best underwater scenery.

About three quarters of the way down the west coast, ask your boatman to stop by a large Japanese ship sunk during World War II. The ship lies on its side in seven to ten meters of clear water, easily visible from the surface. A good view of the craft, home to fish and sprouting coral formations here and there, can be had by snorkelers. While you can easily reach the top side of the ship, peering inside takes unusual lung capacity. Locals maintain there have been no shark sightings, so swimming and snorkeling should be safe.

Heading south from town

While a road is being planned south of Manokwari to the coastal towns of Oransbari and Ransiki, for the foreseeable future travel to those places is by boat only. The paved road out of Manokwari now barely reaches the transmigration settlements at Prafi, some 60 kilometers (37 mi.) away. This road heads south past the airport and hugs the shore of **Lake Kabori**, oval in shape and barely separated from the sea. An old dirt road runs between the lake and the sea but fallen logs and a washed-out bridge prevent vehicles from following this more picturesque route.

From the main road, there's only one viewing spot affording a clear shot of the lake but unfortunately this is next to a garbage dump. The paved road runs above the lake, cutting through limestone hills, before crossing a bridge at **Maruni**, 29 kilometers (18 mi.) from Manokwari. Just ahead, a 6-kilometer sideroad leads to the seaside village of **Mopi**. Just beyond this turnoff, the road swings inland, climbing steeply. If the weather is clear, Numfor Island is visible across the sea. Dropping down from the hills, the road enters a wide, fertile valley containing some

of Irian's best soils. A private company owns huge palm oil and cacao plantations here. A small town, **Warmeri**, is the sub-district capital, 40 kilometers (25 mi.) from Manokwari.

Beyond the town another dozen kilometers of pavement cut across rivers, creeks and oil palms, reaching the oil processing plant and eight transmigrant settlements at **Prafi** — the largest in the Manokwari district. The 15,000-odd transmigrants are mainly rice farmers from Java, with some also from Timor and Flores. About 5,000 Irianese have also resettled here. Each family has been given two hectares by the government as well as a small house, agricultural implements, seeds and a year's supply of food. A smaller Javanese community of 280 families had settled in the vicinity of **Oransbari** on the coast south of Manokwari.

The Anggi Lakes

The best side-trip from Manokwari is to the Anggi Lakes in the Arfak mountains. Backpackers can cover the distance in four days (lop off two days by hopping on a minibus as far as Warmari), but we suggest flying in. Before entering the Arfak mountains, the plane has to fly in a wide circle over the Warmari valley to gain the necessary altitude. Then it's densely wooded, steep-walled valleys, tree tops looking like a blanket of broccoli and huts in the middle of nowhere with cleared patches on impossible slopes.

The tallest peak in the Arfaks, Gunung Umsini, reaches 2,950 meters (6,680 ft.) and five other mountains top 2,000 meters. The flight path crosses the village and landing strip at Manyembow before more mountain scenery, then the flat, swampy, bog-like terrain extending out from one end of Anggi Giji. A tiny outrigger or two might be on the lake to add to the spectacular effect of swooping down over the water just in time for a turn to land on the dirt strip at **Sureri Village**. The scenery along the flight is well worth the price of the ticket.

From paths above the lake, the panorama sweeps over steep slopes covered with ferns or forest tipping into the smooth waters, with the only ripples coming from paddled outrigger canoes. Sunlight, fog or clouds each create a different setting and mood, so it's worth a few days to experience the shifts of atmosphere. Trails connect the various villages for hiking around. With a bit of luck, you can see the large Arfak butterflies, found only in this

Opposite: *Anggi Lake near Manokwari.*

region — with wings beautifully marked by iridescent green patterns. Or accompany bow and arrow hunters stalking wild pigs, the marsupial cuscus or a variety of birds. Delicate, colorful orchids also enliven a forest stroll. Anggi Giji, considered the male lake by the natives, covers 2,900 hectares (7,200 acres) while Anggi Gita, the female lake, spreads over 2,500 hectares.

This lake district and the 12,000-strong Sougb ethnic group living in the area were opened to the outside world by the opening of an airstrip and an American evangelical post at the village of Sureri in 1955. The current missionary, a tall, blue-eyed German chap with 21 years' residence there, has recently completed the translation of the New Testament into the Sougb language. He has also successfully introduced high-protein hybrid corn to supplement the staple diet of starchy sweet potatoes. Other vegetables, now airlifted to Manokwari thanks to special rates by the MAF, include garlic, onions, carrots, white potatoes, celery and cabbage.

Cash is also earned through the sale of the Arfak butterflies, orchids and an occasional sack of smoked fish. While the lakes had originally contained only native eels and minnows, the carp and goldfish have been introduced. Some of the goldfish now grow bigger than a man's thigh. All the fish are caught from canoes with hook and line. Cattle have not fared so well — they went wild, then had to be exterminated.

The Sougb people, now Christians, maintain some of their native traditions. A bride price — ancient beads, store-bought cloth, *ikat* cloth from Flores or Timor, pigs and seashell bracelets — is still required to wed.

All diseases, including the common cold, are believed to result from black magic. Toy pistols are now loaded with potent powder and fired from a hidden position at one's intended victim. The missionary thinks it will take a couple more generations before belief in the efficacy of black magic begins to wane.

Traditional dances are still occasionally performed and can be put on for visitors if given sufficient advance notice. The men dress in red loincloths while the ladies wear black. There are two basic dances, a conga-type affair, single file around the huts, and a linked-arms dance. The missionary does not object to these if a certain decorum is maintained, but unfortunately a certain lewdness creeps into the proceedings.

Most of the Sougb huts are built in the traditional manner, raised a meter or so on stilts, with wood floor, bark walls and thatched roof. Those who can afford it cover their houses with sheets of corrugated metal — not very aesthetic but it ends the chore of replacing the thatching every three or four years. Inside these family huts, the men sleep in bunks on one side while on the other side each woman has an enclosed mini-apartment.

Manokwari Practicalities

All prices in U.S. $; Manokwari city code: 962

Merpati flies to Manokwari from Biak daily, and from Jayapura on Mondays and Tuesdays. These may have changed so check with the airline office.

SURAT JALAN

You can easily obtain this essential travel permit for Manokwari in either Jayapura, Sorong or Biak. If you plan to spend the night outside of the Manokwari subdistrict (*kecamatan*), meaning the town and surroundings, check first with the police to find out if you need an endorsement, then report to the local police on arrival. (For more on the *surat jalan*, see "Travel Advisory," page 150.)

ACCOMMODATIONS

The **Mutiara Hotel**, owned by Merpati Airlines, and another new hotel (not yet named) are planned to open sometime soon. Neither was operating at presstime. The owners are planning them to be the best in town.

Hotel Arfak. Jl. Brawijaya, Tel. 21293 and 21195. With 13 rooms, this former Dutch officers' mess rates as a best buy: quiet, inexpensive with a good view over the bay and the Arfak Mountains. AC $18 S, $27 D; standard (fan and attached bath/toilet) $15 S, $24 D; economy $12 S, $21 D. All meals and service charges included.

Hotel Mokwam. Jl. Merdeka. 12 large, clean rooms. An attached restaurant serves Indonesian and Chinese dishes, ($2.50 to $4). $30-36 S, $36-43 D.

Losmen/Mess Pelabuhan. Jl. Siliwangi. 3 rooms, $3.50-$6.

Losmen/Mess Fasharkan. Jl. Sudarso. 7 rooms, $10-15 w/ meals.

Losmen/Mess Binhar. Jl. Sudarso. 7 rooms. The Ekaria Restaurant is attached. $4-18.

Losmen Apose. Jl. Kotabaru, in front of the Merpati office. 9 rooms. $3.50-$7 S, $9-$12 D.

Losmen Sederhana. Jl. Bandung. 11 rooms, none with attached facilities. Fan-cooled, $4 S, $6 D.

Losmen Beringin. Jl. Sudirman. 8 rooms and 5 non-attached toilet/baths. Attached restaurant has simple rice-based meals (50¢ to $1.20). AC room, $9; fan-cooled $4.50.

DINING

Ekaria. Jl. Sudarso. New, clean place with a wide variety of Cantonese dishes of frog, crab, squid, pigeon, chicken, pork, beef, rice and noodles, $2-$5.

Hawai. Jl. Sudirman. International and Chinese dishes $1-$3. One dining room is AC and one is fan-cooled.

Evaria. Jl. Merdeka. Across from the Hotel Mokwam, Chinese cooking, $2-$3.50.

Kebun Sirih. Jl. Sudirman. roasted fish of several kinds, $2-$4.50 depending on size and species; also serves squid and shrimp.

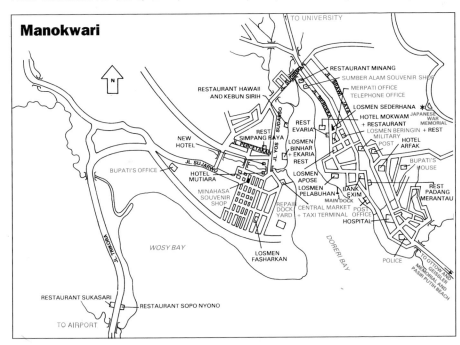

Manokwari

Simpang Raya. Jl. Percetakan. Padang style cooking, $1-$2 per plate.

Minang. Jl. Sudirman. Padang food, $1-$2.

Padang Merantau. Jl. Merdeka. Padang food, $1-$2.

The **Suponyono** and the **Sukasari** are both on Jl. Trikora, across the road from each other, a couple of kilometers from the airport. Both serve Indonesian meals for 50¢ to $1.25.

MONEY EXCHANGE

Bank Expor-Impor. Jl. Jogyakarta #1. open Monday through Thursday from 8 am to 12:30 pm, on Fridays till 11 am and Saturdays till 10:30 am. Takes currency from Australia, Canada, England, Japan, Germany, France, Switzerland, in addition to Yankee dollars. Travelers checks from Visa, Thomas Cook, American Express, Citicorp, Commonwealth Bank of Australia are accepted.

SOUVENIR SHOPS

Toko Sumber Alam. Jl. Sudirman 47. Has lots of porcelain plates (some quite old), along with beads still used as bride price, some mounted butterflies, awful Asmat carvings and still worse penis sheaths.

Toko Souvenir Minahasa. Jl. Pahlawan. Also has a fair selection of porcelain (Chinese, Japanese and Dutch) along with bride price items such as woven *ikat* cloths from Timor and Flores, beads and silver bracelets from Biak. There are also stone axes, bows and arrows, old coins and bills.

For **butterlies**, see Mr. Simandjuntak whose office is on Jl. Sudarso 59, Tel: 21677 or 21045. Home: Jl. Kotaraja 14, Tel: 21139. All butterflies are carefully wrapped in wax paper, ready for export. He knows his prices on the international market.

NIGHTLIFE

Jayakarta on Jl. Jogyakarta

Dinasti on Jl. Kota Baru

Menado on Jl. Sudarso

Kawanua on Jl. Siliwangi

All boring places to drink beer in the company of hostesses from Menado. Not even on Saturday nights do things liven up. At the Kawanua during daytime hours you can eat Menado-style dog dishes. More exciting than the night activities.

EXCURSIONS

Prafi village. Collective minibuses from Manokwari make several round trips each day to Prafi, charging $2.50 per person. Chartering your own minibus for the round trip costs about $45. If you decide to spend the night in this area, you have to report to the police at Warmari with your passport and *surat jalan*. There are no commercial accommodations, so it's either local hospitality or sleeping out.

Mansenam Island. When there are passengers, some craft paddle out to Mansenam Island but we suggest hiring your own motorized canoe for a two-to-four hour jaunt, allowing plenty of time for swimming and snorkeling. The boats hold anywhere from 10 to 15 passengers. Charter prices are negotiable, between $18 and $30 for the ride.

Anggi Lakes. By early 1990, Merpati plans on scheduled flights to the *kecamatan* (subdistrict) capital at Iray, costing some $12 each way. The MAF (Missionary Aviation Fellowship) flights cost $18 one way. Their Cessna flight from Manokwari to Sureri (on Anggi Giji Lake) covers some 80 kilometers (50 mi.) and takes a bit under a half an hour.

While there are no accommodations in the district, either the police, the *camat* or a village chief will help you find a place to sleep. Bring a sleeping bag, sweater and jacket as it can get chilly at night up there at elevations over 1,800 meters. Although some food is available locally, bring a few tins of chow for supplement.

There is a ministore in Iray stocking some of the basics, but due to airfreight charges, prices are higher than in Manokwari. Market days on Iray are Monday and Thursday, from 7 to 8 am. The same hours also for the weekly Friday market at Sureri.

REGIONAL FLIGHTS

Merpati Airlines. Jalan Kota Baru 39, Tel: 21133 and 21153. At the airport, Tel. 21004.

Merpati flies from Manokwari to the following cities (remember that airline schedules change):

Biak	Daily	$30
Jayapura	MThSa	$62
Numfor	WF	$12
Bintuni	MF	$15
Sorong	TuTh	$50
Merdey	M	$12
Babo	W	$19
Kebar	Th	$12
Fakfak	Th	$28

MAF. (Mission Aviation Fellowship) flies a single engine Cessna to many remote strips in the interior. They take passengers on a space available basis.

MAF's hangar and operations are located on the far side of the airport, Tel: 21155.

SEA TRANSPORTATION

Mixed freight/deck passage coastal steamers stop at Manokwari every week or two on their run along Irian's north coast. Pelni Lines' large passenger boat *Umsini* calls at Manokwari every four weeks on its way from Jakarta to Jayapura. (See "Jayapura Practicalties" page 78 for more details on Pelni Lines.)

WEATHER

Unpredictable. Temperatures range from 26 to 32° C (79-90° F). The average year dumps 2,700 millimeters (106 in.) of rain in 124 days.

SORONG

Oil Town on Irian's Western Tip

The town of Sorong is a fading oil center, with rusting tin roofs that stretch along eight kilometers of seashore at the westernmost tip of Irian's Bird's Head Peninsula. There is no center of town — its one long main street runs past government buildings, shops, banks, oil installations and the harbor. Nearby are transmigration settlements: rice farms run by Javanese.

The oilfields off Sorong, one of the reasons the Dutch hung on to Irian after being forced to grant independence to the rest of Indonesia, were first tapped in 1932. While the relative importance of oil has declined in Sorong (just over 10 million barrels were pumped in 1987), the state oil company, Pertamina, maintains major installations in town: storage tanks, a port with docks for tankers and the town's best private homes, on a hill called Kuda Laut ("seahorse").

The numerous foreign oilies who once used to carouse in Sorong have dwindled to a handfull. The foreign community today consists only of a few priests and a few expats working for the timber companies. But there are plenty of guest workers, from other parts of Irian and Indonesia. Sorong's prosperity shows in new bank buildings, shops and a modern shopping center. The town's population is evenly divided between Muslims and Christians. There is a Catholic cathedral, a mosque and several Protestant churches.

Until 1965, Sorong was located on nearby Doom Island (pronounced "dom"). When the town grew too large for the island, it shifted to the mainland. Today, some 45,000 people live in the urban area.

Although the relative importance of the oil industry has declined — it used to be the only source of employment — Pertamina still dominates the local economy. But the timber industry is now a close second. The lumber companies used to ship out entire logs (over 3 million cubic meters) to be processed overseas. But new government regulations require that the milling and processing take place locally, and a plywood factory is being built in Sorong, promising many new jobs.

The mining industry, which has extracted nickel ore from the nearby Raja Empat Islands, has suffered a number of ups and downs. The mines on Waigeo and Gebe have been shut down but the one on Gag Island

remains alive and well.

The seas around Sorong provide lots of fish for local consumption as well as tuna and shrimp for export to the United States and Japan. Frozen shrimp exports run $25 million a year, and tuna accounts for about $2.5 million. The Japanese send home cultured pearls from a farm they manage on Kabra Island. Shark's fins and trepang, shipped chiefly to Hong Kong, are also valuable exports — as are, unfortunately, illegally hunted bird of paradise skins.

Visiting Sorong

Sorong is definitely not a tourist town. While the disco nightlife can be lively, daylight activities are strictly business. Still, the markets are interesting, there are local beaches and reefs, and Sorong is the place from which to visit the Raja Empat Islands, though this is not particularly convenient or cheap.

Mount to the roof balcony of the Kohoin disco and sports (weights and squash) complex to get a view of the islands in the sea to the west — Salawati, Batanta and Waigeo shimmer just on the horizon while the closer, Buaya ("crocodile") and Sop Islands are visible in the blue-green seas. Little boats paddle around, far and near. The road around the Pertamina housing complex on Kuda Laut hill offers a better view of the city itself, and the nearby seas in another direction.

The **Pasar Boswesen** fish market offers a bewildering assortment of local varieties, but you have to get there around 7 in the morning. Later in the day, have a look in the **Pasar Sentral** at the other end of town. This turns into a typical night market after dark with many *warung*-type food stalls.

The best nearby beach lies about 10 kilometers (6 mi.) from Pasar Boswesen, on a decrepit road, at **Tanjung Kasuari**. After a rain, the road is impassable, but it is scheduled for improvements. The large, white-sand beach is favored by locals on weekends and holidays, when food and drinks are sold. Nearby coral reefs offer good snorkeling. On the way to the beach there is a small obelisk erected as a monument to the Japanese who died here in World War II.

A more famous war memorial is in town, on Jalan Arfak, a short ways up the hill near the Cenderawasih Hotel. Most drivers should be able to take you to "**Tugu Arfak.**" To reach this monument to the Japanese war dead, you have to cross the backyard of the local police chief. Some drivers are scared of the chief, others are scared of the chief's dog. Both are harmless, but you have to take the initiative. The house is usually open, so just peer in and ask: "*Boleh ke tugu?*" (Can I go to the monument?). The answer is invariably

Opposite: *Doom Island. Sorong began on Doom, but oil-stimulated growth in the '60s drove the urban center to the mainland in search of space.*

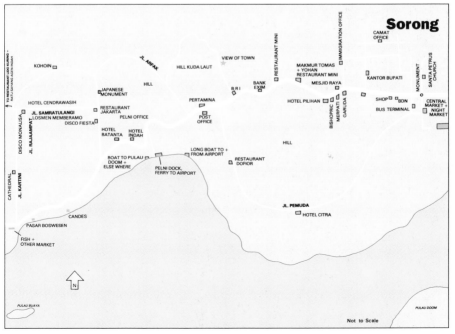

island, there's a large cemetery, with Christians buried on one side and Muslims on the other. Just behind the graves are some "Japanese" caves, used in the war, which locals say have not been visited for years. If you speak Indonesian, try to find an old man living near the graves. The pleasant old chap remembers World War II like it was yesterday, the nearby seas covered with Japanese ships and the huge bombing raid from Sausapor which sank them all. Bodies floated ashore on Doom for days, he said.

The Sorong region

The nearby islands in the Raja Empat group are hard to reach. There are no convenient, regular boats to Batanta, Salawati, Waigeo or any of the further islands. The only possibility for a quick look around Sorong seems to be a full-day tour arranged by the local Makmur Thomas travel agency. Their jaunt takes you to Doom Island, then to Pulau Buaya (Crocodile Island) for swimming off a fine sandy beach. (Don't worry about the crocs. The island takes its name from its general shape, not from an abundance of the critters.) On the way back to Sorong, you can visit other small islands and, if the opportunity presents itself, join some local fishermen.

A more extensive tour takes you to **Kabra Island** to visit a pearl farm under Japanese ownership and supervision. Statistics show that some 20 kilos (44 lbs.) of pearls are exported from here each year, worth close to half a million dollars. From Kabra you continue to **Maton Island** with its white sand beach, for a swim and lunch. With sufficient notice, the organization might be able to obtain scuba gear for rent.

The same travel agency can set up a trip to see birds of paradise and other birds on **Waigeo Island**. This involves some five to six hours of motoring and about four to five days of scouting for the bird perches on the island. You bring a tent or sleep either in local huts. Somewhat closer and cheaper, **Batanta Island** (three to four hours' motoring) has birds of paradise and other colorful endemics, but they are somewhat more difficult to see here than on Waigeo. The best time to see the birds — as well to travel in a small boat on the open seas — is from August to February. The rainy season here runs from March to July.

affirmative. The monument complex includes an obelisk, a bronze Shinto deity and long, thin memorial plaques.

The World War II relics in the area are concentrated on Jefman Island, the site of the current airfield (orginally built by the Japanese). There is said to be a large, intact shore battery, some bombed-out anti-aircraft guns and lots of bunkers. The Allies never invaded here — they just bombed the airfield and sank all the ships, then bypassed Sorong on their way to Morotai.

Doom Island

This is a pleasant little island, close to Sorong, and little outboard-powered boats make the run frequently. Today, the island is one village, with houses hugging the entire shoreline and continuing into the interior wherever the low hills allow them to.

Catch a boat from the beach next to the Pelni dock (20¢ one-way when one of the boats fills, or $1 charter) and in 5-10 minutes you land at a scruffy beach on Doom, next to the big sheet-tin warehouse which functions as a market. The islands' shops are mostly concentrated in this area and a couple of warungs serve *nasi campur* — but forget getting a cold beer. Also forget about walking around the beach, which serves as the island's garbage dump. Instead, make a slow loop around the perimeter road, which will take an easy hour. About halfway around the

Above: *The bronze Shinto diety at Tugu Arfak, a monument to Japanese World War II dead. The memorial is on a hill overlooking town*

Sorong Practicalities

All prices in U.S. $; Sorong city code: 951

Sorong's main airport is on Jefman Island, 20 kilometers (12 mi.) east of town. You have no choice from Jefman but to get in a public "longboat" for the $3 trip to Sorong, or pay $23 to charter a boat yourself. Taxis at the landing site charge $3 to just about any destination in town, but if you are traveling light, a public minibus on the nearby main road is 15¢.

To return to the airport from town, your taxi (chartered or public) lets you off at the Pelni dock. You need a ticket (6¢) to enter the dock area. A ferry usually motors to Jefman Island in the early morning and again in the late afternoon. The one-hour ride costs 85¢ and gets you there in time for your plane. If you miss the ferry, you have to charter a boat ($23).

ACCOMMODATION

Hotel Batanta. Jl. Barito, Tel: 21569. 24 rooms. $9-15 S, $12-19 D. Better rooms with AC. Small dining room only, billiard hall.
Hotel Cenderawasih. Jl. Sam Ratulangi 54, Tel: 21740 or 21966, Telex 77127, FAX (0951) 21966. With 20 rooms, all AC'd, includes breakfast service; $21 S, $24 D. Favored by the few expats around. Large dining room, full menu, various dishes from $1.25 to $4. Singing entertainment on MWS evenings in the dining room and well-stocked bar. Central to the three discos: Mona Lisa a half-block away, Fiesta just down the road, the Kohoin behind.
Hotel Citra. Jl. Pemuda, Tel. 21246. 14 rooms. $12-25 S, $15-28 D. All with AC, with dining room, full menu, dishes from $1.50 to $3.
Hotel Indah. Jl. Yos Sudarso, Tel: 21514. With 33 rooms, ranging from $12 (AC and TV) down to $4.50 for a bare-bones bedroom. Morning and afternoon snack included. Restaurant and car rental. This white tiled, 3-story hotel has an enclosed top balcony which offers a good view of the area. Try to get a room on the third floor.
Losmen Memberamo. Jl. Sam Ratulangi, Tel: 21564. 10 rooms. $17-20 S; $21-22 D. All AC, dining room, pleasant with rattan furniture, fair variety of dishes from $1.25 to $3.
Hotel Pilihan. Jl. A. Yani, Tel: 21366. 15 rooms. $10-11 S, $16-18 D. Better rooms with AC, otherwise fan-cooled. Kitsch figures in entrance yard to amuse guests.

DINING

Dofior. Jl. Pemuda. Chinese, Indonesian food for $3.50 to $7 per dish. A view of the sea; considered by some the best in town.
Lido Kuring. Pertokoan Lido, Jl. Yos Sudarso. Fish and other seafood $2-4, other dishes similarly priced. The Lido's specialty is grilled fish.
Mini. Kompleks Pertokoan Yohan, Jl. A. Yani. Mostly Chinese food and seafood; $1-$7 for the various dishes.
Mona Lisa. (Next to the disco with the same name.) Jl. Sam Ratulangi. Japanese food, $9-12 per dish; international cuisine, same price.
Ratu Sayang. Next to the Lido, same dishes and prices.

MONEY EXCHANGE

Bank Dagang Negara; Bank Expor-Impor.

NIGHTLIFE

Mona Lisa, Fiesta, Kohoin (see map page 89) — all with hostesses and dining available. Local opinion finds the Kohoin the best. There's a $3 cover charge there, none at the others.

EXCURSIONS

P.T. Makmur Thomas. Kompleks Pertokoan Yohan A15, Jl. A. Yani, Sorong, IRJA 98414. Tel: (0951) 21183, 21953, 21594. Fax: 21897. Telex: 77123 MTSON IA. This travel agent, linked with Setia Tours, can arrange tours around the region and offers guides and car service. English-speaking guides, $9 a day. Car rental, from $2.50 per hour.
Doom Island, Pulau Buaya. $30 per person, min. 2 people. Doom Island tour, swimming off a fine sandy beach on Buaya, visit to some of the smaller islands.
Kabra Island. $60 per person, min. 4 people. A visit to the Japanese cultured pearl farm.
Waigeo Island. Approx. $500 per person. This is a trip to see birds of paradise on Waigeo Island. It includes almost a full day at sea, and 4-5 days scouting for the birds. The price varies widely depending on the number in your group.
Batanta Island, other Raja Empat islands. (Variable.) Easier to get to than Waigeo, but birds are somewhat more difficult to see here.

REGIONAL TRANSPORTATION

Garuda. Jl. A. Yani 17, Tel: 21402.

Ambon	Daily	$41
Biak	WS	$48
Denpasar	TWThFSSu	$140
Jakarta	Daily	$170
Jayapura	Daily	$90
Menado	Daily	$107
Ujung Pandang	Daily	$107

Merpati Airlines. Jl. A. Yani 81, Tel: 21344.

Ayamaru	TTh	$23
Ayawasi	Th	$14
Biak	Daily	$40
Fakfak	MWThS	$36
Inanwatan	Su	$14
Kaimana	MWFS	$64
Kambuaya	TTh	$23
Manokwari	TThSu	$46
Timika	S	$93

PART III

Journey to the Stone Age

The lush Grand Valley of the Baliem is set in Irian's cordillera of sharp peaks like a jewel. Coursing down its center is the silt-rich Baliem river, a branching stripe of cafe au lait against the valley's green floor. The valley is a place of almost surreal beauty — the fertile soil is carpeted with rich growth and well-tended plots and on all sides, shrouded by mist and clouds, looms the mountain wall.

The Baliem is home to the Dani, the most populous of Irian's highlands inhabitants. Famous for their ritual warfare and sartorial habits — including bright feathers, nose pieces and penis sheaths — the Dani are also first-rate farmers, the key to their high population density. The Dani's numbers are increasing even today, rising from some 50,000 in the early 1960s to currently more than 70,000.

The Indonesian government and four decades of Christian missionaries have introduced some changes to the Dani lifestyle, but most traditions remain. The grunts of the beloved family pigs can be heard around the thatch-covered hut compounds and the valley landscape is cross-hatched with rectangular mounds of purple-green sweet potato vines.

Most of the men still wear their traditional long, upright penis gourds and the women their low-slung fiber skirts. Elaborate weddings and other ceremonies continue to mark the changes in Dani life. But the stone adze, 25 years after the Dani stepped out of the Stone Age, is now just a tourist item.

Ritual warfare is not quite forgotten, although it has been some 20 years since the last great battles were held. The warriors of Hetegima and Kurima, at the southern end of the valley, still nurse a seething feud over land rights, complicated by women and pig stealing and a variety of old scores. The government sometimes steps in when the number of deaths is even on both sides, but it's hard to keep a lid on things when animosities run so deep. Walking through the Hetegima-Kurima lands, you could well see dolled-up warriors (pig grease, seashells, flowers) armed with spears and bows and arrows, ready for action. Such feuds, now settled on the sly, still claim dozens of lives each year.

The traditional Dani bride price has felt the effects of inflation. Today, the family of a local beauty expects the following: 5 fiber skirts, 10-20 strands of shell money, 30 or so net bags and 10 pigs. But not just any pigs. At least two or three have to be big ones, costing about $300 each. The others, medium-sized critters, cost from $100 to $200 a head.

The Baliem Valley is 1,600 meters (5,200 ft.) high, 60 kilometers (37 mi.) long and 15 kilometers (10 mi.) wide. The valley is surrounded on all sides by 2,500-3,000 meter (8,000-10,000 ft.) peaks. The Baliem River flows into the valley from the north from its two sources near Gunung Trikora (formerly Wilhelmina) and along the Ilaga-Tiom valley system. They join to become the North Baliem, and after disappearing briefly in what is called the Baliem Swallet, their waters cascade to the floor of the Grand Valley. The broad, flat valley bottom tames the rushing tributaries, and the river is reduced to a gentle meander.

After leaving the valley, the river gains speed and rushes south, pouring through the only break in the mountain chain, the earthquake-prone Baliem Gorge. First dropping 1,500 meters (4,900 ft.) in a series of spectacular cataracts, the Baliem is then reduced to a wide, muddy tidal river that slowly empties into the Arafura Sea.

The Dani have gently shaped the landscape of the mild valley into what one author describes as "the only place on earth where man has improved on nature … as close to Paradise as one can get."

Overleaf: *Dawn in the Baliem Valley.* **Opposite:** *A Dani tribesman sporting the traditional penis gourd and a boar's tusk through his septum.*

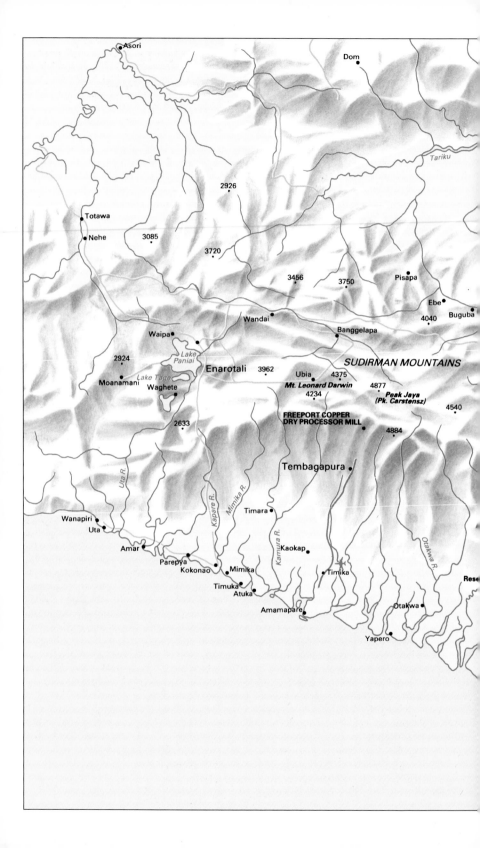

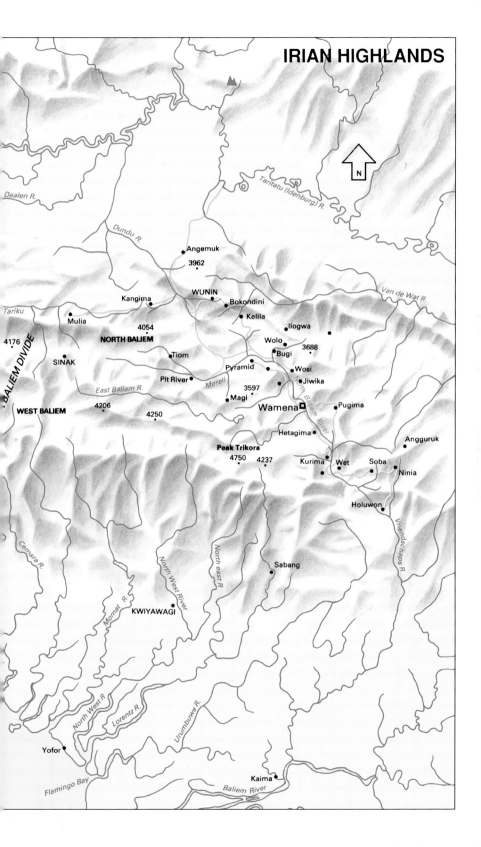

ARCHBOLD EXPEDITION

An American Adventurer in the Highlands

American Richard Archbold, scouting his third expedition to New Guinea, was the very first outsider to lay eyes on the magnificent Baliem Valley. As Archbold peered out of the window of his seaplane on June 23, 1938, the terraced green fields of the valley appeared like a mirage among the rocky peaks.

The 14-month highlands expedition was Archbold's third in New Guinea, all under the auspices of the American Museum of Natural History. The bureaucrats in Batavia (now Jakarta) were at first reluctant to produce the needed permits, but once the Dutch colonial government decided to co-sponsor the trip, the papers came immediately. Soon, dozens of men and tons of matériel were heading for Hollandia (now Jayapura), the population of which at the time was barely 200 souls: government personnel, their servants, Indonesian artisans and Chinese traders.

The area chosen for exploration was the northern face of the Snow Mountain Range — the largest remaining blank on the map of New Guinea at the time. Previous expeditions had explored the southern slope of this impressive range, returning with important biological collections. And though the 1921-1922 Kremer expedition had succeeded in reaching the north slope of the Snow Mountains, Kremer had to abandon his precious collections to the jungle on the exhausting trek back to the coast.

The key to the Archbold expedition's success was a huge flying boat dubbed the *Guba*. The craft was a Consolidated PBY 2, the standard U.S. long-range patrol bomber, that had been specially modified by Howard Hughes for salmon fishing expeditions to Alaska and then subsequently sold. Experts considered it the most air- and seaworthy aircraft in existence at the time. Lift was provided by a 31.7 meter (104 ft.) wing which supported a 20.4 meter (67 ft.) fuselage. And the plane was powered by two 1,000 hp Pratt and Whitney Twin Wasp engines fed from a 1,750 gallon fuel cell and holding 110 gallons of oil in the crankcases. The *Guba* could lift three tons at sea level and cruise for a distance of 800 kilometers (500 mi.), but when taking off from 3,225 meter high (10,580 ft.) Lake Habbema, the payload had to be restricted to just one ton of cargo and a standard crew of four men.

RICHARD ARCHBOLD

The 'Grand Valley' sighted

It was during one of the exploratory flights of the *Guba* that Archbold first sighted the Baliem Valley. Immediately, he realized the importance of his discovery. He was looking at the largest highland valley in New Guinea, as well as the most densely populated. Of course, he did not suspect that the Dani inhabitants were also the highland's most fearsome warriors. Archbold saw the Dani's graceful watchtowers, but could not guess their purpose (keeping an eye out for enemy ambush parties).

Archbold and the Dutch military members of the expedition decided to set up two camps in the interior of Irian: a high one on Lake Habbema at 3,225 meters (10,580 ft.) and a low one in the Meervlakte (the "Lakes Plains" region north of the mountains), 50 meters above sea level. The area to be studied was bounded by Mount Wilhelmina (Gunung Trikora) on one side and the Idenburg River (Taritatu) on the other.

The military arm of the expedition, under the command of Captain Teerink and Lieutenant Van Areken, consisted of 56 officers and men. The porters included 73 Dayaks (the mountainous terrain of their homeland, Borneo, equipped them well for Irian's rugged landscape) and 30 convicts.

The Dutch authorities did not want to lose American lives, and the military men ordered that precautions be taken. Foremost in their minds was an emergency retreat route, should the *Guba* for some reason be unable to pick up the party at Lake Habbema. So men, equipment and supplies were flown up to the Idenburg River, which offered relatively easy river access to Irian's north coast.

Aerial reconnaissance was crucial in determining the best route (about 100 kilometers in a straight line) between Lake Habbema and the Idenburg camp. The military patrols were to leave from each of the two staging areas and meet up in the Baliem Valley. Shortly after Lt. Van Areken's patrol cut upwards from the Idenburg River, the group experienced a pleasant surprise: a large, heavily populated valley and, best of all, a lake, immediately dubbed "Lake Archbold." Located about one kilometer from the Habifloeri River, Lake Archbold measures 1,000 by 800 meters (3,300 by 2,600 ft.), at an altitude of 700 meters (2,300 ft.).

Once the Dayaks chopped down some trees for the approach, the *Guba* could land on the lake to bring in supplies. From Lake Archbold, the going really got tough — steep climbing through vegetation without any

Opposite: *A group of Dani tribesmen at the Baliem River camp. The center tribesman's head ornament is the top of a fruit can.* **Below:** *The Guba on Lake Habbema. Photographs courtesy the American Museum of Natural History.*

native trails.

Once the party began to approach the Baliem Valley, the local people became numerous and friendly. Too friendly. In several villages, Lt. Van Areken was welcomed with food but the tribesmen did not want the party to leave. Only the "utmost determination" kept the group moving. One day, after a friendly reception, the party found their path blocked by a barricade of spearmen. The expedition journal laconically states: "Here occurred the one incident where more than a show of force was necessary."

An unfortunate first encounter

A later missionary account states that two Dani were shot and killed before the party could proceed into the Baliem Valley. The expedition journal says nothing about why the Dani had turned hostile, but it seems that the warriors were trying to block the expedition from moving into enemy territory. Seeing the expedition's resources of valuable cowrie shells (the highland currency), steel axes and knives — all liberally traded for food or offered as gifts — the natives wanted to continue profiting from the strangers' largess, and to keep their enemies from doing so.

Exploring the Lake Habbema area

A total of 105 people had by this time been flown to Lake Habbema in the *Guba,* along with tons of supplies. The military team under Capt. Teerink trekked down from the lake through the Ibele Valley and on to the Baliem Valley. They experienced very friendly receptions but there were no more killings. It was time to set up camp in the valley.

After exchanging locations by radio, Lt. Van Areken and Capt. Teerink rendezvoused in the Baliem. They calculated that an emergency retreat from Lake Habbema to the Idenburg camp would take 14 to 16 days, now that paths had been cut. The two parties exchanged a number of Dayaks before returning to their respective points of departure so that certain men would be familiar with the entire route between Lake Habbema and the Idenburg River.

The men at the Habbema camp got used to sunburn, freezing cold, cracked lips, altitude sickness and thin air. Lake Habbema is in an area of alpine grassland, consisting mostly of limestone bedrock with some large sandstone outcroppings. The lake lies on an upland shelf, 9 kilometers (5.6 mi.) wide. The northern edge of these uplands forms the

rim of the Baliem Valley, and from the southern edge rises Mt. Wilhelmina and the Nassau Range (Sudirman).

The scientists noted that the lake was rich in birds, and the locals hunted ducks there with bow and arrow. Most mammals were pygmy species, with the notable exception of a species of giant rat. The 20 centimeter (8 in.) long crayfish discovered in the lake provided a welcome addition to the explorers' tinned diet. The explorers found a path rising to 3,800 meters (12,500 ft.), in some places worn shoulder-deep by local foot traffic. This communications link was used for both trade and social calls between the peoples of the Baliem Valley and those living south of the mountain ranges.

Once the Lake Habbema region had been explored, the upland party shifted to the Baliem Valley. When the expedition set up camp in the lower Baliem, they were given a huge feast by local Dani tribesmen. Pigs were killed and their livers eaten by the whites and the Dani elders in a kind of initiation ritual. Speeches were made and the pigs' blood was sprinkled on the foreigners. (Sprinkling of pig's blood was the usual way to appease spirits.)

Agriculture practiced in the heavily populated valley was highly-developed: the steep valley walls were terraced using stone and timber retaining walls, and erosion control and crop rotation were extensively practiced. The sweet potato was the staple, but in addition, the expedition notes, the Dani grew bananas, tobacco, taro, sugar cane, cucumbers, gourds, spinach and beans. Peanuts, introduced by the Archbold expedition, soon caught on and are very popular today.

Whenever sweet potatoes, vegetables or pigs were required by the expedition, cowrie shells were used to barter for them. The Dani wanted only the smaller shells, preferably with the back, or convex part removed. Quality — and purchasing power — was determined by the shell's shape, size, ribbing and luster. An average cowrie purchased 10 kilos of sweet potatoes; 6-10 good ones fetched a small pig.

The expedition lasted 14 months, and produced a body of important scientific work as well as a *National Geographic* article that was to pique further scientific and missionary interest in the region.

Opposite: *The Baliem Valley in 1938, as seen from the window of the* Guba. *Photograph courtesy the American Museum of Natural History.*

THE DANI

Gentle Warriors of the Highlands

"The sun had climbed over the valley, and its light flashed on breastplates of white shells, on white headdresses, on ivory boars' tusks inserted through nostrils, on wands of white egret feathers twirled like batons. The alarums and excursions fluttered and died while warriors came in across the fields. The shouted war was increasing in ferocity, and several men from each side would dance out and feign attacks, whirling and prancing to display their splendor. They were jeered and admired by both sides and were not shot at, for display and panoply were part of war, which was less war than ceremonial sport, a wild, fierce, festival."

Peter Matthiessen
Under the Mountain Wall

Of all Irian's indigenous peoples, the Dani have most captured the Western imagination, ever since explorer Richard Archbold's first glimpse of this breathtakingly beautiful oasis of green, dotted with smoking huts and laced with tidy mounds of purple-green sweet potato vines. This "Shangri-La" supports 70,000 Dani, a Stone Age people who have come to be known for their farming skill as well as their fierce and glorious warfare.

Although the valley went unnoticed during the early phases of Irian's explorations, the Dani had been contacted six times by various Dutch teams, beginning with the 1909-1910 Lorentz expedition. J.H.G. Kremer crossed the Baliem River's headwaters in 1921 en route to Mt. Wilhelmina but missed the valley by several kilometers.

The first whites arrive

The sight and news of fair-skinned men begot a legend among the Dani people. Whites and

Dani used to live together in a cave called Huwainmo. The whites, with clothes and guns, emerged first, but went far away over the mountains. The Dani left the cave later, wearing penis gourds, and settled nearby.

During World War II, Allied planes flew over the Baliem, looking for possible airfield sites. An American pilot, echoing Archbold, described the Baliem as "laid out in checkerboard squares as perfectly formed as farmlands of the Snake Valley in Idaho." The pilot dubbed it the "Hidden Valley" and buzzed one of the tall wooden towers, used by the Dani to keep tabs on enemy movements.

A few months later, while Hollandia was being used as a staging area for the Pacific war, American pilots flew joy-rides over the Baliem. One of these planes crashed against the valley's mountain wall, killing seven members of the Women's Army Corps and 14 servicemen. Two men and 20-year-old Corporal Margaret Hastings survived the crash, and an air patrol eventually spotted them near the wreck. Since there was as yet no way to land, a funeral service for the victims was conducted in an aircraft circling overhead, and a Roman Catholic priest, a Rabbi and a Protestant minister read funerary rites over the radio. Supplies were dropped to the survivors and a Filipino team parachuted to the rescue. They built a glider strip and, 47 days after the crash, whisked everybody out in gliders. War correspon-

Right: *A Dani hut compound. The thatched huts stay warm at night and cool during the day. Nearby are the sweet potato mounds.* **Opposite:** *Dani warriors in a traditional frenzied dance.*

dents George Lait and Harry Patterson, who covered the rescue, dubbed the valley "Shangri-La" for its beauty and idyllic setting.

Converting the heathens

The next white face seen by the Dani belonged to Lloyd Van Stone, a tall young Texan missionary from the U.S.-based Christian and Missionary Alliance, who was dropped off by hydroplane on April 20, 1954. After the war ended, the CMA had begun vigorously pursuing its evangelical work in the highlands, claiming "a mandate from heaven to invade the Baliem."

The first mission station, established at Hetegima, was built to U.S. standards using flown-in materials. The houses were "a transplant of American comfort in Cannibal Valley" in the words of one author. It took seven months to build the first airstrip. Later, missionaries discovered an ideal site for a landing field next to what was to become the Dutch government post of Wamena in 1958.

Evangelical work among the Dani proved slow going. One of the missionaries, with experience in other highland tribes, called them the "toughest nuts to crack." Among the many difficulties was the Danis' strong distaste for the whites' body odor. When walking with the Dani, the missionaries were always asked to keep downwind. Various slights to the Dani presented more serious problems, as did two earlier killings by white

members of the Archbold expedition.

Shortly after Van Stone, linguist Myron Bromley arrived. Bromley's studies advanced slowly but he eventually determined that the Baliem Dani could be divided into three dialect groups: north, central and south. While the central speakers could understand the two others, the north and south languages were mutually unintelligible.

A high point of early evangelical work was reached on February 14, 1960. Thanks to sermons by "witness men" — native Christians from the Ilaga area of the highlands — a huge fetish-burning took place at Pyramid, at the northern end of the valley. A pyre over 200 meters long, more than a meter wide and 60 centimeters high, was piled with wooden fetishes which went up in a tremendous blaze. According to one missionary account, 5,000 Dani participated in that particular burn-in; by the same account, 25,000 (out of a total population of 75,000) flocked to hear the "witness men."

Many accounts dismiss the proceedings as another manifestation of the cargo cult phenomenon. (See "Cargo Cults on Biak," page 56.) Many obstacles to the whole-hearted acceptance of Christianity remained. One Sunday service was attacked by Dani. An even greater challenge was presented by the arrival in 1958 of more tolerant and better-educated Catholic missionaries, represented by the Franciscan Order, after which the area

was no longer an exclusive preserve of American Protestant fundamentalists.

Modern anthropological work in the valley began only in 1961, with the arrival of the Harvard-Peabody Expedition, including a film crew, still photographers, anthropologist Carl G. Heider, and novelist-explorer Peter Matthiessen. The crew shot a beautiful documentary film of the Dani entitled *Dead Birds,* and produced a superb book of photographs, *Gardens of War.* Matthiessen's account, *Under the Mountain Wall,* is a poignant and informative blend of novel and ethnography.

A people 'on the edge of change'

The team's anthropologist, Carl Heider, stayed on after the photographers left, completing research for what would become *Gentle Warriors,* his careful and well-written description of the Dani. It was a culture "trembling on the edge of change," he writes.

The Dani remained Stone Age farmer-warriors right up into the 1970s, by which time many tribesman owned a steel axe and were saving up stone ones to sell to visitors. They are still superb cultivators, and tribal warfare now and then occasionally flares up.

Ancestral beliefs remain strong. When conversion to a poorly understood Christianity did take place, it was largely pro forma. The missions as well as the government schools and economic projects are much more successful among the Western Dani, settled along steep valley slopes, than among the Valley Dani who live on a wide, rich alluvial plain.

Dani settlements and habits

Roasted or steamed, the sweet potato, here called *ipere,* constitutes 90 percent of the Dani diet. More than 70 varieties are cultivated. Taro and yams, as well as bananas, various greens, ginger, tobacco and colorful cucumbers are also grown. The high-yield gardens are sustained by sophisticated irrigation works that cover 20 percent of the area. The first ditches were probably dug to reclaim swampland. Now, rich mud from the ditch bottoms is periodically scooped out to fertilize the soil of the raised rectangular mounds where the sweet potato vines grow.

The Dani never form large villages but prefer to live in scattered compounds near their gardens. Clusters of compounds, each holding two to five families, form settlements bound by clan ties. Each roughly rectangular compound is surrounded by a fence and at one end stands a domed men's hut, the *honai,* which serves as the focus of much clan-based ceremonial activity. Several round women's huts, each a scaled-down version of the *honai,* line another side of the compound. On yet another side stands a long, rectangular cooking shed and covered pig stalls.

Men and women sleep separately because sexual intercourse is considered dangerous

and weakening. Taboos also prohibit sexual relations after about the fourth month of pregnancy and three to four years after birth. Only after a child can walk well and take care of itself do the parents resume relations. This keeps the mother from being burdened with several young children at the same time.

Penis gourds and grass skirts

The men's work consists of cooperative digging and maintenance of the irrigation network and fences, and occasional hut construction and repair. They have plenty of leisure time, spent chatting with their fellows. The men also tend the gourds which they "train" to grow according to the shape of the penis sheaths they wish to wear. They also weave armbands and braid fibers into elaborate brides' skirts.

Though unimportant today, in the past one of the chief duties of the men was to stand watch and protect women working the fields from marauding war parties. The women's work is long, tedious and often lonely: planting, weeding, cooking, and tending the pigs and children.

Domestic animals include dogs and pigs, crucial to all rituals. These have the run of the land, crashing into any garden unprotected by a stout fence. A large, locally common spider, which is encouraged to weave on prepared frames, almost qualifies as a third domestic animal. The matted webbing spun by this creature is worked into fabric used for men's caps and magical strips suspended from the neck. The latter protect against spirits, which usually attack at the throat.

The chief item of men's clothing is the penis sheath, called *holim,* and men keep gourds of various shapes and sizes. Married women wear skirts of strong fern fibers. These subtly colored skirts, called *youngal,* are short and slung low on the hips. These are usually made by the woman's nearest male relative.

String bags, called *noken,* are an ever-present part of the women's apparel. The bags are loosely knit, like nets, and carry for sweet potatoes, wood, a child, a piglet — anything that needs carrying. The bags are supported by the forehead like a tumpline and when empty, help ward the early morning chill off the women's backs. The bags are knit from bark fibers that are rolled on the thigh into string. The coloring comes from clay, the outer skin of orchid tubers (orange, yellow and white) and small ferns (red and brown). These materials are imported into the valley by native traders.

Production of stone tools

Some 30 years ago the only tools used were stone adzes, stone and boars' tusk scrapers, knives made from sharpened bamboo, and wooden spears and digging sticks. The wooden implements were readily available, but the stones had to be brought from the bed of the Jelime River, about 150 kilometers (93 mi.) to the northwest of the Baliem in the Nogolo Basin. In 1962, the Austrian explorer Heinrich Harer was the first white man to visit Ya-Li-Me, the quarry at this site. The stone was "quarried" on the river bank, he writes, by building fires on the large outcroppings. The heat would then split small chunks off the larger mass.

There were three types of stone quarried at Ya-Li-Me, of which the greenish *andiba* was most prized. The stone is mineralogically an epidote (or chloromelanite) with a degree of hardness varying between six and seven on Mohs' scale. A bluish stone, called *wang-kob-me* (or *ulu* according to shape) was used for small chisels and adzes. Also used was a black flint called *ka-lu.* This was sometimes brought from the Yamo River, but was not very popular. All of these stones formed part of the bride price. ('Stone axe' in Dani is *ye*).

Trade and economics

The current system of weekly markets around the valley, as well as the permanent one in Wamena, has eased the Dani into a monetary economy, providing steel axes and luxuries like candles, matches, cigarettes and clothing. The traditional long-range trade networks died out a generation ago.

The traditional medium of exchange was seashells (though the Dani possessed no

Opposite: *Dani huts, under the mountain wall.*
Above: *Dani women prepare sweet potatoes and greens for steam baking over hot stones.*

notion of the sea), with the cowrie as the basic unit. Imported items imported included stones for axe heads, furs, feathers, fibers and decorative shells. Traders left the valley with salt from brine springs, pigs and cowries. Status-seeking leaders conspicuously gave pigs and cowries to their followers on ritual occasions. Women were — and still are — paid for with pigs, cowries and other traditional items. But the shells, sewn on fiber strips of varying lengths for display, are now more often sold to tourists. Pigs remain a valued medium of exchange.

The Dani are very aware of economic opportunities and inflation. The Archbold expedition purchased 10 kilos of sweet potatoes for one cowrie shell. Six to 10 good ones would buy a pig. When the Harvard-Peabody team arrived, 24 years later, a shell was worth a potato or two, and no number of cowries could convince an owner to part with a pig.

'Big Men' and ritual warfare

The Dani of the valley are divided into some 30 clans (or sibs) organized into political units that Heider terms "confederations." The Dani believe that men and birds once lived together in harmony, not realizing they were different. As a result of this former relationship, each clan has developed an affinity with a particular species of birds, which are themselves considered clan members.

Leadership, of a highly informal variety, was traditionally provided by so-called "Big Men" — charismatic persons who rose to a position of power through strength and success in war, the pigs and shells they gave away, and the number of wives they could afford. Big men acquired their positions through their skill in manipulating the economic system, but emerged and faded with changing circumstances.

The Danis' ritual warfare, well depicted in the film *Dead Birds,* was a far cry from our usual definition of war. Conflicts, according to Heider, were mostly over pigs and women, with land rights a distant third reason. On a metaphysical level, warfare was waged to placate ghosts who lived nearby and who controlled death, human illness and the diseases of pigs. Some of these ghosts were associated with geographical features, others were ancestors or tribesmen recently fallen in battle. These latter in particular had to be quickly avenged or they would create great mischief. Thus an individual's woman or pig problem — usually theft — was reinforced by the need to stay on the good side of the local

spirits. To win their favor kills had to be made in battle.

Once a confederation decided to wage war, it would seek support from its allies. These confederation-based alliances (of which there were six in the Baliem in 1961) were unstable and subject to kaleidoscopic shifts in composition. Hostilities usually persisted for long periods but were characterized by very sporadic fighting. A major battle every 10 to 20 years usually led to new alliances being formed with ritual warfare continuing along new frontiers.

This ritual warfare consisted of formal battles in designated areas, as well as surprise raids. Tall watchtowers, constructed of strong poles lashed together with vines, dotted the valley to guard against sneak attacks. Most encounters were bloody, but fatalities were rare. The sense of victor and vanquished was at best ambiguous. A handful of wounded warriors was the typical result of a day's fighting.

To the Dani, "a day of war is dangerous and splendid" notes Peter Matthiessen. Formal battles had many of the elements of a pleasure outing. The men rubbed their hair and bodies with pig grease and wore fancy headdresses of cuscus or tree kangaroo fur and feathers of all kinds, necklaces and bibs of cowrie shells or large, spoon-shaped *mikak,* or baler shells. The weapons employed were long spears, measuring up to 4.5 meters (15 ft.), and bows and arrows. Women watched from a safe distance, bringing food whenever the men wanted to take a break from the fighting.

Before the action started, insults were traded. These were often humorous, highlighting the opponents' sexual or other inadequacy. Clashes brought the enemy within arrow range, sometimes spear range. Actual fighting seldom lasted more than 10 or 15 minutes and the battle usually involved fewer than 200 men on each side, though many spectators were always present.

Retreating groups were pursued only a short distance, as reinforcements would be standing by. Some 10 to 20 of these clashes made up a full day's battle — which could always be postponed when it rained. (The warriors were very loath to spoil their fine feathers and furs.)

Dani warfare emphasized competence

Opposite: *A Dani woman has smeared herself with yellow clay as part of a traditional ritual of mourning for a deceased relative.*

and "exuberant exhibitionism." Of course, there was always the possibility of being killed or wounded but an alert warrior dodged incoming spears and arrows. The maximum arrow range was 90 meters, but to reach further that 10 or 20 meters the arrows had to be lobbed on a high arcing trajectory. Except from very short distances, the projectiles wobbled and were easy to see. There was no firing of coordinated volleys.

Heider characterizes Dani battle as aggressive behavior without aggressive emotions. Antagonists were seldom mad at each other. They just wanted to show off. The wounded who could not walk were carried behind the line of battle by friends, there to have the arrows painfully dug out of their flesh. About 10 centimeters back from the tip, the shaft of the arrows was weakened, to insure that the tip would break off in the victim. Deaths were usually the result of infected wounds. When a battlefield death did occur, the body was carried back to the warrior's home compound amidst much wailing. A kill touched off two days of dancing, not so much to underline the victory but to call forth the spirits.

A kill also triggered a cycle of revenge. The enemy now plotted to even the score. If deaths could not be avenged in formal battle, sneak raids would be conducted, without the fun and glory. Children and women were fair game on these raids, and women's digging sticks carried both a blunt point for weeding and a sharp one for defense. Even after ritual warfare ceased under government pressure, these raids continued until scores were even.

Spirits and death rites

Dani religion, like warfare, is based on spirit placation. These spirits are either associated with particular features of the landscape or ancestors. Staying on the good side of the spirits was crucial for survival and prosperity. All ceremonies and pig killings were directed at winning their favor. Sacred objects, called *ganekhe,* which included stones (some Dani try to sell them to tourists today — without much success) can be manipulated to prevent the approach of spirits. Enclosures for ghosts, with bundles of grass representing the deceased, are located far from the villages.

Funerals once were the most important Dani rite. They lasted several years, starting with a cremation to drive the ghost from the living area. Elaborate rituals were held for important men and those killed by the enemy. The ghosts of these men were especially powerful and dangerous. They could be induced to "pre-kill" an enemy — his actual death was then sure to occur in battle.

Sometimes the desiccated corpses of important Big Men were not cremated but kept for supernatural reasons. These are today's "mummies," which tourists can see and photograph (for a fee). Apart from the

ceived initiative, building tin-roofed shacks to get the Dani out of their huts and away from the pigs, has also been abandoned. The houses, it turned out, were too hot during the day and too cold at night. The Dani's thatched roofs and double outer walls keep out the heat during the day, and keep it in at night.

The government has successfully poured money and effort into the Baliem Valley. There are schools everywhere, and roads to several population centers and hospitals. Goats, sheep, and fish have been introduced,

mummies, the Dani show little interest in genealogy. Descent is patrilinial and includes no territorial rights. Nuclear family ties are generally unimportant when compared to wider kinship relations.

One of the adjuncts to the cremation ceremony was the cutting off of a girls' fingers. Anesthetic was crude at best. The fingers (usually the outer two of the left hand) were tied off with string a half-hour before the ceremony, and just before the ax fell, the girls were slapped hard in the upper arm to kill the sensation. The wound was staunched with leaves and the fingers dried for a few days, burned, and then the ashes were buried in a special place.

In Heider's time, every female older than 10 had lost four to six fingers to impress the spirits. Although this is no longer practiced, one can still see many middle-aged or older women with missing fingers. During funerals, Big Men distributed pigs and shell bands among their relatives, reinforcing ties.

Occasionally — every four or five years — the most important man of an alliance would initiate the Ebe Akho. This alliance-wide bash was principally directed at the spirits of the deceased. Formal mass marriages, sometimes more than 200 at once, also took place at this time. The main event was a huge pig killing and feast. The more pigs, the more prestige for the Big Men.

The Dani today

The Indonesian government has taken a lot of heat from journalists for its treatment of the Irianese. Although mistakes were made, the Indonesians have, especially of late, shown a great deal of tolerance in their dealings with the natives. At one time, the government launched "operasi koteka" (*koteka* is the Indonesian work for penis sheath) to get the Dani out of their traditional garb and into "normal" clothes. When the Dani refused, the government wisely relented. Another ill-con-

as well as new crops. Cargo flights are subsidized so most items cost about the same as they do elsewhere in Indonesia. The subsidized items include gasoline, cloth, cooking oil, salt, sugar and other foodstuffs, as well as tinned food and biscuits. While most of these are bought by non-Dani, the locals are slowly acquiring a taste for them.

The problem is that the Dani have to pay for them with money. Although some have found work in Wamena, many of those with junior or senior high school degrees are unemployed. Jobs should be opening up at a new gold mine in the Ok Sibyl region, and some Dani already have jobs at the thriving Tembagapura copper mine.

However, the vast majority of the Dani are still subsistence farmers, growing the staple sweet potato for local consumption. Introduced vegetables — carrots, cucumbers, cabbage, onions and tomatoes — all grow well in the rich highlands soil and the Dani willingly bring them to market. Indeed, the Baliem is one of the few places in outer Indonesia where vegetables are plentiful and inexpensive. Pineapples and oranges also arrive from

Above, left: *A Dani warrior, preparing for (mock) battle, has smeared his face with a jet black mixture of soot and pig grease.* **Above, right:** *Dani mime ritual warfare.* **Opposite:** *A "wounded" warrior is hustled off the mock battlefield by his bemused comrades.*

valleys close to here. The problem is that Wamena and the villages of the valley can absorb only so much produce. The natural market for the surplus would be Jayapura, but the capital receives its vegetables from Javanese transmigrant settlements nearby. A partial solution has been found in subsidized flights shipping vegetables to the mining community at Tembagapura.

The government is also making an effort to introduce rice cultivation as a cash crop to supply local needs, thus eliminating rice imports to Wamena. Dani farmers have created some 80 hectares (195 acres) of rice paddies, with a government goal of 150 hectares (365 acres). A variety of rice from the highlands of Sulawesi seems best suited to the soils and Toraja school teachers, stationed in the valley, impart their technical skill in cultivating the grain. The rice is inter-cropped with soy beans to replenish soil nutrients. Dani farmers can also raise cash by growing high value coffee beans and collecting the highlands' excellent honey, already selling for $6 a bottle in Jayapura.

Dani traditions in flux

Despite 35 years of missionary work and "pacification" by the government, many Dani traditions remain strong. Large-scale warfare has been stopped but small battles with spears and arrows occur. Polygamy is still widespread. The confirmed record number of wives stands at 75 for one wealthy chief, while another claims a whopping 175 — though his memory of deceased spouses is dim. Every five years or so, huge ceremonies combine initiation rituals and weddings with the slaughter of scores of pigs.

It is difficult to judge the effects of present changes. A Catholic priest, with several decades in Irian and a fair knowledge of Dani customs claims Carl Heider's studies, the best available, are too superficial. His church plans to bring in a priest with a PhD in anthropology to study the Dani and develop a rational policy concerning native traditions.

The Dani practice of polygamy illustrates the quandry religious leaders find themselves in. The Catholic priest I spoke to had no objection to this practice, saying that this way every woman, no matter how old or crippled, is part of a household. Dynamic, hardworking men, who can raise the $500 bride price, take extra brides. The priest also says that, according to Catholic hospital birth records, girls outnumber boys three to two.

Arguments against the practice state that many young men can't find spouses because the girls are "bought" by older men with plenty of pigs available for the bride price. Since the men cannot always sexually satisfy all their wives, this leads to extramarital relations. A man caught in an illicit affair, he has to pay a pig-fine to the woman's husband — who uses the animals to buy still more wives.

TREKS AROUND WAMENA

Dramatic Vistas and Dani Villages

Wamena, the administrative and communications hub of the Baliem Valley, boasts a lively market, souvenir shops and relatively good food. But to really see the valley and its peoples, leaving Wamena is a must. Pugima is just an hour's walk away, along mostly level ground. Jiwika is further, about 20 kilometers (12 mi.), but public or chartered bemos take you there quickly. From the losmen in Jiwika, short day-hikes bring you to neighboring Dani villages to see blackened mummies, sweet potato fields, and brine ponds. Kurima, to the south at the head of the Baliem Gorge, offers some of the highlands' most spectacular scenery. Public transport takes you within a couple hours' walk, and a chartered minibus to Sugokmo brings you within an hour of Kurima. Hikes out of Kurima cross rickety suspension bridges and stunning gorges. Longer hikes to the north lead to Lake Habbema, Ibele, Mount Trikora and Pyramid.

Touring Wamena

The town of Wamena is growing by leaps and bounds. Several flights a day, weather and mechanical conditions permitting, bring in tons of subsidized merchandise and gasoline. Air Force Hercules cargo planes bring up Japanese minibuses for $300 each. According to one set of statistics, Wamena's population shot up from less than 6,000 in 1985 to over 8,000 a year later.

Much of this increase is due to Indonesians arriving from elsewhere in the archipelago (mainly from East and Central Java, Menado, Ambon and South Sulawesi) to take advantage of job and business opportunities. The district's only high school and a number of specialized colleges — for example, for teacher training — add hundreds of students to Wamena's population. There's a post office, a bank to change travelers' checks and cash (at a slightly lower rate than in Jayapura), a movie house, and a sprawling covered market. Wamena is a fascinating blend of traditional cultures and progress.

The daily Merpati flight arrives early in Wamena and there's plenty of time to settle into one of the small hotels and still take advantage of most of the day. The central market is crowded with the colorful produce of Dani gardens and equally colorful crowds.

Souvenirs include bows with a bunch of multipurpose arrows (hunting, killing humans), stone adzes, penis gourds and belts of cowrie shell money. You can buy color print film (but not slides) here and bottled water.

Pugima: a taste of Dani village life

Perhaps the first thing to do upon arriving in Wamena, after finding a hotel and having lunch — is to make the two hour round-trip to the nearby village of Pugima for a taste of traditional Dani life. Not even a village actually, Pugima is a series of hamlets or compounds. Each compound is home to from two to six related families. A strong wooden fence encircles several thatch-covered huts: the round men's house, the similarly shaped women's houses and a long, rectangular kitchen adjoining the covered pig sty.

The walk itself travels along level ground (well, there's a tiny hill). A taxi can even drop you off on the far side of the airfield, cutting a half-hour off of the walking time. At **Wesaput**, an Ambonese couple who work in the local department of culture manages a small museum of Dani artifacts. The sign by the road reads "Pusat Alat Seni" (Art Center). With a day's notice, this couple can arrange to have schoolchildren perform a traditional dance. Wesaput was the site of the first Dutch government post in the Baliem Valley.

From Wesaput, you cross the Baliem River on a steady suspension bridge, hike over a small hill and you're in **Pugima**. There are several traditional hut compounds as well as a few "modern" houses scattered around the valley. Have your guide show you around a compound. Some 20 local men have started irrigated rice cultivation here and a market has been built in preparation for the harvest. There's plenty of time to return to Wamena before dark for dinner (try the giant crayfish) and sleep before the next day's explorations.

To Jiwika: mummies and brine pools

The most popular and easy jaunt from Wamena is to Jiwika (pronounced either Djiwika or Yiwika), some 20 kilometers (12 mi.) to the northwest along one of the few roads in the Baliem. A crowded public bemo will take you there for about 75¢. The more affluent can charter a bemo with driver for $6 an hour. It's about an hour each way, and there is a comfortable losmen in Jiwika for overnight stays. During the early morning hours on market days, many Dani walk the road to Jiwika carrying their wares — including firewood, rough planks for hut or fence building, and string nets full of produce.

Overleaf: *Dani warriors, ready for (mock) battle.*
Opposite: *The bustling market at Wamena attracts a mix of tribesmen and townsmen.*
Below: *Using an age-old technique, Dani women soak banana stems to extract salt from the brine pool above the village of Jiwika.*

Along the way, a short side road leads to **Akima Village** and its famous mummy. Men of importance — warrior leaders of an alliance — were not given the usual cremation after death. Their bodies were desiccated and kept in the men's house as a conduit to the supernatural to obtain good health, abundant harvests, wives, pigs and victory in war. No one knows the age of the Akima mummy. (Most Dani don't know their own ages, and consider this unimportant.)

The Akima mummy is the earthly remains of Werapak Elosarek, a powerful warrior and "Big Man." Although the mummy itself is interesting, the people who mill around the compound, strong featured and good humored (especially the old keeper of the shrine), are the highlight of a visit. The keeper, Akima Ulolik, is current chief of the Akima area. After a bit of bargaining, the usual price is $3 per person to have the mummy brought out. When specified, the photo fee includes unlimited picture-taking of the mummy and his descendents. The body, blackened by the smoke, sits in a compact, knees-to-chin pose in the men's hut. It is set on a chair while the men gather around to pose unaffectedly (see frontispiece).

Approaching Jiwika, modern rectangular houses replace the native compounds. These were built by the government in an attempt to give the Dani healthier living quarters, apart from their beloved pigs. Some Dani obligingly moved in while building traditional huts in the back. Eventually they moved into the huts and the "modern" houses were only used for storage and as pig stys.

Jiwika, a *kecamatan* or administrative center, lies a couple of hundred meters off the main road. The market (Sundays only) is a quiet, if crowded affair. Early arrivals grab the shaded spots on long tables inside two open-sided, tin-roofed sheds. Others set their produce on the ground in an open area next to the sheds and wait patiently, gossiping with friends. Sweet potatoes, yams, bananas, red chillies, cucumbers, peanuts, cabbage, fried bananas and an occasional chicken are offered for sale. Most of the sales are to government civil servants living in Jiwika.

The La-uk (meaning hello/welcome in Dani women's speech) losmen in Jiwika, run by a long-term resident Christian Javanese couple, with its thatched roof and dirt floors, has been a hiker's haven for years. The guestbook is full of recent hiking info, and stories and humor from past travelers.

About a hundred yards past the losmen in Jiwika on the main road is a footpath that leads to a compound with another great, gruesome mummy. The price here is about $2 per person for viewing and photography. Another path starts out from the back of the Jiwika market, up a steep mountain side to a saltwater spring called **Iluwe** or **Iluerainma**. The salt pool is about 300 meters (1,000 ft.) above the valley and the steep climb takes about an hour. Beware of the slippery footing.

The brine pool is frequented by the Dani as well as members of Kim Yal and Jale tribes — for whom the trip is a two to three day walk. These last are recognizable by the many rattan hoops the men wear around their waists. The same procedure is used by everyone to gather the salt. Banana trunks, peeled into segments, are soaked in the brine for about a half an hour, then carried home. The saltwater permeates the fibrous trunks which are dried and then burned, yielding salty ash. The ash, wrapped in blocks, was formerly an essential trade item. The quality of the product (the ratio of salt to ash) was illustrated by the type of wrapping.

At **Waga-Waga**, further north from Jiwika, is a limestone cave called Kontilola. Bemos let you out within a hundred meters of the cave entrance. A dark passageway (bring a flashlight) leads from a large chamber to a pool of water and a section of the cave filled with bats. The phallocrypt cavekeeper will charge 75¢ to $1.

South to Kurima: the Baliem Gorge

Some of the Grand Valley's most spectacular scenery lies southeast of Wamena, where the mountain walls part in the Baliem Gorge. Public transportation (about $1) leads as far as Hepoba village, 15 kilometers (9 mi.) from Wamena. Depending on the state of the road and the driver's skill, chartered bemos may go a bit further, either to Hetegima (the site of the first mission in the Baliem) for $12-15, or a couple of kilometers further, to Sugokmo, for about $22. From here, it's an hour's walk to Kurima at the head of the gorge, and the scenery all along the way is well worth the effort.

The easy, level walk from Sugokmo takes you across a long and narrow (but solid) steel suspension bridge over a steep-sided gorge. A bit further ahead, you will have to ford a stream, the Yetni, which is easy when the water level is low, but tough when the river is high. Willing porters carry you across, piggy back. A porter weighing 60 kilos can carry a bulky 85 kilo Westerner. It

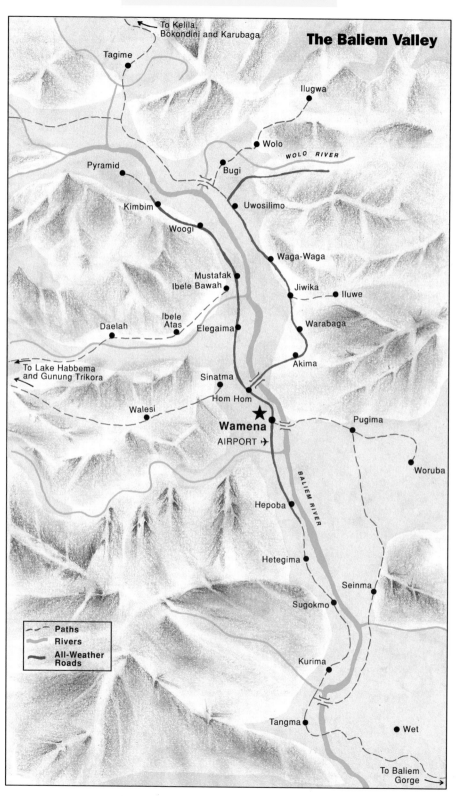

The Baliem Valley

To Kelila,
Bokondini and Karubaga

Tagime

Ilugwa

Wolo

WOLO RIVER

Pyramid

Bugi

Kimbim

Uwosilimo

Woogi

Waga-Waga

Mustafak
Ibele Bawah

Jiwika   Iluwe

Ibele
Atas

Warabaga

Daelah

Elegaima

To Lake Habbema
and Gunung Trikora

Akima

Sinatma

Hom Hom

Walesi

Pugima

★ **Wamena**
AIRPORT ✈

Woruba

Hepoba

BALIEM RIVER

Hetegima

Seinma

Sugokmo

Paths
Rivers
All-Weather
Roads

Kurima

Tangma

Wet

To Baliem
Gorge

may look and feel a bit ridiculous, but it's a lot better than slipping and falling into the rushing current.

Kurima is a tiny, spread-out town with schools, military and police posts and the administrative center of the *kecamatan*. An airstrip and a mission perch on a flat ledge above town. Tuesday is the weekly market day here. If you stay overnight, report on arrival to the police, where your *surat jalan* will be checked and the information laboriously copied down. Possible places to sleep in Kurima include the military post, the police station, one of the schoolteachers' homes or the mission.

Hikes out of Kurima lead to incredible mountain scenery. Good tennis shoes or boots, drinking water, and a porter/guide with knowledge of the local trails are all absolutely essential. The hike described below can be covered in eight hours by experienced mountain hikers, but to photograph and enjoy the scenery you should plan on two or three days.

From Kurima, the trail leads straight up a short but steep mountainside on the western bank of the Baliem River. The trail then levels off, following stone fences and leading past traditional compounds for some two or three hours. Most of the way, the sheer mountain wall on the other side of the gorge looms in the near distance. The steep slopes are blanketed by neat gardens, some on an unbeliev-

able 60 degree slope. The terraces are supported by stone retaining walls or stout Y-shaped branches (sometimes both) to keep the fertile soil from eroding. The rushing Baliem River far below knifes through the bottom of the scene, a silver streak setting off the green slopes.

About one and a half hours out of Kurima, you can clamber down to **Wamarek Village** where a suspension bridge spans the river. Continuing along the Kurima mountainside, a wide panorama opens where the Moki River tumbles down a steep valley to join the Baliem. You feel like you are on top of the world. But then comes the tough part — the path down to the village of **Tangma** must have been laid out by mountain goats. In about 40 minutes, you drop an almost vertical 250 meters (800 ft.) to the airstrip at Tangma (market day here is Wednesday), an evangelical center with irregular weekly flights.

From Tangma, it's about one and a half hours to the highlight of this walk, the **Wet-Pasema suspension bridge**. Here the Baliem River twists and turns through frightening rapids. During the rainy season, the tumbling waters lick the bridge with an occasional wave, giving those brave enough to cross a soaking.

You might be lucky enough to catch a flight out of Tangma, but don't count on it. It's also possible to spend the night here (bring a sleeping bag) with a schoolteacher

or perhaps with missionary-linguist Myron Bromley, an American who was part of the first evangelical team to land in the Baliem in 1954. Otherwise, it's a tough three hour walk back to Kurima.

If you walked from Hepoba or Kurima on the right bank of the Baliem River (facing downstream), switch to the left bank for your return. At Kurima, a suspension bridge crosses the river, then it's an easy two hours' walk upstream to the next bridge, near Sugokmo. About one and a half hours' walk up into the hills to the west of Hetegima, there are salt springs similar to those above Jiwika.

As the Kurima tribes and those of the Hetegima area are traditional enemies, you might see heavily armed, penis-sheathed warriors with their long spears and bows and arrows. Many keep axes to chop up the enemy in close combat. Not to worry. Get out the camera. The warriors have nothing against tourists and will pose happily — for a couple of red hundred rupiah notes.

Unless you have made arrangements for a bemo to pick you up at a specified time and place, walk to Hepoba, where you will probably find one for the ride back to Wamena. But bemos around here do not run nearly so frequently as those to Jiwika.

North to Pyramid and Mt. Trikora

By the time you read this, a paved road may run the entire way from Wamena to Pyramid in the northwest corner of the Baliem Valley. Hopefully the road will even have a bemo service. Otherwise it's a flat, eight-hour walk.

On the way to Pyramid, a side-trip leads to Lake Habbema (where Archbold landed in 1938) and Mt. Trikora, which, at 4,750 meters (15,600 ft.), is one of Irian's highest peaks. Until recently, Trikora (formerly Mt. Wilhelmina) was snow-capped year-round. This excursion requires organization: tents, a warm sleeping bag, food, and porters.

There are two trails to Trikora. One leads

west out of Wamena to the village of Walesi (two hours) then up to Welarek for the first night. From here it's on to Habikmo (good scenery) for the second night, and on the third day to Babilolo village. On the fourth you reach the base of Gunung Trikora. Along the way, you can see Lake Habbema below.

The other route begins by road from Wamena past Elegaima and to the bridge at Ibele Bawah. From here, it's about one and a half hours to Ibele Atas and another three hours to Daelah for the first night. The latter

part of this hike offers beautiful panoramas of terraced gardens dotted with traditional compounds. Daelah is the last village on this trail. From here, it's two days to the shores of Lake Habbema. The base of Trikora is an easy half-day away. The ascent, however, is only for experienced climbers.

There is also a direct road to **Pyramid**, the site of the main highland base and conference center of the fundamentalist Protestant Christian and Missionary Alliance (CAMA). With clapboard houses, lawns and American creature comforts, Pyramid has been called the "most civilized" outpost in the highlands.

If you decide to stay overnight here, ask for a schoolteacher and don't pester the missionaries. A better idea would be to spend the night at **Kimbim**, the district center 5 kilometers before Pyramid. You have to report to the police there anyway. The *camat* has spare beds and so does the school. Figure on $5 for accommodations and meals.

From Kimbim, there is a good trail — about one and a half hours — to the village of **Woogi** where they will pull out the mummy for less than $1. They see few tourists here.

Opposite: *Decrepit suspension bridges like this one span the many rivers and gorges in the highlands.* **Above, left:** *The mummy at Jiwika. The preserved corpses of "Big Men" serve as emmissaries to the spirit world.* **Above, right:** *Pulling off the road to Kurima is ill-advised.*

FURTHER EXPLORATIONS

Spectacular Trek from Karubaga

One of the best ways to see the highlands is to fly to Karubaga, in the home of the Western Dani, and make the spectacularly scenic hike of several days back to Wamena, through friendly highland villages along relatively easy trails.

Weather permitting, Merpati offers a weekly flight from Wamena to Ka.¨ıbaga on Saturdays, for $15 one-way. The window of the Twin Otter displays the highlands in all their panoramic splendor. Tin-roofed Wamena quickly gives way to the valley's neatly arranged sweet potato gardens, here and there dotted by the thatched roofs of Dani compounds. The creamy-brown Baliem River snakes its way along the valley floor. Flying north, the valley floor rises and becomes covered in forest, yielding only occasionally to painstakingly cut agricultural fields. The small plane barely clears the 2,000 meter (6,500 ft.) peaks, and the land below opens again into a huge valley with long missionary airstrips.

Twenty minutes out of Wamena, the plane glides to a bumpy landing on Karubaga's grass-and-dirt airstrip, steeply inclined at an elevation of 1,400 meters (4,600 ft.). An expectant crowd rushes forward to unload the plane, embrace relatives or stare at the white strangers with their strange gear and heavy hiking boots.

Karubaga Town

The tiny town of Karubaga, like the other 12 sub-district centers of the Jayawijaya *kabupaten,* is the administrative center of a wide area and, in this case, a scattered population of some 20,000 Western Dani. Karubaga snuggles just below the mountains at the head of a wide green valley, ending in the distance in steep mountains, shrouded in blue haze. Three rivers — the Kano, the Konda and the Kurege — spring from the mountains in back of Karubaga, flow through the valley, and eventually empty into the Mamberamo River which then wends its way down to Irian's north coast. The town started as a missionary outpost in the 1950s, shortly after the arrival of American fundamentalists. The whites are gone now, replaced by Dani pastors of the Indonesian KINGMI Protestant denomination, overseeing some 50 churches near town and more than 100 district wide.

The legacy of the missionaries in Karubaga and among the Western Dani generally includes an end to tribal warfare, the eradication of diseases such as yaws (a debilitating skin condition), the introduction of a variety of fruits and vegetables, and the end of witch-killings. While in the old days missionaries frowned on penis sheaths and bare breasts, the current and more rational policy permits the native attire, taking into account that many of the Dani are too poor to afford clothes and soap to keep them clean.

Some local pastors allow a bit of the old-style ancestor and spirit worship by some of the few remaining pagans — but only if a fine is paid to the church. Weddings, funerals and even ceremonies connected with the Christian calendar, such as Christmas, are celebrated in the traditional ways. And groups of villages periodically hold huge, several-day-long feasts, in the old style, which result in the slaughter of 500 or more pigs.

Although missionaries have successfully stopped witch-burning, they have not ended a widespread belief in witchcraft. Many of the Western Dani continue to believe in hereditary occult powers. Black witches can become bats in order to eat people, or can become the wind that blows away a whole village. One recently acquired power allows black witches to burn airplanes, but fortunately this technique has not yet been tested. The American missionaries also left a legacy in Karubaga of a more material nature: many neat wooden houses surrounded by lawns and flowers. One of these buildings serves as the best little guesthouse in the highlands. The mission-built complex on the highest part of town gives way to the police and administrative buildings, an army outpost, two primary schools and two junior high schools. The church and government maintain separate school facilities, which include board for children living too far away to make the trek to Karubaga each day.

Arriving in town

The first thing to do is check into the *rumah tamu,* or guesthouse. With five bedrooms, a sit-down toilet and a bucket shower, this is a bargain at $5 a night. Mattresses, pillows, sheets, blankets, mosquito netting (not needed most of the year) and towels are provided. In the daytime, the well-lit living room offers comfortable chairs and a couch, a rug and lots of uplifting missionary literature as well as old *Readers Digest*s and Peanuts cartoons. At night, you can read by candlelight and if it gets chilly, start a fire in the franklin stove.

Opposite: *Crossing the Warom River. While some visitors prefer doing things the hard way, sure-footed porters are always willing to carry their clients across.* **Below:** *A Western Dani couple pauses on the trail above Wunin. Note the Baliem River winding through the valley below.*

The guest house kitchen is equipped with a wood-burning stove (the $5 includes wood) and a full set of pots, pans and crockery. You can cook your own meals or delegate the chore to either your guide or the guest house caretaker, who is available to do all kinds of domestic work for about 10¢ an hour.

After settling in, you should report to the police station, a short walk on the other side of town. They might want to look at your passport but the critical item is your *surat jalan* or travel permit. On the back of this essential document, they will stamp the Karubaga permit, then fill out various forms with an antique typewriter. The clean-cut young policemen are friendly chaps with little to do in life except play ping pong and check out the occasional tourist. Give them a chance to practice their nonexistent English.

Police business over, see to the logistics for your upcoming trek. If you have not brought a guide from Wamena, a local one — as well as porters — can be found, but none can speak English. Even for tough walkers carrying their own backpacks, we suggest at least one guide because trails around villages and gardens can be confusing, requiring frustrating backtracking. If you did not fly into Karubaga with all the essentials, there are a half-dozen small stores around town to buy basics such as batteries, candles, tinned food, biscuits and instant noodles. You do not have to buy food here for the whole trek as vegetables and fruit — including, of course, sweet potatoes — are available along the way. To make the walk enjoyable, hire a porter (about $3 a day). Taking only essentials, one porter should be enough for each person's load, with another for a two-person supply of food and cooking gear.

Karubaga hosts a market on Mondays, Wednesdays, and Fridays, which brings to the town the produce of the subdistrict. The first transactions take place in the uncovered market area around 8 am and by 2 pm, most of the action is over. Peanuts are the biggest local cash crop, selling here for 25¢ a kilo, half the Wamena price. Other marketables include pineapples, 10¢-20¢ per fruit, oranges, red onions, chickens and the occasional pig. Local government employees stock up here, and some of the produce is flown to Wamena at subsidized rates.

The Karubaga market makes a great place for photographs, with lots of Western Dani tribesmen and women gossiping, buying and selling. Outside of the Baliem Valley, you don't have to pay to photograph the locals. They love to have their picture taken. The problem is obtaining natural poses, although this can usually be accomplished with patience and a telephoto lens.

The trail

The trail between Karubaga and Wamena lies along a planned, but not yet built road. The

right of way leads from Nabire (near the coast at the base of Cenderawasih Bay) to Wamena, through the western highlands.

Many sections of this trail have been widened enough to allow sunshine through, drying up the mud below, but elsewhere the trail is just a narrow footpath — especially on the steepest inclines. Even in the driest season, June and July, there is always the chance of a shower, lasting a couple of hours or more. And after a good rain, there will be mud (not very deep). But, unless you have absolutely awful luck, day-long rainfall is most unlikely. On the contrary, chances are better for sunburn. Bring a wide-brimmed hat, long sleeves and pants, and sunscreen.

The level distance between Karubaga and Wamena — through Wunin, Bokondini, Kelila, Tagime and Pyramid — is just 70 kilometers (43 mi.). But this does not account for laboring up the mountainsides or easing one's way down the incline on the other side. A strong hiker can make it in three days (the Danis do it in a day or two), but it is much better to allow yourself four or five days. Then you can enjoy the changing scenery, take lots of breaks and photos, and arrive at your sleeping destination early enough to bathe, relax and dine during daylight.

While tennis shoes will do, hiking boots offer ankle support, keep mud out of your toes and grip better on slippery surfaces. Some rivers are spanned by bridges, but small creeks and mudflats are traversed on a round log or two, which are more likely than not to be slippery. If you don't think you can manage, let your porters give you a hand or carry you across. They are tough chaps, well able to carry even an overweight body across a waist-high raging river with only loose, slippery stones as footholds for their bare feet. (Make sure someone gets a photo!) Even if you can make it across on your own, the lift prevents wet boots or wasted time taking your boots off and putting them on again.

Along the trail there are many places to drink clear mountain water but take a canteen for those stretches of two hours or more under the hot sun. And have your guide bring along some pineapples, delicious at break-time. Keep your camera handy, because you will often meet locals along the way. Only one word of Western Dani language suffices for close encounters: *wah!*

Wunin

Get an early start, 8 am at the latest, and in six easy hours you will reach Wunin. The early start is important — each day begins with an uphill climb (towns are generally in

Opposite: *The spectacular Baliem Gorge, the only break in Irian's high cordillera of mountains.*
Above: *A group of Dani girls. Dani women do not wear the distinctive low slung skirts until they marry. Until then, they wear grass skirts like these.*

valleys) and you don't want to be making this during the heat of the day.

From the edge of the Karubaga plateau the trail drops to a river, with a well-maintained, rattan and cable bridge. Most of the floor planks are in place. After the crossing, be ready for a two-hour climb. The slopes, near and far, are covered with gardens and highlands forests. Once the climb is over, you pass through a village of thatched huts. This signals the beginning of two hours of flat trekking. Towards the end of this part of the stroll, Wunin will appear, but it's further than it looks. First a long drop, then a river crossing on a solid bridge, and finally a short level stretch before Wunin comes back into view. Another short drop and you are crossing the Warom River, the last before Wunin. The river makes an excellent place for a swim before the short climb to Wunin village.

The altitude here, 1,460 meters (4,790 ft.), is just slightly higher than Karubaga. Wunin is dominated by a huge airstrip, flatter than Karubaga's, which receives sporadic MAF flights when building materials or supplies are urgently needed. The village hugs one side of the airstrip. All the buildings are "modern" — clean, tin-roofed and without character. The inevitable church, school and teachers' houses hold together this tiny mission-built village. During clear weather, the upper end of the landing field affords a fine view of the brooding mountains.

At Wunin you can sleep at a schoolteacher's house, but first take a look at the bed offered and agree to a price. Expect to pay about $3 per person, but you might have to bargain. Forget about sit-down toilets — a little outhouse over a hole in the ground is the standard. You can relieve yourself anywhere away from the houses, preferably at night.

Commissioning a Dani festival

There are also several Dani compounds just off the main trail, which starts at the upper end of the landing field, where you can overnight in a *honai* or men's house. The huts have no beds, but soft grass on the floor makes a decent mattress. (Foreign women are also allowed to sleep in the huts.) A central fire, double wood walls, and a number of bodies ward off night time chills. The disadvantages of a Dani hut include the possibility of fleas or ticks. And it can get quite smoky, but it is usually not too bad if you keep your head close to the floor, and stay away from the door. Pay $1-$2 per person for the *honai* stay. Dani guests (your guides and porters)

are usually put up on a complementary basis.

If you are too sore to continue the next day, rest up for 24 hours. Get your legs rubbed with oil and crushed red onions. Have your guide organize a festival. If there are several members in your group, it's not very expensive — say $200. The price depends on the size and number of pigs killed as well as the number of participants.

In the "show" my guide organized, three pigs were killed ($75) and about 140 men and women took part, all in traditional dress. The guide got things going by visiting four Dani compounds at daybreak and by 8:30 am things were underway.

First the tribesmen dug a pit about one meter deep and 1.5 meters long and then, nearby, arranged huge armfuls of firewood into a rectangular pile and covered the pyre with stones. The traditional method, rubbing a tough liana against a piece of softwood, started the fire. When the firewood under the stones was blazing, each pig was held by two men while a third shot an arrow into its heart from close range. Bamboo knives quickly cut up the meat. After the pigs were dispatched, the Dani lined the pit with leaves, and then with stones that had been heated in the fire. More leaves were laid over the stones, and then sweet potatoes and chunks of pork.

While the food steam-baked for two to three hours, the men and women danced and whooped, yelling and singing with abandon. The men organized themselves into two teams and staged an enthusiastic mock battle with plant stems as spears. A few of the men were superbly decorated with soot and pig grease, white lime paint, flowers, cuscus fur and feathers. Everyone had a good time, and I took plenty of photos before the food was cooked and divided among the participants.

On to Bokondini

From Wunin, it's a flat stretch for a half hour before coming to the mountain at the head of the valley. Another half hour and you reach the topside forest and begin a nice, shaded stretch. The trail touches the edge of an artificial lake, a fairyland opening in the high, misty forest. The water is stocked with carp and tilapia. An hour of hiking brings you to the top of the long drop to the Bokondini Valley. If the weather is clear, the looming mountains appear through openings in the

Opposite: *A specially grooved arrow, released at short range, is the traditional way to dispatch a pig. Roast pork is the centerpiece of a Dani feast.*

forest. At the bottom of the mountain is a stream that makes a perfect resting place for weary knees. Then it's flat again for a while before dropping down to the Bogo River below Bokondini. There is no bridge here, but your porters will either built a temporary one or carry you across. A short, steep climb ends at the little town and subdistrict center of Bokondini — six easy hours from Wunin.

The urban "center" of Bokondini resembles Karubaga but with an important difference. A Cessna plane owned by MAF has its home base here, along with its pilot and missionaries. They live in neat wooden alpine houses surrounded by fences, lawns and flowers — in the American style. Don't expect missionary hospitality — they are not in the business of putting up hikers. Try a schoolteacher or the infirmary staff house, just across from the clinic, called *rumah sakit*. Again, look over the facilities and agree on a price before settling in and reporting to the police with passport and *surat jalan*.

Back to Wamena

Try to get the earliest possible start out of Bokondini because there is a long day ahead. The first part is easy: a stroll of some two and one-half hours with little climbing and one solid bridge crossing lands you in Kelila, another subdistrict center where you report again to the police. Kelila has a regular Merpati flight once a week (on Friday) to Wamena, and occasional missionary flights. From Kelila you face the trip's toughest climb, 2 to 3 hours uphill on a wide road to the top of the pass. Here you are on the island's divide. The watershed to the north drains into the Memberamo and the Pacific; to the south all the rivers head to the Baliem and the Arafura Sea. The wonderful view of the southern valley is your reward as your knees take a pounding during the 1.5 to 2 hours downhill to Tagime, a 6-hour day. The pastor in Tagime runs a guesthouse.

From Tagime, it is an easy 3 hours to Pyramid, the missionary center at the head of the Baliem Valley. From Pyramid, you can catch a flight (10 minutes) to Wamena. Or continue to Kimbim, one hour further. The *camat* (subdistrict head) has guest rooms where, for $5 a day, you can room and board. Kimbim requires a police stop.

From Kimbim, Landcruisers and trucks take passengers to Wamena once or twice a week for $2 a head ($60 for a chartered ride). You can also walk, flat but hot, another 4-6 hours to Gunung Susu or Sinatma, where there is regular bemo service to Wamena. Or walk across the valley to the Baliem River, cross on a small raft or a canoe, and from Uwosilimo (often called Usolimo), just on the other side, take a bemo to Wamena. Bemos from Uwosilimo make the run several times a day and the fare is less than $1 (a charter from Uwosilimo is $15-$20).

Baliem Practicalities

All prices in U.S. $

After a 35-minute flight from Jayapura, over Membrano and the Pass Valley, the Merpati airplane touches down at Wamena. Taking a glance out of the holding room at the Wamena airport, all the time and expense to get to the Baliem Valley seems justified. Here are Dani tribesmen, going about their business, sporting yellow penis gourds that, in the words of an American missionary, stand out "like jibbooms, flaunting their maleness."

But the hassles are not over yet. Your baggage has to be searched for alcohol as the Baliem is "dry." And the police have to check your passport and *surat jalan,* the authorization to visit the Baliem. (This paper is easily obtained by tourists at the central police station in Jayapura with 4 passport-sized photos and photocopies of your passport and visa — see "Jayapura Practicalities," page 78.) Once you reach the main part of the terminal, a small army of eager hands (each expecting a tip) grab your luggage to carry it to one of the local losmen.

ACCOMMODATIONS

The best rooms are at the Nayak Hotel, just across the road from the airport. The Sri Lestari has a great location, in front of Wamena's fascinating market. Aside from the Jayawijaya Hotel (3 km out, for tour groups only) the other hotels and losmen are within walking distance. The furthest from the airport, the Baliem Cottages, is just 600 meters away. As soon as you check in, you have to fill out another police form and your *surat jalan* will be re-checked at the central police station in back of the market. Your hotel/losmen can usually send somebody to handle this last detail.

Lodging in Wamena

Losmen Anggrek. Jl. Ambon, P.O. Box 12. The newest and cleanest in town, but unfortunately no attached toilet/baths. 8 rooms. $10.50 S, $15-20 D w/breakfast and tea or coffee.
Baliem Cottages. Jl. Thamrin, P.O. Box 32. Some 600 meters from the airport. 15 thatch covered cottages, a bit run down but spacious. The restaurant on the premises is open only occasionally. $13 S; $19-25 per cottage).
Hotel Jayawijaya. 3 km out of town off the road to Pyramid; 18 rooms, none with attached bath. 5 bathrooms upstairs, 5 downstairs. There are rice paddies and Dani huts in back. This hotel is only for tour groups; $11 per person, with full board.
Hotel Nayak. Jl. Gatot Subroto 1, P.O. Box 1. Tel: 26. 12 rooms with bath. $9 S, $15 D.
Losmen Sjahrial Jaya. Jl. Gatot Subroto 51. Tel. 151. 5 double rooms with simple bath attached. $6 per person.
Losmen Sri Lestari. In front of the central market. 10 rooms. $9-10 S, $15-17 D. A bucket of hot water upon request. Meals in the cafeteria.

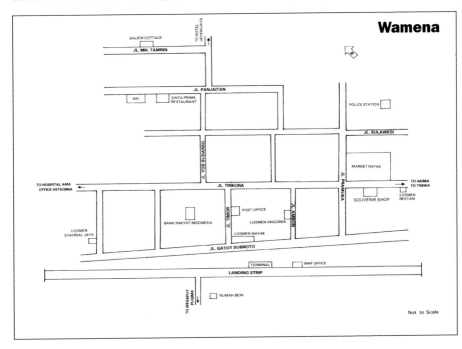

Wamena

Not to Scale

Lodging in Jiwika

Losmen La-uk Inn. On the west side of the main road. $6 for a bed and full board.

DINING

Most hotels/losmen serve meals. There are also many foodstalls around the market, serving quite inexpensive Indonesian food. The **Sinta Prima**, on Jl. Panjaitan, is the best restaurant in town: Chinese food and, when available, huge freshwater shrimp. Meals range from $2 to $5.

In the back of the market are three restaurants. The **Vemalia** specializes in Chinese and Indonesian dishes, $1-2.50. Next door, the **Gembira** serves rice dishes for 75¢-$1. The **Minang Jaya** offers rice and meat for 75¢-$1.

BANKS AND MONEY-CHANGING

Bank Rakyat Indonesia. 8 am to 12:30 pm (Friday till 11:30 am Saturday till 11 am); will change cash of U.S. dollars, Australian dollars, Deutschmarks, French Francs and Japanese yen. They accept American Express, Bank of America, Cook's Bank of Tokyo and Visa Australia traveler's checks.

COMMUNICATIONS

The post office is open from 8 am to 2 pm Monday through Thursday; Friday till 11 am, and Saturday till 12:30 am.The satellite telephone office is on Jl. Thamrin towards the eastern end of town.

HAIRCUTS

Pemangkas Rambut Bangkalan. Jl. Trikora, next to the market. Haircut $1, shave 30¢. A massage is included.

SHOPPING AND SOUVENIRS

At the Wamena market, in the "Souvenir Shop" across the road from the market, or while trekking around, you will be offered various Dani items for purchase. The most popular souvenir is a *horim,* or yellow penis gourd, available in various sizes and shapes. Prices range from 25¢ to as high as $1 if "decorated" by a local (non-Dani) merchant. A bow with a set of arrows, $2-3; net bags (*noken*) $2.50-$5 (depending mainly on size). Strands of shell money, sewn on fibers, cost $2 on up, depending on the quality of the cowries. Long, narrow breast-plates of tiny shells sewn together (*wali noken*) run $10-$18. Determining a fair price for a stone adze is difficult. They range from $4 to $150, depending on the type of stone used: greenish is the most expensive, followed by the bluish hues. Check the binding to make sure the stone won't fall out before you get it home.

TOURS AND TRAVEL AGENCIES

Unless you are traveling on a tour or a travel agency in Jayapura or Sentani has planned your visit to the Baliem, a guide is essential for moving around outside of Wamena, even for those who speak fluent Indonesian. If one of the half-dozen or so unofficial guides who speak "some" English hasn't already latched on to you, your hotel will help you find one.

For those of an unusually adventurous bent, John Wolff's or Sam Chandra's travel agencies can set up long treks outside the Baliem area as well as easier jaunts within the valley. Rudi Willem's agency in Sentani, near the Jayapura airport, provides the same services. All three agencies can arrange exciting traditional dances.

We recommend John Wolff for his pioneering work in opening up many areas to trekkers, his connections with the military in getting permits and the fact that he has himself walked to many places with his groups. He owns the Nayak and Jayawijaya hotels in Wamena, and lives there most of the year. Among his more unusual tours is a 7-day trip to Anggruk/Ninia, $300 per person, to visit the Yali tribe. The 8-day Senggo expedition to visit the traditional lowland tribes on the Brazza River costs $450-525. And he has plenty of long hikes for those in good physical condition.

Only three local agencies handle foreign tourists, and agencies from outside Irian funnel everyone through one of these three experienced local operators.

Insos Moon. Run by John Wolff, P.O. Box 57, Wamena. He can be contacted through Airfast, a cargo/plane rental outfit: Jl. Sam Ratulangi 3, P.O. Box 523, Jayapura. Tel. 21925, Telex 76122 AIRFAST.

Insatra Exclusive Tours. Run by Rudi Willem, Jl. Kemiri, P.O. Box 211, in Sentani. Tel. 094. Or contact through Airfast (see above).

Chandra Tours and Travel. Run by Sam Chandra, P.O. Box 41 in Wamena or Jl. Trikora. Tel: 78 (Wamena).

All the tours go to the Baliem Valley for one or more days and the cost depends on the number of the group and length of the tour. All tours hit at least one mummy and a traditional Dani compound; the longer tours include dances and a scaled-down pig feast.

• 4-day tour (only 1 day in the Baliem), on a basis of a 2 person group, $326/person.
• 5-day tour (2 days in the valley), same basis as above, $410/person.
• 6-day tour (3 days in the valley) $475/person.
• 7-day tour (5 days in the valley) $525/person.
• 8-day Baliem tour from Biak, including Japanese caves in Biak, Jayapura city tour and 4 full days in Baliem, $488.
• 9-day Baliem and Yali tribe tour, $675 to $923 (lots of walking).
• 12-day Asmat tour, $1,200/person.
• 14-day climb of Mt. Trikora from Wamena, $700 — participants have to carry their own food and personal effects for 3 days as it's too cold and tough for the porters during the

actual climb. From the last village, it's about a day or two to base camp from where the mountain can be scaled in about 5 hours, weather permitting. All prices include accommodation, food, transfers, and guides, but not airfare. For all tours, bring a hat, raincoat, canteen, insect repellent, malaria pills, sleeping bag, and sweater.

TRAVEL IN THE HIGHLANDS

Several tourist attractions around the Baliem Valley can now be reached by taxi on a dirt road network from Wamena: Dani villages, mummies, markets, caves. Of course, all the crowds go to these places, the tour groups' delight, with all the implications. You can take a taxi either as one of the (many) paying passengers — or charter one for about $3-$5 per hour. In and around the Baliem (as in life in general), the further you walk, the more rewarding the view, and the more personal, and more unsullied by commercialism, the experience.

To get out of the Baliem Valley, first check with the MAF (Missionary Aviation Fellowship) office in Wamena as to where flights are headed with seats available. Find out if your *surat jalan* covers this area. Fly there then walk back to Wamena with guide/porters to help lug your gear. The local schoolteacher or policeman could help you arrange this. Perhaps even the missionary, but don't count on it as he may absent — or busy. These walks are real adventures, not very difficult if you have time and are in relatively good physical shape. Guides from Wamena might speak some English, but many are just good at finding their way around the highlands.

Porters and Guides

If you arrange your trip through a travel agency, a guide and porters will come with the package. On your own, you can pick up a guide when you arrive in Wamena — either at the airport or at your hotel/losmen. The local guides who speak a bit of English charge $3-10 per day, plus their food and cigarettes. Porters run $1.50-3 plus food and smokes. Although you can hike by yourself, frequently asking for directions, (if there's anyone around to ask), trails often run off into the gardens and you might have to backtrack — often. The guide or porters will carry clients across streams (no wet feet or time-consuming boot removal) and cook for you on any of the longer hikes.

Hiking Tips

Excursions out of Wamena depend on the number of days one can spend in the Baliem, finances, physical ability, initiative and adaptability to local facilities. As long as you stay in the valley, walking is level and easy. If the side valleys require uphill trudges, the scenery makes the effort worthwhile, especially in the Wolo and Wilesi Valleys. Travel agency tours cover several areas of the Baliem but with a little Indonesian and some initiative, you can plan your own itinerary.

The rainy season in the Baliem is from October to December with the driest months (theoretically) being June and July. But it's not worth it to plan your trip for the drier season, when it still rains plenty. When it does rain, it's usually in the late afternoon, at night or early morning. It's much more pleasant to walk under a cool, cloudy sky than the blazing sun, although parts of the trail can get very muddy and slippery. Good soles and nimble feet, plus a walking stick, should solve the problem. In many places you have to clamber over stone or wooden fences but there's always a system of stones, logs and branches where the trail comes up to a fence. Even in the rainy season, take a hat, sunglasses and plenty of drinking water.

For short hikes (2 hours or less) and returning to Wamena or Jiwika to overnight, only a few essentials are required: hat, sunscreen, drinking water, sunglasses, tennis shoes and a waterproof jacket. For longer hikes all of the above plus broken-in, comfortable boots. If you plan to spend the night out in the sticks, either bring a tent or stay with government officials or the natives. A sleeping bag or blanket and insect repellent will be needed in any case. Perhaps a mosquito net. Pay $1-2 for accommodations. Although you can often purchase food (but not meals) in villages, it's best to bring some of the essentials such as rice, tinned fish, coffee, sugar, spoons, plates and cooking gear. Toilets, if any, are of the squat-over-hole variety. Bring toilet paper unless you can adapt your sensibilities to the prevailing water and left-hand method.

Walking Times

One day is about 8 hours of walking:
Wamena to Pyramid: one day
Pyramid to Bokondini: one day
Bokondini to Karubaga: one day
Karubaga to Mulia: three days
Wamena to Lake Habbema: three days
Wamena to Daelah: one day (1.5 hours by taxi to Ibele bridge, 1.5 hours walk to Ibele Bawah, 1.5 hours to Ibele Atas, 3 hours to Daelah)
Daelah to Tiom: one day
Tiom to Karubaga: one day

Dani Greetings (around Wamena)

Nyak to one man; *nayak lok* to several men; *lauk* to one woman; *lauk nyak* to several women.

PHOTOGRAPHY

Penis-sheathed or grass-skirted Dani make for exotic subjects. They will also ask to be paid for participating in photo opportunities — usually with a red one hundred rupiah note. Don't grumble, as this is only direct benefit they receive from foreigners, who spent a lot of money getting to the Baliem to see them. Aside from a few menial jobs in hotel restaurants, tourist dollars flow into non-Dani pockets. Sometimes, if you take a series of photos, the Dani might ask for more money. We suggest going along with any reasonable demand, up to, say, Rp 1,000.

RITUALS AND DANCES

As soon as you arrive in Wamena and where ever you go, ask if there are any ceremonies in the works for the near future. Births, marriages, first menstruation, first wearing of the penis gourd and funerals are occasions for Dani rituals throughout the year. If you happen on any of these ceremonies, find the *kepala suku* (clan chief) or whoever is in charge to obtain permission to photograph. Expect to pay $6-$30 for the privilege. If nothing is going on, you can arrange for a dance in many villages/compounds with a day's notice. Expect to pay $100 to $300, depending on the number of participants and the size of the pigs they will kill with arrows.

AREA AIR TRANSPORT

Merpati: On Fridays, Merpati flies to and from Wamena and Bokondini, Tiom, and Ok Sibyl, and on Saturdays to Karubaga and Kelila. The flights are cheap, $15-30, but prices could go up and schedules change. Book early, check and re-check. Flights can be cancelled for lack of passengers, breakdowns, and bad weather. There could also be flights to other places by the time you read this. Check upon arrival in Wamena.

MAF: The Missionary Aviation Fellowship maintains two Cessnas and flies from Wamena to numerous landing strips in the Irian highlands. Their weekly schedule (Monday–Saturday) comes out the Thursday previous. Check it at their office next to the Wamena air terminal. Their first priority, of course, is logistical support to the Protestant missions. But they also take paying passengers on a space-available basis, at a very reasonable cost. For example, the 60-km flight to Bokondini, usually once or twice a day, costs $13. (On the ground, a tough 2-day hike.) The best way to see areas outside the Baliem is to fly there and walk back. Be sure your *surat jalan* specifies any area you wish to visit outside the Baliem Valley proper.

If money is no problem, you can charter either of the MAF's Cessnas, the model 185 holding 4 to 5 passengers or the 206, turbocharged, carrying 5 bodies. This will cost some $150 per hour and the time charged includes the empty plane's return trip to Wamena unless it can do some business on the way back. Both planes fly at 200 km/hr but the 206 has a higher ceiling and carries oxygen.

Requests for special flights have to be in by Monday to be in the Thursday schedule for the week ahead. Charters can run for less than an hour. If you are flush they have a Hughes 500 helicopter for 4 passengers — $600 per hour.

You can get a rough estimate of both charter and ordinary passenger time and prices by looking at the distance on a map and factoring that by the cruising speed of the Cessnas, 200 km/hr. On a per seat basis, this works out to about 22¢/km.

Note: arriving on a MAF flight doesn't entitle you to missionary hospitality. Missionaries lead busy lives and are not in the field to entertain travelers. Try not to bother them. They will, of course, help you in an emergency.

TOURISM IN THE BALIEM

In 1988, 1,000 foreign tourists visited the Baliem; in 1989, this number was reached by the middle of the year. Still, there is a lack of information about the Baliem and vicinity, because of a lack of promotion by the Indonesian government. This is only justified by the lack of facilities and occasional difficulties in communications due to bad weather or mechanical problems of insufficient planes making the Wamena–Jayapura circuit.

And the fact that MAF does not have enough Cessnas to meet tourist demand to fly to landing strips in the vicinity. For the moment, tourists come in small groups for short periods or else are young back-packers. Most of the visitors are European, for whom the fascinating Dani culture — and the scenery — far outweigh the lack of international class facilities, the expense of getting there and the hassle of travel documents. There are plans to build better hotels but star-rated accommodations are still in the hazy future.

The Dani are profiting from tourism. Groups pay $100 and up to see pigs killed traditionally with arrows and cooked over hot stones while warriors and women dance away. Individual Dani men, sometimes superbly made up with soot and pig grease, decorated with feathers, flowers, shells and cuscus fur, charge for photographs. Other Dani work as porters for tourists at $3 a day. Some Dani, with a smattering of English, are working as guides.

In order to encourage this trend, the local government is planning to exclude non-local guides. The Wamena *bupati* is setting up a yearly mock ritual battle at a traditional fighting ground at Bukit Muliama (also called Gunung Susu) close to Wamena. This would take place just before the 17th of August Independence Day celebrations. If properly carried out, the event could eventually rival Papua New Guinea's annual Mount Hagen bash as a tourist attraction. The *bupati* also hopes that the mock battles will allow traditional enemies to let off enough steam to lessen the several dozen yearly deaths that result from real warfare.

PART IV

The Casuarina Coast

The Casuarina Coast of southern Irian (Casuarina is a genus of tree with drooping branches native to the archipelago) is one of the best-known, but also one of the most inaccessible regions of the island. The Asmat people — superb, world-renowned woodcarvers and formerly ferocious head-hunters and cannibals — dominate much of the area. The coast is also famous because Michael Rockefeller disappeared here in 1961, making headlines worldwide and setting off a large-scale search led by his father, the governor of New York — whether or not he was eaten by the Asmat is still a contested question. Today, visitors no longer need fear for their safety, but many strange practices still exist under a thin layer of acculturation.

Although the Asmat area was closed to visitors when this guide was prepared, as we went to press we found that the town of Agats has been officially opened. Check with the police in Jayapura as to the current situation.

Agats, a small coastal town on the mudflats of stilted huts and walkways, is the capital of the Asmat area. It has a museum of fantastic carvings, many of which were produced before the introduction of metal tools. Otherwise, it is not a terribly attractive place.

Outside influences began penetrating the Asmat region just prior to World War II. Before that, the Asmat fought savagely amongst themselves as well as with neighboring tribes to obtain heads — necessary to their religion and culture. Powerful spirits were honored through inspired woodcarvings — especially the ancestral *bis* poles. Some of these masterpieces are displayed in New York's Metropolitan Museum of Art.

The huge Freeport copper mine located above the town of **Tembagapura** on this coast produces 25,000 tons of ore concentrate a day. The construction of access roads and an aerial tramway leading to the ore deposits found at an elevation of 3,500 meters (12,000 ft.) was one of the world's most difficult feats of engineering. Snow-capped **Puncak Jaya**, Irian's highest peak at 4,884 meters (16,020 ft.), rises just a few kilometers from the mine.

The **Merauke** district, Irian's southeastern extremity, was the first part of the south coast contacted by the outside. To secure their territorial claims, the Dutch colonial government established a post here around the turn of the century. The Marind-Anim groups who live in the area, warriors *sans pareil*, fought frequently with the Asmat to the west and with groups across the border to the east. In the 1930s, the Dutch used the notorious Tanah Merah ("red earth") area up-river from Merauke as a place of exile for troublesome anarchists, communists and nationalists from Java.

The geography of the south coast shows marked contrasts. To the west, a narrow coastal fringe borders the Arafura Sea on one side and the steep southern flanks of the towering Jayawijaya Range on the other. The alluvial lowlands in the east form the world's largest swamplands and, in Irian's southeastern corner, a vast, dry savannah.

The narrow western coastal fringe supports a sparse population living off tubers. New transmigrants from Java are growing rice here with some success. The swamplands and forests up to the mountains provide stands of wild sago trees that are processed into a starchy paste, the dietary staple. Fishing and hunting provide the needed protein, as do the larvae of the capricorn beetle, which are much-esteemed.

The three most important ethnic groups of the South Coast are the Asmat, the Marind-Anim and the Mimika, linguistically unrelated, but culturally quite similar.

Overleaf: *Old and new meet at Amampare, a port carved out of Irian's South Coast mangrove swamps to receive copper from the Tembagapura mine.* **Opposite:** *An Asmat warrior relaxes outside the jew, the traditional men's long-house.*

THE ASMAT

Notorious Warriors and Craftsmen

The Asmat's powerful wood sculptures, coveted by collectors the world over, their reputation for head-hunting and cannibalism, and the well-publicized disappearance of Michael Rockefeller here in 1961, have combined to make the group one of Irian's most famous — and certainly its most notorious.

The Asmat region is inhospitable. Thick tangles of mangrove clot the shoreline, malarial mosquitoes are common, and huge estuarine crocodiles and gray nurse sharks feed along these shores. As this guide went to press, only Agats was open to tourists, but the rest of the Asmat area may open again soon.

The Rockefeller incident

Michael C. Rockefeller, 23-year-old son of New York Governor Nelson Rockefeller, arrived in West New Guinea in 1961 as part of the Harvard Peabody Expedition, to study and film the Baliem Valley Dani. (See "The Dani," page 102.) He shot stills for the group, and rolled sound for the documentary film, *Dead Birds*. On this trip, Michael had the chance also to visit the Asmat area near Agats, and was amazed at the tribe's sculpture. After a short trip back home, he returned with the intention of purchasing as many pieces as he could, for a planned exhibit in the United States.

His partner on this collection trip was René Wassing, a Dutch expert familiar with Asmat art who was to help Rockefeller choose the best pieces. The two hired a couple of Asmat guides, Simon and Leo, and obtained an outboard-powered catamaran. On Saturday, November 18, they set off for Atsj — 56 kilometers (35 mi.) away — where on the first trip Rockefeller had seen many promising carvings. But disaster soon struck.

Right: *An Asmat warrior, in war paint and bonnet, poles down the Aswetsj River.* **Opposite:** *Asmat warriors glide past the village of Amborep.*

Crossing the mouth of the North Eilander River (now the Siretsj), a fierce tide capsized their boat.

Simon and Leo swam ashore to get help, and the collectors spent the night on the upended catamaran. The next morning, Rockefeller became impatient. Although Wassing urged him not to go, the young man was determined, and seeing the shore some 4-7 miles away he emptied the gas tank, strapped it and an empty jerry can together with his belt, and headed for shore. It was the last anyone saw of him.

Wassing was soon rescued, because Simon and Leo had made it to shore and gone for help, but Michael was nowhere to be found. Governer Rockefeller and Michael's twin sister, Mary Strawbridge, flew to Agats to direct the search effort, bringing some 75 reporters in their wake. The press had a field day, reporting that Michael had been eaten by cannibals. No trace of him was found, and Governer Rockefeller and Strawbridge returned to the United States, grief-stricken.

"I don't know what happened to him," Wassing later told a reporter. "But I am almost certain that he didn't get to shore. Even if you are only 30 feet from the shore, you don't stand a chance against that abnormally heavy tide."

Although the rough seas, crocodiles and sharks mitigate against Michael having ever

reached shore, it is at least as likely that the press headlines were correct. After all, the two guides had made it, and Rockefeller was an excellent swimmer. Furthermore, the shark and crocodile hazards, say residents, are overstated.

Proponents of the cannibalism theory, including the Reverend Cornelis Van Kessel, whom Michael was planning to visit on his way to Atsj, offer some intriguing circumstantial evidence. Several years earlier, Dutch police sent to investigate a massive head-hunting incident killed the chief, two warriors and two women in a village called Otsjanep, just up the Siretsj River from Atsj. The normal practice for the Asmat would have been to avenge these deaths so that the chief's spirit could rest. And any member of the white "tribe" who came along would have made a suitable victim.

Otsjanep was Rockefeller's destination, and although it is difficult, given the strong tide, to determine exactly where he may have come ashore, it is possible that he landed in the Otsjanep village's sago harvesting region. Ajam, then chief of Otsjanep, was the son of a man killed by the Dutch police in 1958. Moreover Michael, who had visited Otsjanep earlier to commission some carvings, had then brought along men from Omadesep as guides, unaware that the two tribes were the bitterest of enemies.

A lone white man, tired from a long swim, naked and unarmed, would have made the ideal victim. Rumors persisted among area tribesmen long after the search parties had left, of a pair of spectacles, shorts, and the skull of a white man. The mention of glasses in particular is significant, because other than one local missionary, no one in the area except Michael wore glasses.

Head-hunting and cannibalism

According to accounts from early explorers of Irian's south coast, the Asmat were much to be feared. Captain Cook reported on their lack of hospitality to strangers. One account states that in 1770 he lost 20 men from a landing party that had gone ashore to seek fresh water. The scene of the massacre, now called Cook's Bay, is just a short distance down the coast from the mouth of the Siretsj River.

Following Captain Cook, there were in fact few contacts with the Asmat until after World War II. Their nefarious reputation kept most people away, and the territory remained almost completely unknown. The Dutch explorer, de Rochemont, landed very briefly at Flamingo Bay in 1829. Further down the coast to the east, the Dutch set up a post at Merauke in 1905.

The Asmat themselves traditionally had contact mainly with the neighboring Mimika, a coastal tribe to the west whose heads they hunted as trophies. The Mimikans returned the Asmats' attentions with raids of their

own. Indeed, the Mimikans called the coastal Asmat *monowe,* a term roughly translating as "the edible ones."

During the 1920s, the Dutch brought the Mimikan coast under control and Roman Catholic missionaries began to convert them. Undaunted, the Asmat continued their head-hunting raids — with a particularly successful one taking place in 1928. But two years later they learned that their arrows were no match for Western rifles. An Asmat raiding party of some 400 warriors was at this time completely annihilated by the Dutch police, reinforced by Mimikans bent on revenge. Only a dozen-odd survivors made it to jail.

World War II brought 1,000 Japanese troops to Mimika, and the Asmat area lay

right on the boundary between Allied-controlled Papua and Japanese-controlled West New Guinea. When Japanese troops killed several dozen Asmat, the tribesmen responded in kind.

While the war put a slight damper on Asmat head-hunting activities, they were resumed with a vengeance afterwards. Things soon got out of hand, even for the fearless Asmat. In 1947, more than 6,000 Asmat (out of perhaps 40,000 total) fled to Mimika, and Gerald Zegwaard of the Catholic Crozier Mission at this time opened a school for the refugees and began studying the Asmat language and customs.

Father Zegwaard's diligence paid off in 1953, when he was permitted to settle in Agats. This became the first permanent, and the most important, center of outside influence in the Asmat region. Shortly after the mission opened, the Dutch opened a police post, and a trading company soon began to investigate the economic potential of Jamasj, just north of Agats.

More missionaries soon arrived, including the Protestant Evangelical Alliance, who began proselytizing in a village called Ayam, upriver from Agats. Although the first baptisms were celebrated in 1954, these missionaries lacked a basic knowledge of Asmat social structure and traditional beliefs. Anthropologists came later to undertake field research, but most of what we know about the Asmat comes from the writings of several Catholic missionary-scholars.

Wife-exchange and ritual fellatio

The name "Asmat" has two possible derivations: *asmato-wi,* meaning "we, the true people," or *as-asmat,* meaning "we, the tree people." Asmat men wore no clothing of any kind until outsiders introduced them. While the missionaries were convincing the Asmat to wear trousers, they learned of a custom called *papisj.* This entailed a temporary wife-exchange between two men to cement their friendship as well as to extend their spheres of influence. The wives were required to have been mothers and to agree to the exchange. Also, each husband had to be present in the village at the time and agree on each separate occasion before sex could take place.

The Asmat also practiced public, widespread exchange of women during times of crisis. These orgies would take place during an epidemic, an unusually fierce storm, the arrival of a large ship or any other extraordinary event. This was believed to ward off danger. In the words of one missionary-scholar, an "enormous flow of seminal fluid was necessary to obtain an end beyond the reach of normal behavior."

On several other Indonesian islands, notably Bali, Kalimantan and Nias, carvings with erect penises ward off troubling spirits. Among the Asmat, this is found in art as well as in attempts at stopping enemies through phallic intimidation. Submission often involved ritual fellatio — but not in a homosexual context (although homosexuality was quite acceptable in other situations).

Asmat villages were typically built at the bend of a river to keep a lookout for canoes carrying incoming head-hunters. In order to increase their safety, villages were large, housing several clans with a population in the hundreds. Each clan owned and maintained a large men's house, called *yew* or *jew*, sometimes reaching 90 meters (290 ft.) in length. These long, rectangular houses faced the river and had many doors, each leading to a fire pit located against the back wall.

Each men's house was divided in half, with marriages allowed only between families from each moiety. These men's houses were the focus of all social life, and fulfilled essential religious and social functions. In some Asmat districts, the men's houses were only for bachelors. Temporary "feast houses" were erected on ritual occasions. In all areas, family huts were placed between the men's houses, on high piles or in trees.

Missionaries learned that head-hunting raids were plotted in the men's houses and that the traditional rituals were held there. In spite of this, they recommended that the *jew* be allowed to remain. Such longhouses, the missionaries argued, provided a secure sociological and psychological anchor for the Asmat, who were faced with a bewildering set of new values.

Disregarding this advice, the government ordered the destruction of the *jew* buildings in 1964 (for the sake of morals and hygiene) along with the traditional artwork, and forbade all manifestations of the old religion. Since then, the rules have been relaxed, but few *jew* have been erected to replace the old ones. Everyone lives in family huts. Far upriver, the *jew* houses were never destroyed and still maintain some of their old functions.

Appeasing the spirits

Much of Asmat life and art was directed at appeasing spirits, especially those of relatives killed in head-hunting raids. These spirits demanded revenge. There was a widespread belief that life came from the death of another human. And death in such a hostile, crocodile- and malaria-infested place never came from natural causes. Enemy heads were essential.

The spiritual strength of the village depended on a continuous cycle of warfare, which gave the Asmat the well-deserved reputation as Irian's most aggressive warriors. But this way of life also provided the group with a stable set of values. Abandoning these made for a difficult transition period. In keeping with their traditional beliefs, many Asmat infinitely preferred the powerful and vengeful God of the Old Testament to the defeated and crucified Christ.

In many of the coastal areas, the skull of a deceased relative provided the best protection against malevolent spirits. Along the coast, the head of a powerful warrior of one's own family was considered the most "secure" pillow — it was during sleep that one became vulnerable to the evil influences of the supernatural world and the skull offered a defense.

Some Asmat groups required that the warriors learn the name of an enemy prior to taking his head. This added risk to head-hunting operations, as often the only way to know the name of one's intended victim was to lie in ambush long enough to hear someone calling him. These names were required for subsequent initiation rituals. Attacks usually began at dawn, with bowmen leading the

initial offensive, followed by a spear-and-shield charge.

Life in the tidal swamps

Some 70,000 Asmat today live in one of the largest tidal swamps in the world — 27,000 square kilometers (10,000 sq. mi.) of tropical jungle broken everywhere by contorted rivers meandering slowly to the Arafura Sea. The seas are so shallow and the land so flat that tides reach 100 kilometers (62 mi.)

Opposite: *Asmat initiation bags, woven of bark fiber and decorated with feathers and beads. The bags are worn around a warrior's neck.* **Above:** *An Asmat shield, an item coveted by collectors of traditional art around the world.*

inland. River mouths can be 5 kilometers (3 mi.) wide.

There are no predictable seasons here. In Asmat-land, winds sweep moisture-laden air in from the sea, with frequent deluges depositing up to 5,000 mm (200 inches) of precipitation a year. August is the driest and hottest month, but many years prove an exception to this rule. During the northwest monsoon, from December through March, the sea is often whipped into a mass of waves making sea travel dangerous. The eastern monsoon, June to August, creates the highest tides and hottest temperatures.

Always available, starch from the sago palm is the staple food in the Asmat swamps. Known as *Metroxylon* sp., the tall, stately palm trees possesses trunks of almost pure starch. In addition to its food value, the sago tree provides building materials, fibers for thread and harbors the delicious grub of the capricorn beetle — a local delicacy which also serves ritual functions. Much of Asmat daily life and religion in the days before contact with the West depended on this unique plant, which was — and remains — a sure food source. A family can obtain close to 50 kilos (110 lbs.) of sago flour in half a day from just one tree. The job consists essentially of scraping the pithy trunk and separating out the starch from the fibers.

The rights to harvest stands of sago trees were held by a man's family and handed

down to sons. However, marriage gave the husband lifetime rights to harvest a part of his in-laws' sago, along with fishing privileges. Many an ambitious man became polygamous in his search for sago — as widely extended harvesting rights led to a wealth of food which could be given away in potlatch ceremonies marking the man as a leader.

In order to marry, however, a hefty bride price had to be paid in items of high traditional value: stone axes, dogs' teeth necklaces, daggers (preferably of human bone), animal furs, bird of paradise and cassowary feathers, and weapons — hundreds of lethal arrows and spears. With all this wealth at stake, it's no wonder that wars were waged over sago territories.

The tidal swamps completely lack stones, so the Asmat obtained fully-formed stone tools from upriver tribes, trading sago, shells, jewelry, lime (for coloring), cassowary bone tools and bird of paradise feathers for the precious items.

The cargo cult of Ayam

As in many other Melanesian societies, the forced imposition of Western rules and values traumatized the Asmat. Under the threat of superior weapons, they were forced to abandon head-hunting, one of the central aspects of their lives. A new religion, somehow linked in their minds with military might and material goods, proposed a new lifestyle, but negated the very ancestral and other spirits that were the key to life in the Asmat world. At the same time, the new religion did not necessarily even produce the desired goods — metal tools, lamps, tobacco sticks and tinned food.

There were other disappointments. Many initial promises by the missions and government were not kept. Teachers from other islands beat the children and made fun of the illiterate adults, calling them animals. The Asmat were sometimes forced to work in logging operations, then cheated of their money — or not paid at all. Powerful, self-confident warriors were treated as inferiors and idiots.

"Cargo cults" sprang up among the Asmat. These movements, common to many parts of Melanesia, combine traditional and Western elements in varying degrees into a kind of messianic creed that promises a better life — a utopia wherein Western material goods are available through ritual and without work. (See also "Cargo Cults on Biak," page 56.)

The best-documented Asmat cult formed in the village of Ayam, 40 kilometers (25 mi.) upstream from Agats on the Asewetsj River. Before Agats was established as a mission center, Ayam was the most powerful center in the area. When Westerners arrived, the Asmat from Ayam were the first to accept their ideas.

Ayam, clean and orderly, became one of the most progressive villages. The first cooperative in the region was established here, as well as the first native-owned store. Father Delmar Hesch of the American Roman Catholic Mission settled in Ayam, followed by his Protestant counterpart. The schools were well-attended.

Then, in 1970, Father Hesch renounced the priesthood, married a local girl and took her to the United States. He had been the parish priest since 1959. As logging activities increased, so did the overpricing of merchandise, cheating on large bills, and general inflation. Worse still, some local logging operations were carried out by a trader who then refused to pay. When the men would not cut more ironwood logs, they were whipped.

Things finally came to a head when some of the men of Ayam initiated large-scale ritual sex, an activity that, according to the traditional belief, would ward off danger in a time of crisis. When word of the orgies got out, the leaders were arrested and whipped by an official with the serrated tail of a stingray. Soon after that, many families left the village to live in the jungle. The government went after them, but the soldiers were repulsed with a shower of arrows.

The wife of one of the Ayam leaders then saw visions of a crocodile that, in various

episodes, talked to her, had sex with her, and swallowed and regurgitated her. The crocodile promised freedom for those heeding its instructions and death for the now-hated schoolteachers and outsiders.

After a small detachment of soldiers was unable to bring the Ayam rebels back from the jungle, the government planned a larger military operation. To forestall a bloodbath, a certain Bishop Alphonse Sowada, who knew the Asmat well, was permitted to go alone to visit the renegades. When all his arguments failed, he made use of his extensive knowledge of Asmat culture. Sowada addressed the principal leader: "Since you do not believe me and have no confidence in me, when you defecate tonight, I'll eat your feces to prove my sincerity."

That did it. The leader agreed. But first he begged for forgiveness — in the traditional manner. "He went down on his knees and began to kiss the tennis shoes on my feet, proceeded up my trousered legs and into my groin," the bishop writes. "For a moment I was nonplussed but fortunately considered that the thin line between success and failure was too uncertain for me to become squeamish."

Bishop Sowada brought enough people back to Ayam to forestall a military operation scheduled to begin the very next day. Later, a formal meeting with high government and military authorities sealed the reconciliation.

JULIE CAMPBELL

Opposite, below: *An Asmat* bis *ancestral pole stands guard in front of the regional museum near Abepura.* **Opposite, above:** *Village women of Per, clad in skirts of woven grass, perform a traditional dance.* **Right:** *This Asmat father wears a headdress of dog and cuscus fur.*

ASMAT ART

World-Class Traditional Woodcarving

Asmat art is ranked by scholars and collectors among the world's best traditional carvings. These wooden sculptures have powerful lines and bold schematic motifs that appeal strongly to the contemporary Western eye. Collectors today pay thousands of dollars for good Asmat carvings. Chief among their admirers was the young Michael Rockefeller. "The key to my fascination with the Asmats is the woodcarving," he said. "The sculpture which the people here produce is the most extraordinary in the primitive world."

Asmat culture places no particularly high value on the aesthetic beauty of the sculptures, nor did it encourage innovation. The general forms appear highly stylized, and individual creativity could function only within accepted norms. To the Asmat, these carvings essentially served to connect them to the world of spirits, to facilitate contact with the ancestors. The best carvers acquired status equal to that of great warriors, but this was a function of their technical skills, not of their aesthetic sense.

Another prime function of these sculptures was to serve as reminders of vengeance. Only after a spirit had been avenged could it rest in a tranquil, supernatural realm called *safan*.

Carvings range from humble sago pounders to tall, intricately carved totem poles, called *bis*. The 3-5 meter (10-13 ft.) *bis* are the best known expressions of Asmat sculpture. Carved from mangrove trees, they represent decapitated clansmen crying out for revenge. The carved figures are delicate yet strong, culminating in a stylized phallus. These were carved when village leaders decided it was time for a head-hunting raid.

Bows of canoes are decorated with ancestor figures. Bottomless canoes, or soul ships (*uranium*), containing a variety of figures, were once used in initiation rituals. Working canoes, with finely sculpted bows, are hollowed out of a single log up to 20 meters (66 ft.) in length. The handles of the long paddles (the Asmat stand erect in their canoes) were formerly carved into the form of an ancestor's head — and not just any ancestor, but one who had been killed in an enemy raid. The face was thus a reminder of a death that still needed to be avenged.

Rectangular shields, up to 2 meters high, are decorated with bold motifs designed to terrify the enemy. Many shields sport a small ancestral figure or a penis sprouting from the upper side.

Drums, while all of the same hourglass shape, show unique decoration. The handles may be carved with intricate, abstract lacework or shaped like humans. According to an Asmat creation myth, mankind was first carved from wood and brought to life by a spirit beating a drum.

Other art objects include decorated skulls, spears, paddles, water containers, pipes, bowls of all shapes and sizes, club and axe handles, masks and body costumes.

When Irian Jaya was first integrated into Indonesia, some over-zealous officials, anxious to "civilize" the Asmat, burned down the men's houses, forbade rituals and destroyed many sculptures. The Catholic Church stepped in, buying carved items for safekeeping. The church's plan was to preserve the Asmat's cultural heritage and sense of identity so that later a revival of the carving traditions would still be possible.

This policy eventually led to the creation of the Asmat Museum of Culture and Progress in Agats, officially opened in 1973. By then, the government's attitude toward local art had changed considerably and high officials were commissioning the work of Asmat carvers. There was an embarrassing moment in 1971 when a local government employee set out to burn some drums — until he found out they had been commissioned by the police commander in the district capital of Merauke.

When tourists began visiting the Asmat in the 1970s, demand for the carvings increased and they became an important source of cash income. A marketing scheme was devised by the Department of Small Industries, but neither the tourists nor the government put much emphasis on quality. Often, the prices paid were ridiculously low, encouraging bad work. Fortunately, the Catholic Church still encourages quality carvings.

Opposite: *A small Asmat war shield.*

VISITING THE ASMAT

A Life of Tidal Rhythms in Agats Village

NOTE: At presstime, in late 1989, the government began issuing surat jalan again to visit Agats. The rest of the Asmat area was still closed, though there was talk of re-opening it soon. Check with the police in Jayapura to find out if the situation has changed.

This land barely keeps its head above water. About 5,000 millimeters (200 in.) of rain fall each year, and ebbtide exposes a band of coastal mudflats a mile wide to the hot sun. Mud is the bane of everyday existence.

Upriver, in the rainforests, enormous ironwood trees, sago and nipa palms, ferns, orchids, creepers and thorny rattan vines grow. The forest teems with wild boar, cuscus, squirrels, flying foxes, snakes, and noisy birds of every hue — cassowary, jungle fowl, kingfishers, hornbills, parrots and cockatoos.

Spirits dwell in all parts of the Asmat environment. Animals often take on human form and humans assume animal forms. Ancestors inhabit carvings, and masks become infused with spirits of the dead.

Visiting Agats

Agats, founded in the 1950s, is the administrative and mission center of the Asmat coast. The little town faces the Aswetsj River, which not far from Agats empties into Flamingo Bay. Coconut trees lean at odd angles in the soft mud. When the tide is in, small canoes and outboard-powered launches weave through a small network of canals.

Walkways of dubious strength link the town landmarks — two churches, a mosque, five schools, Catholic mission offices, a post office, a police station and several government huts. A few shops sell basic hard goods — hammers, nails and the like — as well as rice and tinned food. Some 1,500 people live in huts along the rickety walkways.

The **Asmat Museum of Culture and Progress** in Agats, planned and developed by the American Roman Catholic Crozier Fathers mission, houses some of the best carvings and artifacts from all over the region. The pieces were collected by the fathers during the 1960s, when the Indonesian government, desperately trying to eliminate head-hunting, banned tradional practices, including woodcarving.

Inside the museum, *bis* poles carved with ancestral figures almost touch the ceiling. Spirit masks and war shields line one wall. The strong, geometric motifs are from Brazza; the more sweeping designs, including human figures, are from the south. Human skulls form a macabre display — some sport beaded headdresses and others red seeds plugged into their eye-sockets. Many have gaping holes from which the victim's brains were removed — a special treat for the clan chief and the elders.

Spirit ships, a miniature bone house, drums, spears, and canoe prows are more pleasant artifacts. The museum's assistant curator, Mr. Yuven, comes from the northern Asmat village of Jamasj and will answer questions and tell stories from his childhood.

Beside the museum is **Pusat Asmat**, a carving center where top Asmat carvers display and demonstrate their work. There is a theater here also, where tribal dances and singing are performed. The building is festooned with well-carved Asmat motifs, and the walkway passes beside raised gardens containing beautiful orchids.

Near the old losmen is an artifacts store, the only place to buy carvings here if one is unable to visit the outlying villages. Small pieces cost $15, with more elaborate carvings costing considerably more.

Trips out of Agats

When the tide is out, the walkways here get crowded, as people wait for the incoming tide. The tides rule life in Agats. Small outboard-powered boats can take you to nearby villages such as Yepem, Per and Ows — centers of carving activity. Longer trips, 2-4 days, can be arranged up the Siretsj River to the villages of Amborep, Jaosoikor and Atsj.

One can even walk to **Syuru**. Dilapidated walkways lead there past dormitories where students from neighboring villages stay while attending the mission high school. In Syuru, typical Asmat houses balance on stilts. Women sit on bark benches outside their houses fashioning bags from sago fibers. Children and mangy dogs are everywhere.

The small patch of land that remains dry at high tide is used for canoe-building. At the river's edge, men pull up in their canoes from the jungle loaded with wrapped sago starch, roots and sour fruits. Women bring crabs and fish from the river.

Villagers wait at the dock for the dugouts to appear. The up to 9-meter (29 ft.) canoes jostle for space at the mooring steps. A foreign visitor attracts a lot of attention here, but if one doesn't mind the stares, Syuru is a very interesting place to visit and photograph.

The walk back takes one past the *jew*. To see this longhouse, one must cross the tidal flats, balancing delicately on logs, sticks and chunks of rotted bark that serve as a "bridge" across the muck. Myriad orange and blue mud crabs scatter before you and curious little mudskippers — thumb-sized fish that are just as much at home on the flats as underwater — hop and slither out of your way.

Feasts and the *jew*

The *jew* was the cultural and political focus of an Asmat village before it was banned in the 1960s. The ban is not longer in effect, and the *jew* has now regained something of its former prominence in village affairs. The building is long, with a doorway and a fireplace for each clan in the village. It is at these fireplaces that the men meet to smoke, exchange news and gossip, make spirit masks, and plan feasts — these last, today, often including as much Christian lore as traditional Asmat myth.

The initiation ceremonies are still held. From age 14 to 17, all boys live in "bone houses" — small huts formerly made of whale bones collected from beached carcasses, but now made of wood and sago fronds. The house is 4-5 meters long (13-16 ft.) and 3 meters (10 ft.) high. During this period, the boys are instructed in the mysteries of the tribe by elders. For 3 months before the initiation feast, the boys eat just one meal a day.

Just before the feast, paints are prepared — mussel shells are burned and ground and mixed into a white paste. Ochre, traded from the north, is mixed into a yellow paste and heated over a low fire until it turns bright red. Charcoal is ground into a black slush. Village men paint special shapes and symbols on the boys' bodies with these pigments, and crown the initiates with white feathers.

After secret, private instruction, the boys are made to lie down on a slatted platform outside the bone house. Here, hidden under the boards, are village elders, who slash with razors at each boy's upper thighs and chest. Then, dancing and leaping, the boys join the village in front of the *jew* for a great feast. The feast, nowadays, ends with a special church service.

— Julie Campbell

Opposite: *An Asmat war shield, from Brazza.*
Right: *The Asrama Putera, a rooming house for children from outside the area who are attending the Catholic Church–run high school in Agats.*

TEMBAGAPURA

A Giant Copper Mine in the Sky

In the shadow of glacier-capped Puncak Jaya, Irian's highest peak, steel jaws travel along the world's longest single-span tramway carrying 10-ton loads of ore across some of the most inaccessible terrain on earth. A huge refining mill and the world's longest slurry pipeline then transport the copper concentrate to a port on the malarial mangrove flats 80 kilometers (50 mi.) away on the coast.

The Freeport copper mine at Tembagapura has already provided the world with 25 million tons of copper, in the process leveling a huge mountain — the largest outcropping of base metal the world has ever seen. The mine is far from tapped out, however. At least as much copper still remains to be harvested from the rich rock below.

Called Ertsberg by the Dutch and Gunung Bijih by the Indonesians (both names mean "Ore Mountain"), the site was discovered in 1936 by Dutch geologist Jean Jacques Dozy. The huge, jet-black knob of copper then reached a height of 179 meters (586 ft.) above a grassy meadow situated at an altitude of 3,500 meters (11,600 ft.) in Irian's highlands. High-grade ore lurked in the rock below to a depth of 360 meters (1,181 ft.). This huge chunk of mineral had been carved out from the much softer limestone by the irresistible force of creeping Ice Age glaciers.

Freeport's ore now comes from underground mines with tens of millions of tons of proven reserves, though only a deep pit remains where the high dome of Ertsberg once towered over a small meadow. And although world copper prices have for periods dipped below the high 55¢ a pound break-even mark for Freeport, with copper futures now topping $1 a pound, the mine is highly profitable.

A melting pot of ethnic groups labor in the mines. A Javanese welds and reshapes the huge steel teeth of a monstrous ore crusher. A Buginese from Sulawesi checks the rollers under a long conveyor belt that brings blasted chunks of ore to the crusher. A highland Irianese rewires a complicated fuse-box. And a team of two men from Biak efficiently maneuvers a pneumatic drill at the far end of a side tunnel to prepare a section for blasting.

From the mill, it's 10 kilometers (6 mi.) to the town of Tembagapura ("Copper City")

about 1,000 meters (3,500 ft.) straight down. The road cuts through thick, dripping vegetation and tunnels 850 meters (2,786 ft.) through the western flank of Mount Zaagham, which forms a spectacular backdrop to Tembagapura.

The Sudirman Range, within which Tembagapura is nestled, was first called the Carstensz, then the Nassau before assuming its current name. There are two other peaks in this range with names that will never appear on any official maps. Helicopter pilots during the construction of the Freeport mine dubbed one nearby mountain "Jane Russell" for its well-endowed twin peaks; and two Jewish American climbers baptized a heretofore unnamed mountain "Kike's Peak."

Ertsberg discovered

In the early 1950s, the chief exploration geologist for Freeport Sulphur of Louisiana, a man by the name of Wilson, was researching profitable mining areas. He chanced across a report by Jean Jacques Dozy published by the University of Leyden in 1939 then forgotten in the upheavals of World War II. Although Dozy wrote that it would be hard to imagine a more difficult place to find an ore deposit, Wilson was thrilled: "My reaction was immediate. I was so excited I could feel the hairs rising on the back of my neck." In 1936 it had taken Dozy 57 days to reach Carstensz Top after a parachute drop. Wilson

was determined to view the marvel himself and to take enough samples to determine if mining operations would be justified.

Taking advantage of post-World War II U.S. military organization and financing from Freeport, Wilson sent in an advance party and hopped on a chartered plane from Biak. He landed on the south coast of what was then Dutch New Guinea — the landing strip was a former Japanese airfield used for bombing raids on Darwin, Australia.

Wilson's party canoed as far upstream as possible, then hiked in with mountain Irianese as porters. These folks, paid in axes and machetes, were used to eating "anything that walks, creeps or crawls," the mining engineer writes, including humans which they called "long pigs" and found much juicier than pork.

It took Wilson 17 days to reach Ertsberg, scaling a sheer cliff face 600 meters (2,000 ft.) high where the tramway now smoothly ferries passengers and ore. The trek was worth it — as he chipped through the stone's oxidized layer he saw the gleaming golden color of chalcopyrite, a sulfide of iron and copper. Spending several days at the

Opposite: *The ridge road to Tembagapura was painstakingly cut by flown in bulldozers.* **Below:** *Tram cars at the Freeport mine carry 10 tons of ore at a time along the world's longest single span tramway to the refining plant below.*

Ertsberg collecting samples, Wilson also saw malachite stains on a distant cliff, part of what is now called Gunung Bijih Timur or Ore Mountain East.

Wilson's initial estimates, relayed excitedly by radio, proved quite accurate: 13 million tons of high grade ore lay above ground and 14 million tons more below. But, as he describes, this was "perhaps the most remote, primitive and inhospitable area in the world." The copper was there all right; the problem was getting it out.

Wilson even had problems getting out himself. Not only was he (understandably) apprehensive of his cannibal porters, but he wore out his seventh and last pair of boots before reaching the canoes. But he made it, bringing back with him several hundred pounds of samples which confirmed his opinion of their high copper content.

Technology and politics

Freeport needed more samples before investing the millions of dollars required to build the mine, however. One problem —insurmountable at the time — was transporting the huge diamond drills needed to take deep samples. Even disassembled, the parts were too heavy for choppers in the early 1960s, which could then lift only one passenger and 113 kilos (250 lbs.) to a height of no more than 3,600 meters (12,000 ft.).

Clouds of political instability combined with technical problems to block the project, as President Sukarno began a military campaign to wrest Irian from the Dutch. The project was put on the back burner in the hopes that eventually the situation would change.

After Suharto took over the reins of government, a 1967 Foreign Investment Law once again encouraged investment in Indonesia. Freeport hired Ali Budiarjo as a consultant and things began to look up. Budiarjo was a Dutch-educated Indonesian, a patriot who opposed colonialism, but most importantly, a Javanese well connected to the Jakarta scene.

Wilson and a legal advisor were among the first foreign businessmen to be welcomed back to the country. When they arrived at the Hotel Indonesia, there were only 15 guests attended by 1,800 employees. Freeport's contract with the government was the first to be signed under the new investment law.

In 1967, the last phase of testing was carried out. Helicopter technology had by then advanced such that there were craft available that could lift half a ton to the required altitude — enough to ferry in the diamond drills needed for core samples. When the deep cores were analyzed, the results confirmed Wilson's estimates.

Financing was the next problem. Wilson had to convince Freeport's board of directors, understandably nervous after Fidel Castro's nationalization of their operation in Cuba, that Indonesia was a safe place to invest. A consortium of Japanese and German lenders finally backed Freeport and the project got underway.

Bechtel was chosen as the prime contractor, but even these famous can-do engineers were nearly overwhelmed by technical problems at Tembagapura. Bechtel stated categorically that the mine was the most formidable construction feat they had ever undertaken.

Building the mine

Men and supplies were ferried in from Australia in a PBY seaplane (Howard Hughes had earlier converted it to fish salmon in Alaska but later lost interest). A seaport was hacked out of the mangrove swamps with chainsaws at Amamapare, at the mouth of the Timika River. Men sank up to their waists in mud sawing through a 15-acre morass of mangrove roots, praying all the time that the racket would keep the crocodiles at bay. The squawking of sulphur-crested cockatoos joined the din, as did the noise of the great hornbill, whose flight sounds like a chugging steam locomotive.

Temporary landing pads for the helicopters were carved out by lowering chainsaw-wielding men on lines from the hovering craft. The men, dangling in the air, cut the tops off the trees to get through the thick canopy and, once on the ground, chopped up enough trunks to make a landing platform. Helicopters ferried men and supplies everywhere. Six choppers were on the job by August 1971, shifting 1,604 tons of supplies inland in that month alone.

The 100-kilometer (63-mi.) road from the Tipoeka River to the mill site was the toughest challenge. Eighty kilometers (50 mi.) from the port, the least abrupt incline rose at a 70 degree angle. The mountain was not only steep, but razor-backed — a two-foot wide ridge, with sheer drops on either side. At first, tiny D4 bulldozers, slightly bigger than a lawn-mower, were flown in to carefully shave off the top of the ridge and make room for the slightly larger D6s, which in turn cleared space for the D7s, followed by the

D8s. By the time the monsterous 25-ton D12s were done, 12 million tons of earth had been moved, altering the angle of the slope from 70 to 25 degrees — the maximum that could be negotiated by fully-loaded trucks. Not even the steepest streets of San Francisco have such a steep grade.

A hundred Korean coal miners were flown in to dig a 1,105 meter (3,627 ft.) tunnel through Mt. Hannekam for the first section of the road, at 2,600 meters (8,500 ft.). From there, the road dropped to 1,800 meters (6,000 ft.) at the site of Tembagapura, then shot up through another tunnel to the future mill site, located at 2,900 meters (9,500 ft.) up, 10 kilometers (6 mi.) from Copper City.

To move ore from the mine to the mill, an 800-meter (2,500 ft.) tramway was constructed through the rain and fast-moving clouds of the highlands. Each of the cars, humming along on dual cables, carries 10 tons of partially crushed mineral to the bottom, dumps its load, and then returns to the top in a never-ending procession.

Construction of the unsupported, single-span tramway began when a helicopter towed a 3,000 meter-long (10,000 ft.) nylon rope from the valley to the mine site. Once this was strung, it was used to pull up progressively stronger rope and finally, the heavy cables. But once in place, heavy oscillation derailed the ore cars, flipping them against the rock wall and down into the valley. An expert mathematician was brought in from Switzerland to solve the problem. After a serious of precise measurements he carefully calculated the resonances of all the parts. Then, he made some small but crucial adjustments to the system which resulted in a smooth ride. "A tramway is like a violin," the mathematician said. "It has to be tuned."

Pipeline to the sea

At the mill, the ore is crushed to a fine powder, and the valuable mineral is separated from the base rock. A concentrated slurry is produced, then pumped into a 120-kilometer (74 mi.) pipeline that follows the contours of the land to the port of Amamapare on the coast, where it is deposited in ore ships.

The pipeline gave engineers headaches at first. It repeatedly ruptured until a pump speed of just over 3 miles per hour with and a fairly wet slurry of ore with 64 to 67 per cent of water was used. At Amamapare, the slurry is dehydrated to the required 36 percent moisture content for shipment to Japan.

There are no roads out of Amamapare. All travel is by boat, across the ocean or up the river. From Amamapare inland through the mangrove swamps to the lower end of the road is 18 kilometers (11 mi.). Timika, where an airport receives Garuda jets, is 22 kilometers (14 mi.) from here. The road then runs flat and straight for 40 kilometers (25 mi.) to the base of the mountains, by the ricefields of Javanese transmigrants. From the base of the mountain to the 2,600 meter (8,500 ft.) ridge is a quick, switch-back climb. Once at the top, the road follows the ridge before heading through a tunnel to Tembagapura — 101 kilometers (63 mi.) of incredible engineering.

Above: *Gunung Bijih, a mountain of nearly pure copper ore, has been harvested — leaving an open pit. Hundreds of thousands of tons remain to be unearthed.* **Right:** *A skilled Irianese miner wields a jackhammer to break up ore-bearing rock.*

On Christmas Day 1971, the first convoy of trucks arrived at Tembagapura. A year later, the first shipment of copper concentrate was already on its way to Japan. In the meantime, about $200 million had been spent.

In March 1973, President Suharto gave Tembagapura its name and officially opened the operation. At the same time he ordained that the name of the province would henceforth be Irian Jaya ("Victorious Irian") instead of Irian Barat ("West Irian"), a decision which obliged the Freeport officials to send the dedication plaque back to the United States for re-engraving.

Although the initial investment in building the mine was recovered in just three years, low world copper prices kept profits to a minimum until 1979. From the start of operations until the end of 1980, some 521,000 tons of copper concentrate were shipped out, containing 6 million ounces of silver and 463,000 ounces of gold, resulting in $772 million in gross sales.

Community relations problems

The local Irianese were at first simply astonished by all the activity, then began to resent the huge disparity of wealth that existed between themselves and the Freeport mine people. At times they claim ownership of the mine, saying that their land had been unfairly expropriated. Some Irianese work at the mine, but with no education they are offered only menial jobs. With proper training some do rise higher, but many feel that everyone should receive equal wages, a demand the mine owners find impossible to oblige.

At one time, the Irianese — who considered the mountain sacred — put up *saleps,* hex sticks in the shape of crude half-meter-high wooden crosses, all around Copper Mountain. Today displeasure still surfaces in the periodic appearance of hex sticks around Tembagapura.

A cargo cult further complicates the situation. A self-promoting leader among the natives near Tembagapura once proclaimed that he would be able to open the warehouse inside the mountain where the whites and Indonesians obtain their wonderful possessions, with only a special rodent's tooth. The tooth didn't work, but this longing for material goods was used by separatist rebels to recruit some natives near Tembagapura, including a few of the company workers. The rebels, who since 1963 have been fighting the government, used the convincing argument that the Indonesian government was blocking the flow of Freeport cargo to the locals.

When the conflict came to a head in a six-week period in the summer of 1977, the slurry pipeline was cut in several places, power lines were ruptured, an explosives magazine was burned and several trucks returned with arrows in their radiators. The company has had fewer problems since, but sporadic fight-

ing still occurs not too far away. Inter-tribal warfare is still occasionally practiced in the highlands. At Tembagapura, a chief once came into the company hospital with 11 arrow wounds, some still stuck in his flesh. After he was treated, his only thanks was to say that it was a good thing for everyone that he had survived. Had he died, he said, there would have been trouble. The hospital routinely treats arrow wounds.

Some villagers near Tembagapura took plywood from the mine and used it to make shields, which they hung around their necks with electrical wire. With this formidable defence against arrows, they defeated and nearly wiped out the enemy.

Several years ago, a company truck hit a little girl and broke her leg. Her incensed future husband demanded reparations, and after some bargaining settled for two medium-sized pigs, which had to be flown in by helicopter. On another occasion, a jilted husband demanded a helicopter to pursue the adulterers. His request was diplomatically turned down.

Two shanty towns have sprung up just outside of Tembagapura. The incredible wealth of the company has attracted opportunists from villages as far off as several days' walk. These squatters live off Tembagapura's garbage, steal whenever possible and remain a sore point with Freeport as well as the government, which is trying to convince the squatters to return home or settle in the transmigration site at Timika, 70 kilometers (43 mi.) away in the steamy lowlands. At one time, there were 1,000 squatters outside of Tembagapura, but today this number has been reduced considerably.

Working at the mine

For the workers, Tembagapura is a pleasant place indeed. As an Irish expert said: "All you have to think about is your work — everything else is laid out for you." And very well laid out, with modern homes following the gentle slope of the creek-split valley. After a heavy rain, 50 waterfalls spring from the tropical vegetation or bare rock on a spectacular vertical face of Mount Zaagham.

Freeport maintains houses for Indonesian staff, foreign experts and their families, and dormitories for the 2,000-odd miners and assorted workers. Facilities include schools, tennis courts, a soccer field, a complete indoors sports complex, the latest videotapes, a subsidized store, clubs and bars — including the so-called "animal bar," frequent-

ed by workers. Hard liquor is taboo, but copious quantities of beer are served. Only the staffers are allowed to take booze home.

Within the relatively narrow valley, real estate is at a premium. This means that many of the married workers cannot bring their families to Tembagapura. Some families live in shantytowns nearby but the majority remain home. This makes for a lot of lonely men. A practical soul once suggested that some ladies of pleasure be "imported" and periodically checked for disease — a practice in many Indonesian company towns. But the idea was shot down.

Although the management of Freeport includes a number of foreigners, mostly Americans, the workers are Indonesians, joined by about 350 Filipino miners on a temporary basis. The company is scrupulously fair in allotting the two items in shortest supply: private housing and jeeps. Job title and seniority are the only criteria that count.

Tembagapura has changed drastically since the early days, when a German visitor exclaimed, "Mein Gott, Stalag 17." But it is still an isolated, tight-knit community. As a Javanese jokingly said, "Irian is the Siberia of Indonesia." He was referring to being so far from home, cut off from familiar surroundings. But in Tembagapura, he could also have been referring to the cold weather. The camps of Siberia never had the creature comforts of this town, however.

Most of the Indonesians at Tembagapura are content with their lot. The high wages and opportunities for training and advancement counter the stress of being apart from families and lovers. They are allowed two leaves per year of two weeks' duration each, and the company pays one round-trip fare.

Opposite: *"Copper City" nestles in a 1,800-meter-high valley.* **Above:** *Separated from loved ones in isolated Tembagapura, mine workers entertain themselves with spirited soccer games.*

LETTER FROM MERAUKE

Adventure on the Casuarina Coast

The following are excerpts from letters written by Charles V. Barber to his wife, during a visit to Merauke, the trading and political center of Irian's southeast coast, in the summer of 1987.

Hotel Asmat, Merauke
Friday, July 17

Dear Cardamom,

Well, yesterday was a long day. I was up and out the door of my hotel in Jayapura by 5:00 a.m., on the plane by 7:00. Fantastic flight south; the high mountains were completely clear, and I took some good (I hope) pictures of Mount Mandala and its snows. After a good deal of passport checking and paper shuffling at the airport, I made my way over to this weird hotel, in which I seem to be the only guest. After taking care of business most of the day, and borrowing a Honda bebek ("duck") motorbike, I took off to explore the town and environs.

Merauke isn't so bad. Spread out, dry, and it'll never win any architectural prizes, but the weather is fantastic — dry and clear like Sumba — and the surrounding countryside is beautiful, unlike any I've seen in Indonesia. Basically, it's Australian tropical savanna, complete with eucalyptus and lots of trees, wide areas of tall waving grass, kangaroos, cassowary birds, and thousands of deer.

The Arafura Sea is indeed a "bilious swill," (i.e. shallow and brown) as a silly Rolling Stone article on Irian called it, due to three nearby river mouths, but the beach is made of row after row of white sand dunes — quite beautiful. Lots of immigrants live on the outskirts of town, from Sulawesi, Ambon, and, of course, Java. I got lost, covered in dust, took pictures, cruised all over on this silly bebek bike. A good time.

Sunday, July 19

Well, yesterday was an exhausting, but fascinating day. My guide for the day (a tall, skinny, cadaverous-looking Marind who laughs a lot) and I headed out at 8:00 a.m., both of us packed onto a 125cc trail bike, making for the Salor area to the Northwest. To get there, you start by loading your bike onto a prahu (launch) to cross the wide, bilious Maro river. Then, after five kilometers or so on a narrow road, you hit the beach. Wow! It was low tide, so we could ride on the fine, hard-packed sand. The distance between the high and low tidelines is 3 kilometers (2 mi.). When it's low, you can't see the water at all, but when we came home at 5 p.m., there was a sea where we had ridden earlier. A really wide-open-spaces kind of coast, fringed with palms.

Eventually we got river #2, and crossed in the same fashion, by rickety *prahu*. Then, off into savanna-land, on a dusty, bumpy road. There are no rocks anywhere in southern Irian, not even a pebble. It was about 50 kilometers (30 mi.) through empty, eerie, and beautiful country. Grassland, punctuated by bizarre trees I've never seen, and some thickets of forest. I think I spotted more bizarre and beautiful birds in that one day than in all the rest of my life combined. Good lizards, too, but by far the strangest sight out there is the hundreds of termite mounds made of outrageously sculpted mud, some as high as 6 meters (20 ft.), reminding one at time of cathedrals, Monument Valley mesas, or of disturbing but beautiful dreams from childhood. Indeed, I had strong feelings of deja vu all day, for what reason I can't fathom. You rarely see deer and kangaroos, as they are shy of hunters. We did have deer for lunch, though. We made it back to Merauke by dark, extremely stiff and sore, and I was dead asleep by 7 p.m.

After Friday's adventure, Saturday was relatively tame, except for the evening. After finishing all of my various appointments and duties, I wandered on down to a shop that is a general store, bar, and Asmat carving trading post, all-in-one. I got to talking with some cargo pilots, Asmat traders, and various other local characters, and began to drink their favorite local brew, which is a mixture of Drum Brand "whiskey," Orang Tua ginseng wine, various local mind-bending roots, and

Opposite, Above: *Transportation along the mudflats of the Casaurina coast is by dugout or covered outboard.* **Below:** *Charles' guide, a good-humored Marind-Anim, takes a break while the men and their sole means of transportation, a 125cc trail bike, are ferried across the Maro River.*

Talking with cargo pilots, Asmat traders, and various other characters I began to drink their favorite brew, a mixture of "whiskey," ginseng, mind-bending roots and deer fetus wine — strong, if a bit weird tasting

Chinese-style deer fetus wine (yeah, I know — Bleah!). It is ladled out of a jerry can at Rp 500 a dipper, and it is strong, if a bit weird tasting.

Welcomed boisterously by the jovial Javanese Ibu who runs the place and a crowd of locals, I began drinking the local poison, and the whole event took on the complexion of Anthony Burgess's tales in The Malayan Trilogy. Me getting vaguer and vaguer, various locals and Bugis telling me about their sex lives, brushes with the law, etc. I think I was trying out bows and arrows, and I know I bought a lot of Asmat carvings, which one of the obliging cargo pilots is bringing back to Jakarta (expect some big packages at the house soon!). A bit of luck, meeting him. Somewhere along the line, a guy pulled out a dead bird of paradise and tried to sell it to me for Rp 15,000. I gave him an eloquent lecture

(or so I thought at the time) on nature conservation, and told him that dead birds were generally stuffed for sale; this one was just dead — for some time — and really stunk. There was some singing I think, and both the motorbike and myself made it down the street to the hotel at some point, or so I surmise.

Needless to say, I feel a little under the weather this morning, but it's a clear day, and the flight back to Jayapura should be beautiful. Jayapura will seem like a real metropolis! Well, Merauke may never displace Kuta Beach as a tourist attraction, but — hey — where can you get a deer fetus daiquiri in Kuta?

Love
Charlie

Travel Advisory

While a trip to Irian Jaya still requires some planning, the good old days of cannibals, fierce warriors and deadly diseases are past. There's no longer a chance to see a cannibal feast and ritual warfare has almost disappeared. Although there are probably a few small, uncontacted groups in the Mamberamo River basin in north-central Irian, your chance of being the first Westerner to meet them is just about nil.

All this doesn't mean Irian is now like Bali. A visit to the Baliem valley is truly a unique experience — there is literally nowhere else on earth like it. Irian is far from developed as a tourist destination. Much of the island is impassable. Travel requires flying on small propeller planes and walking. Roads are currently being built to link the inland villages to the important coast cities, but the incredibly difficult terrain makes a road network something for the distant future. Few other places in Indonesia reward initiative as well as Irian.

It is almost impossible to describe an area as huge as Irian, especially within any kind of reasonable time frame and budget. The travel sections of this book include only areas where access is easy, and tourism is encouraged. It is hoped that later editions of this book will cover other areas, especially the Asmat region, once wider travel receives government approval.

Anyone traveling to Irian Jaya should fly to Wamena and spend at least a few days in Dani country. It would be a shame to come here and miss the best known, and most accessible of the highlands tribes. Right in Wamena, the administrative center of the valley, there are more traditional (non-Christian) villages than in the more outlying parts of the valley. Diligent and persistent inquiry might scare up an invitation to an authentic ritual, but luck seems to play at least an equal role. But dances, quite good ones, can be arranged for a fee. And for a truly dramatic exhibition, you can arrange a ritual battle (though this is not inexpensive.) Consult the Baliem Valley section of this book for more details.

ARRIVING BY AIR

From the United States. Garuda Indonesia's twice weekly or, during the summer months, thrice weekly flights from Los Angeles and Honolulu stop at Biak on their way to Bali. From Biak, it's but a short hop to Jayapura (the capital of Irian) or to the other coastal cities.

From Australia. unfortunately, there are no direct flights and visas are required if one comes through Papua New Guinea on the weekly flight from Wewak to Jayapura. From Down Under, you have to fly to Bali first then backtrack east to reach Irian. There's talk of a future Garuda flight from Kupang to Ambon (Maluku province) whence frequent flights leave for Irian. Nothing definite as of this writing.

From Europe and Asia. at the moment, it's only the rather expensive Garuda flights — heading east from Jakarta, Bali or Ujung Pandang — that land you in Irian. It's worth trying for the "See Indonesia" Air Pass. There are rumors of an upcoming Philippines — Menado flight (North Sulawesi) whence to Ternate and Ambon.

Visa Formalities

Nationals of the following 30 countries are granted visa-free entry for 60 days. For other nationals, tourist visas are required and can be obtained from any Indonesian embassy or consulate.

Australia	Austria
Belgium	Brunei
Canada	Denmark
Finland	France
Greece	Iceland
Ireland	Italy
Japan	Liechtenstein
Luxembourg	Malaysia
Malta	Netherlands
New Zealand	Norway
Philippines	Singapore
South Korea	Spain
Sweden	Switzerland
Thailand	United Kingdom
United States	West Germany

To avoid any unpleasantness on arrival, check your passport before leaving for Indonesia. You need at least one empty page for your passport to be stamped. Passports must be valid for at least six months upon arrival and you should have valid proof of onward journey, whether return or through tickets. Employment is strictly forbidden on tourist visas or visa-free entry.

Visa-free entry to Indonesia means not exceeding a stay of two months (60 days). This is not extendable and is only valid when entering via Biak or any of the following airports: Ambon, Bali, Balikpapan, Batam, Jakarta, Kupang, Menado, Medan, Pandang, Palembang, Pekanbaru, Pontianak and Surabaya.

Customs

Carrying narcotics, firearms and ammunition are strictly prohibited. Advance approval is necessary to bring in transceivers. On entry 2 liters of alcoholic beverages, 200 cigarettes, 50 cigars or 100 grams of tobacco are allowed. There is no restriction on import and export of foreign currencies in cash or travelers checks, but there is an export limit of 50,000 Indonesian rupiahs.

All narcotics are illegal in Indonesia. The use, sale or purchase of narcotics results in long prison terms and/or huge fines — this applies to all foreigners as well as to Indonesians. Once caught, you are immediately placed in detention until trail and the sentences are very stiff.

Keep your cool

At a government offices like immigration, talking loudly and forcefully just does not make things easier. Things in Indonesia may take a little longer to accomplish than you are used to. Patience is a virtue in Indonesia that opens many doors. Good manners and dress are also to your advantage.

ARRIVING BY BOAT

Pelni. Pelni (Pelayaran Nasional Indonesia) is Indonesia's national shipping lines. Pelni Line's huge 1,700 passenger *Umsini* calls at Jayapura every two weeks. The same line's *Rinjani* stops at Sorong twice a month. First class cabins (two passengers) run some 25% less than airfare and dormitory class (the least expensive) is about one-third of the first-class rate. These ships are meant to move Indonesians around the archipelago, but foreigners are welcome in any of the five classes. The food is decent, the ships are clean and for those with a few days to spare, this is a wonderful, inexpensive alternative to flying.

Travel agencies do not work with Pelni so you have to pay and pick up the tickets yourself or have a friend do this for you. Inconvenient, but worth the effort. Around Indonesian vacation times, the ships tend to be crowded and advance reservations are advised.

Pelni's main office in Jakarta: Jl. Angkasa 18, Tel: (21) 416262, 417136 and 417319. Telex: 44301 and 44187. Mailing address: P.O. Box 115, Jakarta. Ticket sales: Jl. Pintu Air 1, Tel: 358398.

In Sorong: Jl. Yos Sudarso 176, Tel: (951) 21860. Telex: 77114 1A PELNI SORONG.

The *Umsini*'s route: Jakarta, Surabaya, Ujung Pandang, Bitung (Menado), Ternate, Sorong, Jayapura and return the same way. The trip takes exactly two weeks, leaving and returning on a Thursday.

The *Rinjani*'s route: Jakarta, Surabaya, Ujung Pandang, Bau-Bau, Ambon, Sorong, Ambon, Bau-Bau, Ujung Pandang, Surabaya and back to Jakarta. The trip takes 11 days, leaving every second Wednesday and returning Saturday.

Visa free entry to Indonesia is possible at the following seaports: Ambon, Bali, Batam, Jakarta, Manado, Medan, Riau, Semarang and Surabaya.

THE *SURAT JALAN*

Outside of Sorong, Biak and Jayapura, you need a travel document called a *surat jalan* (literally "travel letter"). This permit can easily be obtained — for much of Irian — at the central police stations in the three towns mentioned above. It takes one to four photos and half an hour to half a day. Local police stations will check this permit anytime you spend the night in this area — in fact, you are *required* to report to these police posts, although they won't shoot or jail you if you are just walking through and don't report.

Some areas of Irian Jaya are formally closed by the government. The areas are, at the time of this writing: the border fringe with Papua New Guinea, the Asmat lands (with the exception of Agats), the Mamberamo River, and the Paniai Lakes and adjacent highlands, including Puncak Jaya.

In any case, we strongly recommend against trying to travel in the closed areas. They are not so exciting anyway. Just to properly visit the open areas, particularly the Baliem highlands, would require months.

There is, perhaps, one way around the travel restrictions. Given enough time, some travel agents, with connections perhaps to the military, could arrange a trip — including getting a *surat jalan* — to the south coast areas around the Asmat and other less acculturated tribes to the north of the Asmat territory. The trips are expensive (chartered plane) and a few travelers we have talked to who have taken one of these trips said they were disappointed as they did not see enough to make the price worthwhile. We suggest exploring the rest of Irian first.

TRAVEL IN IRIAN

International flights and most flights from within Indonesia land in Biak, which is the hub for flights around Irian. On Garuda you can fly to Jayapura ($36) and Sorong ($41) and on Merpati — always 10% cheaper than Garuda — you can fly to Fakfak ($80), Jayapura ($31), Kaimana ($47), Manokwari ($26), Merauke ($84), Nabire ($27), Serui ($15) and Sorong ($37). Many of these same cities, as well as a few others, are served by Garuda and Merpati from Jayapura (For more on flights from Biak, see "Biak Practicalities," page 68; from Jayapura, "Jayapura Practicalities," page 78 — also check the destination "Practicalities" section). Garuda is slowly transferring their smaller routes and planes over to Merpati, so be alert to changes.

Garuda Indonesia. In Biak: Jalan Sudirman 3, Tel: (961) 21416. In Jayapura: Jalan Percetakan 2, Tel: (967) 21220.

Merpati. In Biak: Jalan M. Yamin, across from the airport, Tel: (961) 21213. In Jayapura: Jalan A. Yani 15, next to Hotel Matoa, Tel: (967) 21111.

The only airline with a regular flight to Agats, on Irian's south coast, is the Catholic American Missionary Alliance (AMA). They make the flight in a Cessna 185 (maximum 4 passengers and 400 kilos total weight) at least once a week — $120, one-way.

AMA. In Jayapura, near the Sentani airport. Tel: (Sentani) 26. Contact: Bosco Fernandez.

Flying in the highlands

The fastest way to reach the Baliem Valley is to fly into Biak, catch the next flight to Jayapura to get your *surat jalan,* overnight in Sentani near the airport, and fly from Jayapura to Wamena on Merpati's daily 7:00 a.m. flight ($25).

Once in the highlands, Merpati and the Missionary Aviation Fellowship fly small planes to a number of highlands airstrips. Every Friday from Wamena, Merpati flies to and from Bokondini, Karubaga and Kelilia ($15-30). The MAF posts a weekly schedule of flights to a number of highlands strips, and their prices are very reasonable ($10-30). The list goes up Thursdays for the next week's flights. With enough notice MAF will accept a charter of one of its Cessna 185 or Cessna 206 airplanes, carrying 4-5 passengers. The rates are around $150/hour which, at the usual flying speed, works out to a reasonable 22¢ per kilometer.

The offices of both airlines are at the Wamena airport. (See "Baliem Practicalities" page 124 for more details.)

Travel by sea

Pelni, Indonesia's national shipping line, has several mixed passenger/cargo ships that run occasionally along Irian's north coast. Prices are very cheap, and this can be an interesting way to see the small coastal villages. Check in Jayapura for schedules and fares if you are interested (to Sorong, one week with many stops in between, $10.)

Pelni. Jayapura: Jalan Halmahera 1, Tel: (967) 21270.

Yotefa Shipping, a cargo outfit, has deck space for up to 50 passengers on a monthly run to Sorong (2 week cycle). Yotefa also runs a coaster along the south coast between Merauke and Fakfak.

Yotefa Shipping Lines. Jayapura: Jalan Percetakan 90A, Tel: (967) 21823. Contact: Jack Saenen. (See "Jayapura Practicalities" page78 for more details.)

In many places in Irian small boats make regular runs (e.g. from Biak to Supiori Islands) and the fares are quite minimal. Chartering small outboard powered launches and outriggers is also possible in many places, with fares ranging from $10-30/hour depending on the size of the engine and capacity of the boat. Keep in mind that Irian is not really set up for tourists, so don't expect fixed prices and all kinds of services to come with your boat.

LAND TRANSPORT

In the relatively few places in Irian with developed road systems — major cities, some of the smaller villages and parts of the Baliem Valley — the standard Indonesian form of mass transport, the "Colt" or minivan, plies the road. Along the regular route, these vehicles are quite cheap, but since their drivers usually wait for at least a half a load before departing, and often swing through populated areas to round up passengers, the eager tourist might find them a bit slow for his schedule.

These vehicles can almost always be chartered, however, and the best way to do this is have your hotelier round one up for you. There's no harm in bargaining a bit for rates, but expect to pay $5-10 per hour. Irian is off the beaten path, and things like truck parts are expensive.

MONEY

Best to carry travelers' checks of two leading companies as sometimes, for mysterious reasons, a bank won't cash the checks of a company as well known as, say, American Express. U.S. dollars — checks and cash — are accepted in all banks which deal in foreign exchange, as are Australian dollars and (usually) Japanese yen, deutsche marks, French and Swiss francs. Carrying cash is not a good idea. Aside from the possible loss, banks won't take the bills unless they are in perfect condition. Rates in Jayapura are about 5% to 7% better than in Wamena.

Prices quoted in this book are in U.S. dollars and were noted in September, 1989. The Indonesian rupiah is being allowed to slowly devalue, and prices stated in U.S. dollars are more likely to remain accurate.

Exchange rates as of late 1989, were:

US $ = Rp1,783
£ sterling = Rp 2,776
Aust $ = Rp1,353
Sin $ = Rp 904
Mal $ = Rp 661
Dfl = Rp 799
DM = Rp 901
FFr = Rp 267
HK $ = Rp 228
Yen = Rp 12.15

The highest denomination bill is the Rp 10,000 note, which makes for bulky wads of money. About $600 at the time of this writing made you a millionaire in rupiahs — nice feeling but conceal the loot.

Bargaining

Other than airfares, package tours, prices for prepared foods and most hotels/losmen, a price in Indonesia is a relative thing. At the market, however, "How much?" is not a question needing a short answer, but the beginning of a conversation. Bargaining is a highly refined art, but there are a few simple rules.

1) Never lose your temper or your sense of humor. A smile is an essential weapon.
2) Always agree on a price *before* accepting a service.
3) Feign indifference to the charms of an item if you really want to get a good price.

4) Don't be shy about denigrating the item you want to buy: "Is this a scratch?" "But look, it's faded here."

5) It's not worth bad feelings just to knock a few cents or dollars off. You've come a long way to see Irian, why spoil it?

HEALTH AND HYGIENE

It is a good idea to take anti-malaria pills, starting three weeks before arriving in Irian and continuing the dosage for the same time span after leaving. Various malaria pills can be purchased locally, but your defenses should be up before arrival. Malaria in Irian is neither rampant nor nonexistent. There are no other major health problems here. Still it's always a good precaution to take a basic first aid kit and quickly treat any cuts or scratched mosquito bites — infections take hold quickly and tenaciously in the tropics.

It is a good idea to bring a medicine kit. A good assortment might include: A variety of bandages, antiseptic wash (Betadine, Dettol), Aspirin/Tylenol, antacid tablets, antiseptic cream (for local infections), antifungal cream (Tinactin), soap, cotton swaps (Q-tips), tweezers and a small pair of scissors. Also a good bet, more important for a longer trip, are antibiotic tablets and cream, (available over the counter in Indonesia) but do not take these unless absolutely necessary.

Also put some good sunscreen in your kit, and don't waste your money on anything less than SPF#15. Don't forget a hat.

Absolutely essential is a strong insect repellent, such as Cutter's or extra-strength Off, and (for the inevitable bites) a small jar of Tiger Balm, a camphorated salve famous in Asia but less well-known in the Western world. Good insect repellent is very hard to find in Indonesia. Mosquito nets are also hard to find, and another good item to bring along.

Keep in mind that personal care items like contact lens solutions, prescription drugs, even dental floss are impossible to find in a place like Irian Jaya. Bring what you will need.

In the larger towns. especially Jayapura, there are decent government hospitals and medicines are widely available. Some doctors even speak passable English. The highlands aren't this developed. Like anywhere in the world, medical facilities decline in direct proportion to the distance from urban centers. Missionaries are usually equipped for medical emergencies — but at least pay for whatever medication/help you receive from them.

MOUNTAIN CLIMBING

Access to Irian's highest peaks lies through Tembagapura. If you have permission to stay there, it is only a question of acclimatization and a one-day trek from the mine site to Puncak Jaya and other peaks in the area. There is also a roundabout way in from Beoga, but this requires permits from the police and military and chartered missionary light planes.

Those interested in climbing in Irian should contact the Indonesian Mountaineering Association. Rafia Bontoh will be most helpful and he has scads of experience with bureaucratic red tape, logistics and actual climbing. His club, MAPALA, is connected with the national university.

MAPALA. University of Indonesia, Jl. Pegangsaan Timur 17 Zaal, Jakarta Pusat, Indonesia, Tel: (21) 333223.

To climb Puncak Jaya, along with the other peaks, your cost with MAPALA will run about $100 a day (plus airfares) for roughly 15 days. There are lots of peaks to climb in the area, and they are the most challenging in Irian, requiring ice/glacier as well as mountaineering skills and equipment. In comparison, Irian's other peaks are easy. Trikora Mountain, accessible from the Baliem Valley, is exclusively a rock climb. Mandala Mountain presents no technical problems, although access is difficult because it is in a security-conscious area.

DIVING

We have seen some excellent sea gardens for snorkeling around Yapen and Biak islands, and reliable sources vouch for excellent scuba diving as well as snorkeling off the coast and other islands in Cenderawasih Bay. Unfortunately there's no scuba equipment for rent at the moment and no travel agency handles arrangements for diving tours. But this may change, and initiative (and language skills) might very well be rewarded.

NATURE RESERVES

Irian is full of interesting and strange wildlife, and there are many unspoiled reserves. Visiting most of these, however, requires time, money and some knowledge of the Indonesian language. And, of course, the surat jalan. If this sounds like a lot of hassle (it is), keep in mind the rewards. In addition to the many species of birds, Irian is home to marsupial mice and cats, bandicoots, ring-tailed opossums, pygmy flying phalangers, cuscus, tree kangaroos and wallabies. Patience, time and good organization are needed to see many of the mammals, most of which are quite shy. The birds are easier, once you are in the right place.

Cenderawasih Marine Reserve
Wandiwoi/Wandammen Reserve

These are located on a mountainous peninsula jutting into Cenderawasih Bay, and include a large surrounding marine area, between Nabire and Manokwari. The peninsula is home to many bird species: parrots, lories, honeyeaters, birds of paradise, flycatchers, kingfishers, and the unusual bower birds. The male bower bird constructs a nest decorated with any brightly-colored object he can find. In the areas modern man has reached, batteries, ribbon, and bits of plastic packaging do as well as flowers and rushes. The western shore of the peninsula has several villages where one can find boats, guides and porters. The steep cliffs of the uninhabited east coast offer spectacular views of the bay.

Near the peninsula, the coral Auri islands are feeding grounds for sea turtles and the dugong (*Dugong dugon*), a plant-eating sea mammal that resembles a walrus without tusks. The islands are also nesting sites for terns, boobies, frigate birds, night herons, and cormorants. The best way to reach this area is to fly to the mission landing strip at Wasior from Manokwari, Nabire or Biak. Remember to get your *surat jalan.*

Gunung Meja Reserve

A small reserve with kaleidoscopic parakeets and lories and many other feathered creatures — a birder's dream. The reserve can be reached by road from Manokwari on the north coast of the Bird's Head. This part of Irian is quite dry, and the soil is rocky and alkaline, mostly coral limestone. A very rare orchid, *Gammatophyllum papuanum,* grows on the coral rock. A boat trip from here along the coast, where limestone cliffs jut straight upward, can reveal huge leatherback sea turtles (*Dermochelys coriacea*) laying their eggs. Far inland are the Arfak and Tamrau mountains (formally a closed area), where many very rare animals lurk, but this trip is best left to a very well-financed, and politically well-connected expedition. The wettest months in the Gunung Meja Reserve are January and February, and it is dry again by March. The seas are rough during the *wambrau,* the local name for the southeast monsoon, May to October.

Lorentz Reserve

From the Arafura Sea to Indonesia's highest peaks, this reserve covers 1,675,000 hectares (4,087,000 acres) at altitudes from sea level to the tip of ice-capped Puncak Jaya, the nation's tallest point. Practically all of Irian's animal and plant life can be found in this reserve. The vegetation is particularly strange, as the altitude and tropical climate combine to produce peculiar tree ferns, epiphytic flowers, and other strange plant life. (This is a closed area, see MOUNTAIN CLIMBING above.)

Mamberamo Reserve

This is a huge area — 1,752,500 hectares (4,276,100 acres) — located along the Mamberamo River and its two principal tributaries, the Taritatu and the Tariku. This is Irian's largest river system, extending 400 kilometers (250 mi.) inland. The reserve includes Lake Rombebai, 50 kilometers (30 mi.) inland, and the Foja mountains, whose gorges have been cut by the Mamberamo some 120 kilometers (75 mi.) from the coast. This reserve includes ecological zones from sea level to 2,103 meters (6,900 ft.), from inaccessible peaks in the Foja group to the Meervlakte or "Lake Plain" — a huge, low-lying basin extending from near the coast to 150 kilometers (90 mi.) inland. A huge variety of birds is found here: black night herons, bower birds, cassowaries, cormorants, crowned pigeons, darters, egrets, five species of birds of paradise, golden-headed beos, hornbills, lorikeets, parrots, swamp hens, terns, white cockatoos, and the endemics, including a ground flycatcher, a rail, a thrush, two honey-eaters and a warbler. A brightly colored species of tree kangaroo, *Dendrolagus matschiei,* lives in the Foja mountains.

The best way to see this reserve is by boat. Start from either Sarmi or Teba, at the delta, or at one of the Meervlakte airstrips. You may be able to get a ride from one of the Summer Institute of Linguistics' planes, or charter one, from the institute's base camp at Bira (Holmes) Lake. Accommodations with missionaries or locals might appear, but bring food and essentials along. Seasons here are meaningless.

North Biak/Supiori Reserve

These two islands are separated by a channel so narrow they are almost joined. One bridge over the channel has been built and washed away, but another, stronger one is under construction. This will give land access from Biak to Supiori. The trip is now a 5-hour boat ride from Biak town. There are lots of endemic bird species here, but they are not easy to spot.

Pulau Dolok Reserve

Some 600,000 hectares (1,464,000 acres) on an island called Yos Sudarso (formerly Frederik-Hendrik.) The wet season is the best time to visit — during the dry season, this area is a morass of mud, to which the locals have adapted but to which you might not. Besides, the wet season — November through April — is the best time to see the many waterbirds and migratory species here.

During the rainiest months, January through March, the sea is calm and boats travel everywhere. To reach this reserve, fly to Merauke and then hire a boat to the island. Alternately, fly from Merauke to the government station at Kimaan on Yos Sudarso, then on the the reserve.

Raja Empat Reserve

The area covers the western portion of Waigeo Island and nearby seas, along with parts of Batanta and Salawati Islands close to Sorong. Ever since Wallace's time, this area has been a magnet for naturalists because of the unusual endemic species and the long coastlines, which allow for short walking trips inland. The wildlife of Waigeo, thanks to long isolation, is most unusual. Birds include frilled flycatchers, lories, kingfishers, and the red and Waigeo birds of paradise. The island's endemic marsupials include the large spotted phalanger, mice and bandicoots.

On Salawati, one can find the 12-wired bird of paradise, an endemic species of myna, the orange lori and the white-crowned koel. A noticeable dry season takes place on Waigeo from July to about October. To reach the reserve, you must fly to Sorong on the tip of the Bird's Head, then charter a boat to any of the Raja Empat islands. There are a number of boats to charter to Salawati and Batanta, but it is more difficult to get out to Waigeo. In Sorong, try the following agent for charters to the islands:

P.T. Makmur Thomas. Kompleks Pertokoan Yohan A15, Jl. A. Yani, Sorong, IRJA 98414. Tel: (951) 21183, 21953, 21594. Fax: 21897. Telex: 77123 MTSON 1A.

Prices range widely, depending on the destination, the number of days to be spent there, and the number of people commissioning a boat and guide. Figure $30-60 a head for a day trip to a nearby island, $500 or more for 4-5 day trips to far off Waigeo. (See also "Sorong Practicalities," page 91.)

Rawa Biru/Wasur Reserve

This reserve, adjacent to the border with Papua New Guinea, is contiguous with the Tonda Wildlife Management area of PNG. Savannah woodlands surround a blue lake (Rawa Biru means "Blue Swamp"), and here you can see giant termite mounds, long-grass, paper bark trees, acacias and eucalyptus — much like Australia. The waters shelter crocodiles and the curious dugong, and birds such as cranes, ducks, geese, ibis, pelicans, spoonbills, storks and waders. Other area birds are cockatoos, parrots, crowned pigeons, and the fierce cassowary. Native wallabies and the rusa deer, introduced in 1913, thrive in the area. The deer are hunted, and some of the venison ends up in Jayapura. The reserve is 60 kilometers (37 mi.) from Merauke, and the best way to get there is by jeep during the dry season. This part of Irian, the southeast corner, receives almost no rain between June and the end of October, making for little chance of getting bogged down in mud.

WEATHER

Due to Irian's mountainous body, the climate is subject to a great deal of variation. The one constant rule is that temperatures drop one degree centigrade with every 100 meter rise in elevation. In general, lowland temperatures fluctuate around a mean of 27 degrees centigrade with an annual range seldom exceeding 8 degrees centigrade — less than the night/day difference.

During the northwest monsoon, from November to April, heavy rains fall on the north coast. During this monsoon, the heaviest rains in the highlands pour down from December to March, with a second peak in August. The least precipitation here (but don't count on this) occurs during July, and September. The southeast monsoon, from May to October, dumps 6,000 mm (230 in.) of rain on the slopes, leaving the coast relatively dry.

As a general rule, expect hot and muggy climates on the coasts and cold in the highlands. Variations from this are more a matter of luck than careful planning, especially on the north coast which is rainy, but has no real season.

The seas are more predictable, July and August are the best times to navigate off the north coast. January to March and June to October are the dangerous months for sailing off the south coast.

PHOTOGRAPHY

The cardinal rule in travel photography is never take new equipment on a trip. But get plenty of film — at least twice as much as you think you'll need. While 35 mm color negative film is sometimes available in the bigger towns, the stock may be old and the color balance ruined by heat and humidity. Slide film and black and white negative film is very difficult to find.

Don't load yourself down with equipment. The most sophisticated gear available does you no good if it's too bulky and cumbersome to have always at hand. We recommend bringing just two lenses, one wide-angle for scenics, and one longer lens for details and flattering portraits. Handled properly, it is possible to shoot an entire article for *National Geographic* with just these two lenses.

If you shoot Kodachrome, of the two processing plants in Asia — Japan and Australia — our experience is that the plant in Japan has the best quality control.

Although slow film is generally safe from airport x-ray machines, in general it's better to have the attendant hand inspect your film. Keep it in a separate bag, ready to be pulled from the rest of your luggage for inspection. Resist the urge to process film in Indonesia to avoid the inspection machine — bad processing has ruined more film than x-ray machines.

If you travel by boat, at the first hint of sea spray either move or pack up all camera equipment immediately. A little rain is no problem; a little seaspray can turn a fine machine into a piece of junk.

Heat and humidity are general problems in Indonesia. Obviously you shouldn't leave your camera — especially if it contains film — in the direct sun. But humidity is harder to avoid. Keep in mind that condensation is worse than humidity, and moving a camera from hot, steamy outdoors to a cool, air-conditioned room can cause problems. Keep the temperature change gradual. Another good habit is to run rolls of film through your camera quickly, and pack them up in a cool, dry place.

Further Readings

Aggressive cannibals combined with malaria to keep travel writers away from Irian's shores until well into the 20th century. Alfred Russel Wallace's *The Malay Archipelago* for the first extensive description of Irian's wildlife, as well as culture and trade. Naturalist D'Albertis followed, and left a fascinating account of his explorations of the Bird's Head and the Fly River. (The best contemporary account of Irian's wildlife is Brongersma's *The Animal World of Netherlands New Guinea*.)

Peter Bellwood's *Man's Conquest of the Pacific* and *Pre-History of the Indo-Malaysian Archipelago,* and a helpful essay in Peter van de Velde's *Prehistoric Indonesia,* summarize the state of anthropological knowledge of Irian's prehistory.

American explorer Richard Archbold, who discovered the Baliem Valley, published a detailed description of his expedition in *The Bulletin of the Museum of Natural History* (which sponsored his trip) and a popular article in *National Geographic.*

Leopold Pospisil's *The Kapauku Papuans,* is an excellent work on the Ekari (then called the Kapauku). Missionary accounts began appearing at this time, perhaps the best of which are Don Richardson's *Lords of the Earth,* about missionaries among the Yali, and *Peace Child,* set among the Asmat.

The Catholic Fathers of the Crosier Mission compile the *Asmat Sketch Books,* containing assorted articles on the history, art, culture and difficulties of Asmat life. [contact Crosier Missions, 3204 East 43d Street, Minneapolis, MN 55406. They also have *Asmat Images,* a catalog of the excellent collection in the Asmat Museum of Culture and Progress in Agats.]

The Harvard-Peabody expedition to the Baliem Valley produced a great documentary film, *Dead Birds,* and *Gardens of War,* a book of still photographs. Carl Heider, who accompanied the expedition and stayed on after it left, wrote a thorough treatise on Dani life. The literary talents of Peter Matthiessen provide the beautifully written *Under the Mountain Wall,* a moving account of the Kurelu Dani. German anthropologist K.F. Koch wrote in English about the Yali in *War and Peace in Jalemo.*

The problems of the Dutch and Indonesian over Irian have resulted in countless pages of polemics. For a clear overview, try R. C. Bone's *The Dynamics of the West Irian Problem,* or Henderson's more recent analysis.

Two authors deserve a separate category. Tobias Schneebaum, a gay, Jewish New Yorker, visited the Asmat and documented secret Asmat practices and his personal sense of fulfillment in the excellent *Where the Spirits Dwell.* Robert Mitton's *The Lost World of Irian Jaya* is truly outstanding. The author, a young geologist-explorer, was possessed of intelligence, humor and a keen eye. Mitton died tragically at 30 years of age, and the book was compiled from the author's photographs, maps, diaries and letters to friends.

Archbold, Richard. "Results of the Archbold Expedition," *Bulletin of the American Museum of Natural History.* Vol. 88, Article 3.

— "Unknown New Guinea," *National Geographic.* Vol. 89, 1941.

Asmat Sketch Books, Vols. 1-8. Crosier Missions: Minneapolis.

Baal, J. van. *West Irian: a Bibliography.* Dordrecht, Netherlands, 1984.

Bellwood, Peter. *Pre-History of the Indo-Malaysian Archipelago.* New York, 1985.

Bickmore, A. S. *Travels in the East Indian Archipelago.* London, 1868.

Bone, R. C. *The Dynamics of the West New Guinea Problem.* Cornell, 1958.

Bromley, M. "Ethnic Groups in Irian Jaya." *Bulletin for Irian Jaya Development.* 2-3:1-37, 1973.

Brongersma, L. D. *The Animal World of Netherlands New Guinea.* Gronengen, 1958.

D'Albertis, L. M. *New Guinea.* London, 1880.

Gardner, R. and C. Heider. *Gardens of War.*

Gibbons, Alice. *The People Time Forgot.* Chicago, 1981.

Harrer, Heinrich. *I Come from the Stone Age.* London, 1964.

Heider, Carl. *The Dugum Dani.* New York, 1970.

— *Grand Valley Dani, Peaceful Warriors.* New York, 1979.

Henderson, William. *West New Guinea: the Dispute and its Settlement.* Seton Hall University Press, 1987.

Hitt, Russell T. *Cannibal Valley.* New York, 1962.

Kamma, F. C. *Koreri.* The Hague, 1972.

Koch, K. F. *War and Peace in Jalemo.* Cambridge, 1974.

Matthiessen, Peter. *Under the Mountain Wall.* Penguin:New York, 1987.

Mitton, Robert. *The Lost World of Irian Jaya.* Melbourne, 1985.

Pospisil, Leopold. *The Kapauku Papuans.* New York, 1978.

Richardson, Don. *Lords of the Earth.* Ventura, California, 1977.

— *Peace Child.* Glendale, California, 1974.

Schneebaum, Tobias. *Where the Spirits Dwell.* New York, 1988.

Temple, Philip. *Nawok!* London, 1962.

Velde, Van de Peter, ed. *Prehistoric Indonesia.* Dordrecht, Netherlands, 1984.

Wallace, Alfred Russel. *The Malay Archipelago.* New York, 1962.

Wilson, F. *The Conquest of Copper Mountain.* New York, 1981.

Index